Beyond Toasted Ravioli

A Tour of St. Louis Restaurants

by Joe & Ann Lemons Pollack

D0329579

Copyright © 1998 by Joe and Ann Lemons Pollack

All rights reserved. No part of this book may be reproduced in any form or by any electronic or mechanical means, including information storage and retrieval systems, without permission in writing from the author, except by a reviewer, who may quote brief passages in review.

ISBN 1-891442-06-6

Library of Congress Catalog Number: 98-060429

Virginia Publishing Company
4814 Washington Blvd.
St. Louis, MO 63108
(314) 367-6612

Acknowledgments: Copy Editor: Anna Ross. Cover Design: Roger Kallerud. Back cover photo and photos of Joe and Ann by Herb Weitman. Proofreading and research: Ami Norris.

Table of Contents

Note: Restaurant reviews are listed alphabetically below.
To find a restaurant by **food type**, see index page 205.

For each other.

Joe's Preface

Oscar Wilde once wrote a fairy tale about an imaginary land called Serendip and the handsome prince who lived there. Every day, when the prince went walking through his kingdom, he saw things on the ground, and picked them up, and they turned out to be interesting, or beautiful, or educational. Wilde's story brought the word serendipity, and its relative, serendipitous, into the English language.

It's one of my favorite words. Not only does it roll nicely off the tongue, but it's also true that serendipitous things happen, to me and to everyone else. Look for them. Take advantage of them. They're fun.

A large part of my life, looking at and writing about the restaurants of St. Louis, has been a serendipitous adventure. I had just joined the *Post-Dispatch* as theater and movie critic, in the summer of 1972, when my boss, Joan Foster Dames, then the features editor, asked me if I'd like to write about restaurants. The paper had had a restaurant critic, its first, but he had gone on to other things.

"Why not!" I said, as I often did when someone suggested a potentially serendipitous adventure, and suddenly I had a new career. In truth, I had another career, as in one more, but that's a different story. As luck would have it, St. Louis restaurants leaped across the twentieth century that year, and the assignment became even a greater joy, allowing me to follow the adventures of our local chefs as they changed things for the better and brought new dining experiences to everyone in the city.

But in the autumn of 1995, after writing more than a thousand restaurant pieces for the *Post-Dispatch*, it was time to retire in the company of a new bride, Ann Lemons, a curious and intelligent eater, an excellent cook and a writer of elegant, distinctive prose about restaurants and food.

Retirement is wonderful. Ann and I have traveled three continents, eaten superb meals on all of them. But as we rolled through 1997, I began to notice that St. Louis restaurants, many of which had been dozing quietly for a decade or so, were beginning to stir. New foods, new flavors, new ownership, new chefs, new investors were arriving, and the local restaurant scene was brightening. It took a while, but I realized we were about to re-create the early '70s, and maybe surpass them.

We weren't breaking ground in other areas. St. Louis remains the last stop before a fad reaches the scrap heap. Other cities build theatres and concert halls and museums. We build a museum but keep the public out. We let the rich people renege on their promises—in writing—to refurbish a splendid auditorium and theatre. In this city, the leadership considers Planet Hollywood both a cultural and a culinary step forward, and we lust to have our own Hard Rock Cafe, even if ours is one hundred and twenty-ninth on the list. In our glorious tradition of being able to screw up a two-car funeral, we schedule two major events into our city's biggest meeting site on the same weekend.

But new restaurants were opening all over town, without help from Civic Regress or 2004 or anyone else. And they were good.

Voila!

The last book about St. Louis restaurants was published in 1992, and it was time for another, taking advantage of Ann's culinary expertise and writing style. We have told many people that ours is a relationship of specialization—she cooks, I eat. More of a joke than the truth, as you will note, but the unaltered fact is that neither of us can resist a good line, even if it may bend the truth.

To provide a basis for comparison, the so-called "Class of 1972," a centerpiece of the earlier books, included Anthony's, Balaban's, Duff's, the Jefferson Avenue Boarding House and Yen Ching. Anthony's and the Boarding House are gone, Duff's and Balaban's remain, with the latter having expanded into West County. Yen Ching missed the cut in 1992, but is in the higher ranks again.

Looking geographically at the city and county, the Hill, where Italian restaurants congregate, and the Central West End, along with Downtown and the University City Loop, are still primary dining areas. But they have been joined by Clayton, first choice for the upscale and the trendy, and South Grand Boulevard, home to bargains and ethnic diversity. There is even greater sprawl of places to eat, but eating is not necessarily dining.

St. Louisans have more—and better—choices for lunch and dinner than they had in 1992. Most of them, however, represent the United States, especially the southwestern United States. At the same time, we have better and fresher seafood, better and fresher bread, more locally grown vegetables, fruit and herbs. Far more choice is available for those who prefer Chinese cooking, or the tangy cuisine of southeast Asia, or the multitude of styles from the Mediterranean Basin. More Caribbean and South American dishes are coming to local menus. We still need an elegant Chinese restaurant serving classic dishes in the Cantonese and Shanghai styles, and our choices would be improved with great restaurants serving the foods of eastern Europe, Germany and the Iberian peninsula.

When it comes to dining, Ann and I are adventurous and eclectic. The restaurants listed here are ones we usually enjoy, for one reason or another, primarily the food. We have avoided chains and franchises for obvious reasons, and we will accept the blame for errors and omissions. Prices listed are approximate for one person having appetizer, entree and dessert. Drinks, tax and tip are extra, and be warned that drinks will make check totals leap higher than a young trout chasing a fly.

We don't believe in cutesy emblems to rate restaurants. We are literate people of strong opinions, and we hope both of those attributes come through clearly in our prose. We start to get impatient after waiting twenty minutes for our table, and we wish you, our readers, good meals, good dinner companions and good health.

Ann's Preface

If there's one question Joe and I hear more than any other, it's "What's your favorite restaurant?" We wrote this book, in part, to answer that question.

Foodwise, we come from two very different backgrounds. Joe grew up in a world of sour pickles, Chinese food and Nathan's hot dogs. His Brooklyn-based family was composed of legendary eaters, both male and female. Forays into the land of crab cakes to visit a Baltimore aunt and uncle had a permanent effect on him, as you will see. Initially attracted to Missouri by its journalism school and its policy of licenses-by-mail for underage drivers, he spent a brief, and fortunately, unremarkable period as a fry cook in college. After stints in the Army, graduate school, the St. Louis Globe-Democrat and the front office of the St. Louis Football Cardinals, eating well on the Bidwills' budget, he went to the St. Louis Post-Dispatch. In August 1972, he began writing restaurant reviews, in addition to his duties covering film and theatre. When he retired in 1995, he didn't stop eating.

As for me, I've publicly admitted that I spent my early years as a picky eater. Raised in Desloge, Missouri, I lived in a world without sour cream, cilantro or fresh blueberries. The nearest Chinese restaurant was sixty-five miles away. After I moved to St. Louis as an adult, my eating and cooking skills were honed over varying degrees of protest from my children, Terry and Jennifer. My existence as a food writer began by accident when an acquaintance, a food writer in New Orleans, published one of my personal letters to him in his newsletter. When I complained that it wasn't intended for publication, he replied, "Write me something I can use, then." So I did.

I eventually became a restaurant critic for the late St. Louis Dining and wrote a cooking column for St. Louis Home. I currently write about shopping, cooking and eating for the Post-Dispatch and St. Louis Magazine. Food also led me to Joe.

When we married in 1994, while Joe still was reviewing restaurants, the most asked question then was, "What's he like to cook for?"

The answer to that brings us to the realm of restaurant cooking versus home cooking. The gap between the two never has been wider. From the least expensive fast-food restaurant to a temple of haute cuisine, restaurant-style food never has been less apt to be seen on a kitchen table. Who do you know that makes French fries at home? Even hamburgers show up only when we're grilling outdoors. The little joints that serve meat loaf and—oh, hallowed hall—real mashed potatoes are practically nonexistent.

Classic French cuisine was put within reach of the home cook by Julia Child and Simca Beck, but momentum quickly moved back to restaurants. By the time Americans had mastered souffles, French nouvelle cuisine had popped up. By now, it has influenced almost every commercial table in the United States above a certain price level. Ingredients are more exotic, and a lot more available in St. Louis now than only a few years ago. Improbable culinary matches occur hourly. ("Just remember," as Fran Lebowitz said, "if you're the very first person to think about combining lime juice and scalloped potatoes—there must be a reason.")

But it's more than just ingredients. In almost every course at today's restaurant, a plate of food involves a number of separate operations. An entree is not just a piece of meat with a vegetable next to it. There may be a marinade, a stuffing and a sauce for the meat, all of which are preparations or cooking jobs of their own. The vegetables are no longer steamed broccoli and a baked potato, but often several kinds to be prepped and cooked. Perhaps they come with a sauce of their own, which means more preparation and cooking.

After all that work, it's still not ready to leave the kitchen. At all but a handful of high-end restaurants, the food must be assembled on the plate. The exceptions, by the way, are part of a wonderful but dying breed where food is finished and brought to serving temperature by the captains working over a burner on a serving cart. Trained chefs put high value on "plating," placing the food and the garnish in a particular way, bringing a visual aesthetic to add to the taste and smell and feel of what we eat.

Garnish and plating are nice, but the competitiveness is getting silly. Deep-fried spaghetti wands towering out of a dish like antennae? And "dust," the confetti of vegetables or mixture of spices that circle the rim of a plate, now looks dated. Vertical food, the style of piling ingredients into a tower, isn't amusing when a diner has to topple the construction to get to the food, and a scallop or a strawberry flies onto the chest of the person across the table.

Home cooking, mostly, isn't like this at all. American home cooking these days is simpler, with fewer courses, lots of prepared or semi-prepared food and not many desserts. One-dish meals are supplemented with packaged salad greens. People who cook from scratch are as apt to recreate the comfort foods they remember from childhood as they are to experiment with the latest in exotic cuisine.

At our house we do some of each. Despite the seeming disparity between Brooklyn and Desloge sharing a table, our tastes are usually quite similar, which makes life a lot easier. We are close to omnivorous. We're both suckers for spicy cuisine, good soup and Wicker's Barbecue Sauce. One of us considers broccoli a burden on society and feels ketchup has a place in the diet; the other eschews green peppers and fenugreek and prefers her burgers with mustard.

Our tastes tend toward big red wines and very dry sparkling wines, with happy excursions into British-style apple and pear ciders. We take our steaks medium-rare, ditto our lamb. One of us is maniacal about hot foods being hot and cold foods being cold; the other allows for things like the wonderful almost room-temperature soups of Italy, but only in specific situations.

When it comes to restaurants, we love the temples of haute cuisine and the little one-of-a-kind places that dish up gumbo and tamales. We haven't found a cuisine yet that we both dislike, although one of us is tepid with Ethiopian and the other cool to Japanese. We make an exception for sushi, which we both enjoy to an indecent degree.

The food on our table at home is exactly what we spoke of before. Sometimes it's meat loaf and baked potatoes, the latter cooked until the outside is chewy-crisp. Other times it's a risotto, a curry or a tuna casserole that combines the best of both worlds—dried Chinese mushrooms and Old Bay seasoning is how. To answer the question: He's a pleasure to cook for because he eats almost anything.

Eating out in St. Louis is, mostly, a delight. We continue to insist it's an underrated restaurant town. It's not in the league of New York or San Francisco or Chicago (which, by the way, is as good for food as it is for theatre). St. Louis doesn't have the distinctive regional cuisine that marks New Orleans or Santa Fe. Nevertheless, you can eat very well here, at prices that make folks on both coasts gasp with delight.

Another crop of restaurants is springing up these days. Restaurant people are coming back to St. Louis because they love the town where they or their partner grew up, and they bring expertise from fine kitchens across the country.

It's an exciting time to be eating out, and the book you hold reflects that, we hope.

But that doesn't answer the question about our favorite restaurant. The answer, which will disappoint some people, is, "It depends." On a given day, do we want lobster or hamburgers, spicy or simple, cozy or coddled? Do we feel like a ride in the car, or just a fast bite? There is no simple answer for us, or for anyone who truly likes to eat. But here, we feel, are our current thoughts on the subject.

Some Basic Thoughts On Visiting a Restaurant

What do we expect when we go to a restaurant? More important, what should you expect? Pollacks' First Law of Eating Out is: **Restaurants set their own standards by the way they price themselves**. It is foolish to judge a small lunch spot by the same criteria used for white-tablecloth temples of cuisine. But if you're eating at the most expensive place in town, it ought to be the best place in town.

Pollacks' Second Law is: **Food should be fun**. This doesn't mean that restaurants ought to be treated like Six Flags. It means that the grim-faced eater trying to determine what's wrong with everything needs to rethink his life. It means that we're in it for pleasure—gastronomic, visual, social—and we hope you are, too.

What about reservations? We're prejudiced in favor of them. It may seem silly to call at six-thirty for a table for two at seven. But if the restaurant turns out to be full to the gills and says, "Sorry—how about eight?" or if an unannounced party of twelve is coming in the door, or if the restaurant is closed for vacation, religious holidays or a broken gas line, you'll be awfully glad you called. A preliminary call saves us hassle several times a year. You will, of course, show up after calling with a reservation. No-shows aren't as much of a problem here as they are in the restaurant meccas, but it's just plain rude, an attitude the world currently sees far too often.

In other cities, Ann has occasionally walked into elegant restaurants (who've told her on the phone they had no tables) and asked politely if she could be fed if she were willing to wait. This works surprisingly well, but if you try it, be aware the odds are better at a large restaurant.

Speaking of such adventures, restaurants dealing with solo diners sometimes need reminding that it's called the hospitality business for a reason. Interestingly, we're hearing more complaints from men who eat alone than we used to. Women have always run into difficulty at times—twenty years of being single makes Ann particularly conscious of this—but now, as things seem to be improving for them, men are acknowledging getting the cold shoulder, too. Firmness, dignity and charm are what the single diner needs in such situations. If the service persists in being awful, you're quite justified in lessening your tip. And if you're a woman (because of the stereotypes about women being tight-fisted tippers), as you're leaving, ask for the manager and quietly say, "I stiffed my waiter and I want to tell you why."

At any restaurant more elegant than a hamburger joint, people should be greeted when they walk in the door, even if it's just, "Hi, sit where you like and we'll be right with you." By the time you get to the price point of a reservation book and a desk where it rests, greeting becomes mandatory. If no one's there because a party is being shown to its seat, that's understandable. But milling around waiting for several minutes is not conducive to a pleasant evening.

We don't have many hangups about so-called good tables. We've been put in Siberia in other cities (and occasionally this one), and it's no big deal unless it's a quiet night and they seem to be doing it out of spite. You're quite entitled to ask for a table with a view, if there's one available, or one on the terrace. If you're willing to wait for your preferred seating, say so.

Much of the stigma about being seated near the kitchen has disappeared now that restaurant-as-theater is here. We think it's great fun, of course, and have enjoyed the view at places from New Orleans to Honolulu. Much more disagreement occurs over thermal incompatibility, when part of a group finds a restaurant suffocatingly hot and the rest fear frostbite from the gusts of frigid air entering with each arriving diner. Don't expect solutions on this one from either of us; we battle it even at home.

After you're seated and the menus arrive, the specials should be discussed. How many times have you decided on minestrone and the pasta carbonara when the waiter returns and, instead of taking your order, begins to discuss specials—such as an appetizer of roasted peppers and a veal piccata, both of which you happen to love?

When the specials are offered, *prices should be given*. Customers should not have to ask, nor should they be treated as if they are on unlimited budgets. This is far too common in St. Louis these days, and it needs to stop.

Questions about the menu? Feel free. Menus have become so wordy in some places that the old questions like "How are you cooking those ribs?" is superfluous. But customers are entitled to know these things. There's no sense in pretending to be familiar with a cuisine you know nothing about, and even in the tiniest ethnic places, asking, "What are samosas?" is not impolite. Obviously, if you have an intolerance for certain things, you're entitled to know if the food contains them. Waiters must be honest and say, "I don't know, but I'll ask the chef if this contains peanut oil." The kitchen has the same obligation, but the buck stops there, and "We're not sure," is preferable to having to call 911 for anaphylaxis.

And speaking of honesty, the menu has an obligation in that area, too. We're more than a little bothered by finding margarine called butter, frozen fish referred to as fresh, and "home-made" food that never saw the inside of a private residence. If the food is made on premises, "our own" or "house made" is quite acceptable, but don't stretch our credulity any further, given health department regulations. Probably the commonest example right now is "fresh season-able vegetables," a.k.a. "seasonal vegetable medley." Zucchini, yellow squash, broccoli and carrots, the most frequent flyers in this hot air balloon, are available in grocery stores year-round, so don't get us thinking we might actually be getting summer corn and tomatoes in August and fresh peas in the spring.

People who wait on tables have various titles—servers, waitpersons, and so on. We have no personal preference, although we cringe at "Oh, Miss," and turn purple at finger-snapping. There's a fight going on now about who originally came up with the answer to this problem. George Lang, proprietor of Cafe des Artistes in New York, and Joe Baum, who helped open the Four Seasons, are each claiming credit for creating that cliche of restaurantdom, "Hi, my name is Bruce and I'll be your server tonight." This is a battle of the titans in a teapot, and some patrons think they both deserve to suffer for it.

Whatever they're called, the people who serve your food are mostly hard working. They all are underpaid because Federal minimum wage laws don't apply here, and they frequently don't have health coverage. Many work two jobs. It's hard on the feet, it's hard on the back, and the income is erratic. Weekends, and sometimes holidays, are spent working. It's a rough way to earn a living.

In St. Louis, we don't see the between-engagement actors you find in New York and Los Angeles, so for years, we had a good, if rather floating, pool of talent. Recently, as the number of restaurants has boomed, the dilution of the pool is evident. We hear rumors of a certification program for servers at St. Louis Community College at Forest Park, which could prove to be a significant help.

Servers of whatever gender have an obligation to avoid condescension. This means no veiled sarcasm if the customer mispronounces felafel (emphasis on the second syllable, if you wondered), and no talking down to anyone. At a fine-dining restaurant, we heard a tuxedoed waiter in his thirties repeatedly address a woman in her fifties as "young lady." A couple of friends of ours who are blind are frequently ignored by servers as their companions are asked, "What do they want to eat?" And senior citizens are consistently addressed as "Darling" or some other inappropriately intimate term. Bubble-headed actions like that are apt to severely inhibit tipping. And they should.

The customer's obligation is to be specific about what he or she wants, particularly when it comes to the question of cooking meat. You can and should say things like, "I want it pink inside, but not red." The waiter may reply, "Here at the Beef Barn, we call that medium," but at least you'll know the restaurant's definitions. The same thing applies to how hot you want your spicy food. Very mild is okay; so is our habitual "Somewhere between medium and as hot as it gets." (One waiter grinned and said, " Oh, you mean Indian medium.")

So you have a table, a waiter, and an order working its way through the kitchen. What should you expect now?

Bread baskets have become a lot more interesting in the last few years. There is no crime in using an outside source for the bread. The emergence of small bakers like Companion helped pave the way to bread-awareness in this town. While researching this book, we realized that the local standard has been raised so high that it's now a real disappointment when ho-hum bread appears at a restaurant priced above a certain level.

Soups should arrive hot, just short of mouth-searing, and they should be hot all the way through, not just on the edges. Deep-fried appetizers should have no visible grease, and if they leave none apparent on your fingers or lips, so much the better. Specific utensils aren't absolutely necessary—we can live without oyster forks—but you shouldn't have to ask for a spoon for your soup. Chilled forks for a salad seem sort of pretentious to us unless the alternative is hot from a dishwasher.

For years, Joe has muttered and written about one-fork restaurants, the kind that removes your soiled fork from your appetizer plate and puts it on the table instead of giving you a clean one. Except in the case of the tiny restaurant starting out on a shoestring, this is a stingy gesture. The offense is much worse, however, if the utensil is placed on a bare table or plastic tablecloth rather than on a paper placemat or tablecloth that is replaced after each party. It's simply a question of hygiene.

When it comes to salads, no matter what kind of greens you're served, they should never be brown. Fine restaurants shouldn't be serving iceberg lettuce; indeed, the wider variety of greens in a salad, the better. Carrot shreds are a cliche.

Dressing should be available on the side if requested. St. Louis has two regrettable tendencies regarding salad. One is overdressing, leaving a heavy coating rather than just a glaze. Puddles in the bottom of the plate, whether water (greens should be dry) or dressing, show carelessness. The other is the tendency to put sugar in house salad dressings. We're not sure where this began, but it seems like something designed to get kids to eat their rabbit food. Sugar has a place in some salads—slaw, German potato salad, that sort of thing—but not on lettuce.

When the main courses arrive, there should be no "Who gets the trout?" routine. However, if it's a very large group or a great deal of ordering irregularly, some confusion isn't the end of the world. After a few bites of your meal, the server should return and ask if everything is satisfactory. This saves craning your neck when you discover the duck is burnt or you need a salt shaker.

And speaking of salt shakers, please taste your food before you add salt and pepper. A few restaurants, mostly high-end, don't put them on the table. St. Louis restaurants that follow that practice will bring them if requested, unlike Charlie Trotter's in Chicago, which refuses to bring them to patrons, insisting that the food doesn't need it. Not the sort of place we care to patronize, we'd add.

When do you send food back? When it's over- or under-cooked despite your specific instructions, or when it's spoiled, not when you just don't care for it. If a waiter notices you're not eating, you confess you just don't care for it; if offered something else, then you may accept.

If something is truly awful, sitting back with your hands in your lap and with a stricken look on your face does quite nicely at all but the most casual of restaurants.

When the main course is done and the table is cleared, a process that shouldn't begin until everyone is finished, it's really much nicer to hear, "May I tell you about our desserts?" than "Can I get you anything else?" The latter sounds much more like you're being hurried along. Coffee is sometimes not offered until after dessert, but it's quite acceptable to ask for it alongside. And feel free to hear about desserts, or inspect a dessert tray and decline after all.

Checks shouldn't come until summoned. Certainly, the harassed waitress at a hash house has other things to worry about and so do we. There's a lot less leeway, however, in an elegant bistro when it's a quiet night hours away from closing. Then an unrequested check is very clearly the bum's rush.

Splitting the check? Many places, bless them, will take two credit cards and divide the balance. You ought to have some rough idea of how much you owe for your share if you're paying in cash.

About tipping: Pollacks' Third Law says **Bad food is not the waiter's fault**. You can't penalize a waiter financially if the chef thinks pasta can stay on a steam table for a day and a half. Fifteen percent is the minimum, unless you had an experience that you can use to liven up a dinner party. If you tied up the table a long time with a small check and it's busy, tip more. If they've put aside the last serving of your favorite mocha cake in case you want it, tip more. If your dinner companion accepted your proposal—or your proposition—tip more. Be kind. It makes you a better person.

Good Morning...Or Is It?
Breakfast & Brunch Restaurants

Chris' Pancake and Dining, 5980 Southwest Avenue, 645-2088
Delmonico Diner, 4909 Delmar Boulevard, 361-0973
Goody-Goody, 5900 Natural Bridge, 383-3333
Kopperman's, 386 North Euclid Avenue, 361-0100
Majestic Restaurant, 4900 Laclede Avenue, 361-2011
Museum Cafe, St. Louis Art Museum, Forest Park 721-5325
Obie's of Soulard, 728 Lafayette Street, 231-2401
Parkmoor, 6737 Clayton Road, Clayton, 863-2430
Pumpernickle's, 11035 Olive Street Road, Creve Coeur, 567-4496
South City Diner, 3141 South Grand Boulevard, 772-6100
Uncle Bill's Pancake and Dinner House, 3427 South Kingshighway, 832-1973; 4000 Lemay Ferry Road, Mehlville, 845-0660; 4196 Manchester, 394-1416

Whatever happened to the Great American Breakfast? Are children going to grow up thinking that waffles come out of the freezer and orange juice from McDonald's?

We know. Life is busier.

But it's more than that, as far as restaurants are concerned. Certainly, restaurants have prospered because of our busy lives. People eat out more frequently. In the restaurant business, however, breakfast is a whole different kettle of kippers. It requires a group of people willing to get up early, and restaurant folks tend to be night owls. It's a completely different menu, calling for items that use capital and storage space but that are only able to produce revenue for about three hours a day. A breakfast kitchen needs fry cooks, which is an area of expertise not even taught at the Culinary Institute of America and its kin.

One would think that here in the Midwest, with its tradition of hearty farm breakfasts, we'd have lots of good places. It isn't true. You have to seek them out, unlike California and New York. Breakfast is practically a religion in California. And in New York, we're not just talking bagels here, bubbie. Salami and eggs ... caviar omelets ... apple pancakes so big they flop over the side of the plate. Things like that.

Too many places still have sour coffee. Nobody squeezes orange juice to order. We can't count the number of places that use frozen hash browns. The menus are, for the most part, achingly boring. It's a real drag.

Despite how depressing things *sound*, we have to say we've been pleasantly surprised by the number of places we've found doing good and interesting breakfasts.

You know you're getting old when the album you trembled for as a teenager is part of a nostalgia-themed decor. That doesn't keep us from enjoying breakfast at the **South City Diner**. This is, as far as we know, the only place in town that serves a meat loaf omelet, to the gurgling delight of the senior partner, Mister Meat Loaf. Huevos rancheros, eggs smothered in salsa with refried beans and tortillas, are pretty good, too, and so is the hangtown omelet with oysters, bacon and cheddar cheese.

Maybe the best thing, though, is the country fried steak. It's The Real Thing, not the extruded semi-plastic stuff, with a crunchy exterior, slightly chewy meat, and the right dose of black pepper. The breakfast comes with milk gravy (no resemblance to library paste here), eggs, toast and mashed potatoes. Yes, mashed potatoes for breakfast. Oh, yeah, as Kramer would have said appreciatively, these are *fine* in this combo, amazingly fine. Actually, SCD's breakfast potatoes are deep-fried chunks, and are about the only part of the breakfast that doesn't quite make it for us.

The **Majestic** is St. Louis' equivalent to the classic Greek-American diner. They offer omelets on that axis, with feta cheese, spinach and such. They also have gyro meat as a breakfast meat. It's the only place we've seen offering brains and eggs for breakfast. Potatoes are real potatoes, new spuds thinly sliced and pan-fried. The bacon servings are generous and the pancakes, which at one time seemed to contain wallpaper paste, are vastly improved. The silver dollar blues—great name—are very thick but tender and homey-looking. The coffee is diner coffee, but on the whole the Majestic comes out a winner.

Menus that get cute are an early warning sign that the food leaves something to be desired. **Pumpernickle's** is the exception that proves the rule. Breakfast is served all day on the weekends, until 10:30 Tuesday through Friday mornings, with food that makes you makes you want to stand up and shout *Oy!* Salami and eggs comes both as a scramble or as an omelet. The omelet is immense, five or six eggs, browned but not too much, and the chunks of salami folded inside it are small but numerous and dense, a fairly fine grind that's moist without seeming fatty. Alan King once wrote a book called, Is *Salami and Eggs Better Than Sex?* The point is well made; the combination is truly magnificent.

There's matzoh brei, the egg scramble with matzoh in it, an eastern European version of migas. French toast is made with thick slices of challah and the syrup has a little spice in it. There are latkes as well as hash browns. The hash browns are standard frozen ones, crisped within an inch of their lives. The latkes, potato pancakes for those who haven't been introduced, are even crisper, made of shredded potato with a lot of onion. (Extra points for that, we say.) They come with both applesauce and sour cream, so you don't have to choose, and are available as a side dish, as well as a main course. The same goes for the blintzes, the thin crepes with cheese filling. These have cottage cheese, but the cheesecake-like taste is right there. Other fillings, like fruit, are also offered.

Lots of smoked fish, sable and lox and whitefish, and whitefish salad, one of the delicacies that gave delicatessens their name, is available, too. Weak coffee, another delicatessen tradition, but zippy service.

The good news at **Chris' Pancake and Dining** is that salsiccia and chicken-fried steak are listed as breakfast meats. There is a sunny glassed-in porch area, and people eating breakfast at 11 a.m. is a good sign. The bad news is that the potatoes are diced and deep-fried, and the chicken-fried steak seems to be pre-formed out of chopped beef and soy protein. The breading is crispy and the patty well-drained, but it lacks the resistance to the tooth that CFS classically offers. There are buckwheat pancakes under the heart-healthy menu. (We don't know if this means less fat or just more fiber.) They're tangy and tender but the syrup fails abysmally, with fake maple flavoring and not even the basic comfort of sugar. How can you have an unsweet syrup? The gravy with the CFS was milk gravy, but of such gloss and smoothness that we suspect something other than flour for a thickener. It was tasty, though; one of the best we've had. Coffee, too, was good, fresh and not sour.

Goody-Goody, which is celebrating fifty years of feeding folks, is a family spot. Breakfast, every morning but Sunday and all day Wednesday and Saturday, features a wide variety of traditional foods with a clearly Southern influence. Fish croquettes, grits or rice, biscuits, all make you expect to hear waitresses address customers as "y'all." The fish croquette is well-seasoned and pan-fried to a soft crunch. Potatoes are home fries with onions and six additional spices.

Homemade bread for toast, thick slices of ham sliced from the bone, tender pancakes with lots of butter and decent syrup all fly past to fill up the crowds. Saturday brings lots of families and lots of folks who know each other and the staff. This sparkling-clean joint in northwest St. Louis makes you believe the answer to St. Louis' racial problems may be reached with good food.

The **Parkmoor's** Sixties Redux interior always charms us. Their blueberry pancakes do so, too, huge, slightly misshapen, tender babes that go with good syrup (and margarine, we think) and very good bacon. Diner coffee, as always, but on the other hand, the people-watching and the eavesdropping are great.

No breakfast discussion about St. Louis would be complete without including **Uncle Bill's**. Neither of us has been really crazy about it, feeling like it was pretty much a cliche. We went back in the spirit of scientific investigation, and were pleasantly surprised. The coffee-pot elves had been at work scrubbing, and the coffee was some of the better we've had at restaurants like this. Bacon was thick, crisp and quite lean; eggs are, as usual, mostly very competently handled. (Softly-scrambled is always a battle, of course, here as elsewhere.) Pecan pancakes are good, but immense, four huge irregular discs sprawled over the edges of the plate. Order them as a short stack unless you're a lumberjack heading out for work. (We've always meant to ask about the difference in the tropical syrup in the Panama banana pancakes and the Hawaiian syrup in pancakes Hawaii—we did research on this topic at Eggs 'n' Things in Honolulu.) A person could do a lot worse around here, especially if you're into 4 a.m. sociological research.

Kopperman's has more tables than ever, both inside and outside. On a pleasant morning, watching the passersby on Euclid is an entertainment bonus. (Pay particular attention to some of the parking maneuvers you see.) Pretty good coffee, although not terribly strong, starts you off. The menu promises freshly squeezed orange juice, and it is, although the machine uses the whole orange, so the result is more like frozen concentrate than that from juicers that ream out just the inside.

This is a large menu, lacking only pancakes to make it complete, from smoked fish to croissants. There is, however, French toast made from French bread. Salami and eggs were a scramble, not overcooked and with lots of still-moist salami, very good indeed. The corned beef hash is house-made from kosher corned beef, more meat than potato, with fresh parsley and onion bits, very different from canned hash, but tasty, especially when the bite includes some potato. Eggs over easy were respectfully cooked, an essential attitude when dealing with eggs.

Kopperman's deep-fries its latkes. They drew mixed reviews. Joe thought they were good, Ann thought they were gummy and lacked potato taste. Applesauce is $1.95 for a small side dish of the house-made product, dark with cinnamon and smooth and very sweet. We squeezed in a little lemon juice to punch it up, but at that price, it shouldn't need help. Speaking of additional charges, cream cheese was a good-sized wedge, an extra seventy-five cents but worth it, compared to the prepackaged squirts you receive at some other places. The low-fat version was one of the best we've found.

If breakfasters want some wine, Kopperman's will uncork any bottle they sell on their wine racks for $3 over the retail price, a considerable saving over most dining-spot markups. Champagne, my dear?

"Oh, my," Ann kept murmuring at the **Delmonico Diner**. This is serious African-American (or Southern) breakfast stuff. A steam table with what was said *not* to be country ham … but it sure looked like it. Salmon croquettes, smooth inside, crisp outside, and with a little spiciness. Thick, potato-chip crisp bacon. Fried bologna, for heaven's sake. Big link sausages cut in quadrants the long way. Rice. Grits. Stewed apples with cinnamon. Biscuits. The best breakfast potatoes we've found, cooked with salt and pepper and plenty of onions, soft and not real, pretty but so good with over-easy eggs you want to stand up and testify. There's some pie and bread pudding around, too, in case desserts strikes your fancy.

The big, slightly cavernous room is cozied up with dining room tables that look like they came from someone's home and lots of pictures and photos. Gentlemen at a window table conduct a Bible lesson while toward the back, another group hums over the neighborhood news. Business people enter to get takeouts for meals at their desks. Oh, my, indeed—this was a good one.

And a few words about brunch....

We've written before that this is a heavy-brunching town. We write about the brunches at the Adams Mark, Balaban's, the Bristol, Harry's, Oh, My Darlin' and the Ritz-Carlton in the entries for those places. We also visited a couple of places just for their brunch.

Several restaurants close to Soulard Market are offering Saturday brunch. At **Obie's**, which faces it on the south, we were greeted promptly with reasonably good coffee, declining their offering of bloodies and mimosas. After 11 a.m. they add lunch offerings, too, but we wanted morning food. A Denver (known elsewhere as a Western) omelet came properly cooked and generously stuffed. The Monte Cristo, a sandwich rather unknown in St. Louis but basically a French-toasted ham-and-cheese sandwich, came with the oddball traditional side of something sweet, in this case currant jelly (another relative stranger on St. Louis' tables and we're missing something; it's nice and tart) and maple syrup. The jelly was just the ticket, curiously pleasing.

Agonizing over whether to try potatoes and onions as one of the three potato choices, we went with the southwestern au gratin potatoes, long slices of Yukon golds layered with cheese and peppers, and particularly tasty they were. Not everyone can tolerate that sort of a jolt in the morning, but the senior partner loves it, and he was beaming. Biscuits and gravy were fine crumbly biscuits and well-seasoned gravy.

This is a good place to recover from the strain of deciding which stand's strawberries look best.

Maybe the nicest setting for brunch on a rainy Sunday morning is the windowed side of the **Museum Cafe**. There's something about sitting by windows in museums on rainy days that lowers the metabolic rate. The place gets a crowd evenly divided between multigenerational groups and the artsy and would-be-artsy young. It's run by Catering St. Louis, and the help seems well-meaning but poorly organized.

Juice is not included here in the one-price ($12.95) buffet. But the coffee is good when it finally arrives, and the buffet well mixed between safe items kids can eat and interesting things for grownups. Ham is carved to order, and there's a chutney available for it as well as mustard. The sausage, we overheard, is turkey, and looks baked rather than fried. It's not going to fool a farmer, but it's pretty tasty, and probably low in sodium. Potatoes are incredibly bland, but the pepper cheese grits more than make up for that. A corned beef hash is very meaty, but surprisingly sweet. Creamed spinach is extremely flavorful, and so is a rigatoni salad with Asian seasonings. Avoid the couscous, a real snoozer. Biscuits are homemade, and there are a lot of tea breads, muffins and rolls. The dark brown round things are a cross between a beignet and an apple fritter, quite charming.

After we were nearly done, a waitress with a tray of pancakes flew across the room. We hadn't seen or heard anything about pancakes. Neither had the people around us (we eavesdrop a lot in this line of work). Just then, a twosome seated nearby had their drink orders delivered. "And would you like some pancakes?" asked their waitress.

Chalk it up to confusion. But the food's pretty good. And check out the fabulous glass chandelier as you come in.

Almond's

Mostly-modern New Orleans, Southern

8127 Maryland Avenue, Clayton
725-1019
Lunch Tuesday-Friday, Dinner Tuesday-Saturday
Credit cards: All major
Wheelchair access: Satisfactory

Downtown Clayton, within a block or two of the County Courthouse, is the victim—or beneficiary—of a restaurant crush that has threatened to absorb every location in the business community. Almond's, in a small storefront just outside the immediate area, brings updated American Southern cooking in a space small enough that reservations are a necessity.

The site formerly was Twigs, and some of the tree decor remains, but it blends well with the new original art on the walls. The cuisine emphasizes New Orleans, but the adherence to those styles is fairly loose, and includes items like garlicky olive oil for the good bread. The menu arrives on small chalkboards, appetizers on one side, entrees on the other; obviously it's a bill of fare that may change two weeks, or even two days, hence.

Almond's proves itself in something as simple as soup. Mushroom soup was rich and earthy with the taste of several succulent fungi. And speaking of mushrooms, pastry triangles stuffed with them were crisp and flaky, offering fine balance. Crawfish etouffee was mild until a bit of jalapeno pepper came along, but the dish was extremely flavorful and well balanced with the bell pepper, onion and celery that Paul Prudhomme calls "the Holy Trinity" of Cajun cooking.

For main courses, the wonderful fried chicken at the late Redel's has reappeared—Tony Almond brought aboard the cook who masterminded this titan of the table. It's seasoned, breaded and pan-fried, and it isn't like Grandma's, but more like one of Grandma's friends who had a more adventuresome hand with the seasonings. It comes with mashed potatoes that offer a hint of garlic, and some green beans. Alas, these are not Grandma's green beans. They go beyond al dente to tough, particularly disconcerting when the plate deserves country green beans, cooked with ham until they're falling-apart tender. The color on those beans was a lot drabber, but the flavor certainly was much brighter.

New Orleans barbecued shrimp is a descendant of the great stuff they serve at places like Pascal's Manale way down yonder. They're not grilled, but sauteed or roasted in a butter-based sauce with lots of spices, and served in shell, making for messy fingers and a good excuse to use bread to mop up the pan juices with the taste of shrimp, butter, pepper and beyond. We like Almond's version, which isn't as tongue-tingling hot as some, but one of our shrimp was quite rubbery and several others were considering the Michelin plant as a bunkhouse. A gumbo was available, and there are always several fish on the menu.

The wine list is interesting and modestly priced, with several bottles under $20, and good by-the-glass choices. Dinner is in the $25 range, and service is solicitous, both for first-timers and the large crowd of regulars whose comings and goings are given a great deal of happy notice—just like at Grandma's.

Al's
Steaks and Chops
1200 North First Street
421-6399
Dinner Monday-Saturday
Credit cards: AE, MC, V
Wheelchair access: Satisfactory

Years ago, before task forces and committees told St. Louisans that living downtown was a good thing, people really *did* live downtown. As a small boy, Al Baroni lived with his family at First and Biddle Streets, over the family restaurant.

"Mostly Sicilians," Baroni recalls. "We lived along Cole Street and Franklin Avenue. It was a neighborhood. The Lombards lived on the Hill, but we had all the things we needed right here."

Al's Restaurant was, and is, one of the great and unsung, old-fashioned steak-and-chop houses, not only in St. Louis but in all of America. For decades, when baseball was only played during the day, and there was no major league baseball west of River City (a situation that held forth until the mid-1950s), Al's was a popular stop for athletes, sports writers and umpires. Yes, even umpires, who often ate here after the game or on their way to Union Station on getaway day.

In the 1960s, when the Football Cardinals were here, New York writers often congregated at Al's on Saturday nights. And somewhere along the line, someone dreamed up a cross-country, all-NFL dinner. Al's provided the salad.

Al's is famous for its meat and for having no menus. It's a steak house straight out of, say, the Johnson administration, with lots of protein and people drinking "bourbon and branch" in big, comfy chairs. Limousines are parked outside, while businessmen entertain out-of-town clients inside. Male customers are required to wear jackets, another touch of tradition. Prices are traditional, too, ranging upward from $30, and the wine list will take it higher. All this in an industrial neighborhood a few blocks north of a downtown area that some p.r. star named Laclede's Landing.

Italian bread sticks are arranged in flower frogs on each table, but the bread is much better, especially covered with a flavorful feta cheese spread that also includes some nuts and a few herbs. The stuff is addictive; good ballast for drinking, but apt to fill a person up. Self-discipline is important.

The waiter recites a long list of first course possibilities. Variations of shrimp—from cocktail through de jonghe—with many stops in between, including scallops, smoked salmon, oysters in season and chicken livers wrapped in bacon. Prosciutto and melon involves thin slices of perfectly ripe cantaloupe, nuggets of strawberry for garnish, slices of pink ham and a half lime. Lime is great on cantaloupe, and it does marvelous things to the strawberries, too. The ham is smoked, very moist, without the deep taste that one associates with prosciutto, which is cured. Still, it was so good, all was forgiven. Flash-fried soft shell crabs come with a lemon butter garlic sauce to be added at will. The crabs were lightly battered and ungreasy, but could have had a little more flavor.

Now the serious floor show begins. A large tray of raw materials arrives (a teaching tool, as well as a menu). Strip steak, big filet mignon, slightly smaller filet. Provimi veal, veal scallopine. A rack of lamb. Norwegian salmon, sushi-grade tuna, swordfish, all thickly cut. Dover sole and a lobster tail the size of a submarine sandwich. At previous dinners here, we've seen quail, pheasant, chicken, duck, other fish and game.

Each item and the methods of preparing it are discussed. Diners who might want the sauce from the salmon on the veal chop, for example, are encouraged to speak up. It's a time to ask questions, because this staff has the answers. In fact, customers must participate, because without some sort of dialogue, it's impossible for waiters to help diners decide what they want.

After the entree is chosen, and the method of cooking and the sauce are determined, come the decisions among three salads, some alternatives and a wide array of side dishes. Al's has all sorts of green vegetables—plain, in combination and with variations. Potatoes, of course, in usual and not-so-usual methods, such as Italian fried. Superb onion rings, the only ones we've seen arrive on a doily. (This is the reason for discipline earlier.)

Al's salads are immense, with an excellent variety of greens, all bite-sized, accompanied by a giant green olive, an Italian pickled pepper, a monster shrimp with a little Russian dressing draped around it like a veil, and a couple of chunks of tomato. The tomatoes had the unique ability to taste good even though they didn't look quite ripe. Maybe the Italians have something—the big, fat red-ripe babes that we love in mid-summer, they find fit only for sauce. Tomatoes for salad still have a little green on the top, and are firmer and more tart than what Americans prefer. The house dressing is an Italian vinaigrette, lightly seasoned and with a lower ratio of oil to vinegar than some. Joe considers the dressing about perfect; Ann realizes she's moving toward preferring it a little less tart.

Exercising options, we tried the sirloin strip as a pepper steak, rolled in peppercorns before broiling. Exquisitely trimmed and flavorful, it was just as seriously rare as had been requested. Salmon was broiled, cooked through but not a second longer (no question about degree of rareness), and covered with a buttery hollandaise more French than Creole in ancestry. Luxuriously rich, it was a great pairing. The onion rings are huge, flaky monsters crispy-tender and perfectly drained. Blue ribbon winners. Grilled eggplant came in thin slabs cut vertically, very moist and seasoned with olive oil and a little garlic. The main flavor was that of the eggplant, tender and quite charming.

Desserts are considerably less complicated: berries, strawberry shortcake, cheesecake, chocolate cake, ice cream, although the lemon ice is more like a sherbet, the texture is reminiscent of a real Italian gelato.

Andria's
Steaks and Chops
6805 Old Collinsville Road, O Fallon, Ill.
(I-64 east to exit 12, north on Illinois 159, right at Salem Drive (first stoplight),
to Old Collinsville Rd. (4-way stop), then left. The restaurant is just across
railroad tracks on the right)
(618) 632-4866
Dinner Monday-Saturday
Credit cards: All major
Wheelchair access: Passable

If we had guests coming in from, say, California or New York, people who needed a proper introduction to our great Midwestern red meat, this is probably where we'd take them. They might look down their noses at driving by a collection of mobile homes or the pleasant, rather simple dining room located well within earshot of the Illinois Central's finest. But they'd jerk to attention with the first bite of their entree.

Andria's is a steak house in the great tradition, a simple menu with mostly classic items, competent servers who know their jobs well, and guests who are there for Real Food and willing to spend above $25 a person to get it. Knowing a salad and side dish come with the entree and, suspecting their sizes, we split a small cup of marriage soup, chicken broth with pasta pearls, small meat balls and spinach. Tasty, but not earthshaking.

Salads come with a sweet and sour house dressing, or other standards. St. Louis diners seem to be facing a growth of sweet-toned dressings to join the several-years-old trend of creamy ones. Too often, a basic vinegar-and-oil dressing becomes the diner's responsibility. The huge salad plate holds mostly iceberg lettuce, with some romaine and a little spinach. Adding to that were a small pepperoncini, croutons, a few elderly raw mushrooms whose flavor had disappeared, some red onion and a pair of olives—one, unfortunately, a tasteless black monster from California.

The wine list doesn't list vintages, and the house was out of one of its two red zinfandels. With a few exceptions, the list covers mid-range, mid-price Californians; the house wine, from Round Hill, was eminently agreeable.

The large sirloin strip sprawled alluringly on one plate, nuzzling some steak fries and a spiced crabapple. On the other plate, a pork chop almost three inches thick was poised and waiting. Its partner was an immense Idaho baker, probably weighing a pound. The waitress expertly pinched it open, ripping its cocoon of brown wrapping paper. The white flesh poured steam like an old engine on the nearby track

The steak itself was succulent, thick, tender and juicy, cooked as requested and not a blink longer. The outside was brushed with the house's sauce, which makes a brief, delightful appearance in your mouth, then bows out to let the steak do its magic.

The junior partner in this book is unashamedly a pig lover. Pork may not be fashionable, but when done right, it's one of the great pleasures of the table. Hog farmers, to your swine! Grow more meat! If the greater world gets hold of chops like this little piggy, the demand will skyrocket. The chop was juicy, a hint of smoke, and full of porcine goodness. This is the best pork chop in the area. Admittedly, it will not please those that insist that the meat be gray all the way through. The current professional advice says 140 degrees at the center, and this matched. The meat remains slightly pink inside, so be prepared.

The baked potato, with lots of butter and sour cream on the side, was perfect, and could have been a meal in itself. The steak fries, grainy and slightly greasy, need work.

Dessert, house made, included a strawberry-rhubarb cobbler, which was the kind of cobbler that has a light layer of cake batter poured over it. Nothing against strawberries, but they take up space that could be used for more rhubarb. The cobbler rewarmed nicely, and was tart-sweet. A German chocolate cheesecake was a thin layer of cheesecake, a layer of dark chocolate cake, extremely moist, and the traditional frosting. Pretty good, but not much beats rhubarb.

And ace service from both the waitress and an alert busboy.

For many years, Andria's didn't take reservations; a policy Joe remembers criticizing. That's changed, except for Saturday night. "That's our walk-in night," they say. Walk in and eat well, we say.

Annie Gunn's

Old and New American Cuisine

16806 Chesterfield Airport Road, Chesterfield
532-7684
Lunch and Dinner, Tuesday-Sunday
Credit cards: All major
Wheelchair access: Passable

The first—and worst—thing about Annie Gunn's is that it's practically impossible to get a yen for the food and be eating it before the urge passes, unless the itch hits in mid-afternoon. The restaurant takes reservations for up to half its tables; the rest are doled out on a first-come basis.

And it often seems that everyone within a dozen miles is there every day. When the parking lot invariably fills, people park on the sides of the road and in the driveways. They jam the bar; they've even been seen eating outside on the picnic tables belonging to Annie's next-door sibling, the Smoke House Market. The last time we called for a reservation, the nice lady said the best they could do was "three or four weeks." A drop-by on a Tuesday night around 8 p.m. produced news of a ninety-minute wait.

We like Annie's a lot. But the policy is inhospitable. It also produces a place with hordes at the bar, many of whom are fueled to speak not only without style or taste, but also without volume control.

It's been this way since Thom and Jane Sehnert reopened the restaurant (which was named for Thom's great-grandmother) after the whole world watched a chopper pluck him from its roof during the Great Flood of 1993. Why? Because Sehnert runs a great restaurant. He hires outstanding people, like chef Lou Rook, CIA graduate and serious eater, and a front-of-the-house staff that look cute but are as efficient as IBM. Sehnert serves good food. And he enjoys doing it.

The menu has two kinds of food. One is simple, like hamburgers and ham sandwiches, French fries and apple pie. The other is not so simple. Things like duck breast with a bacon and juniper glaze, venison with fresh figs and eleven (yes, we said eleven) different kinds of potatoes.

The simple food is very good, much of the raw material coming from the market next door. Besides a complete list of sandwiches, which start at $6.25 for smoked ham and go to $8.95 for smoked salmon, there are lots of steaks, chops and fowl among the dinner entrees (between $15 and $23), and accompanied by one or another of Rook's peerless potatoes.

The not-so-simple, however, is sufficient to make the lame not just walk, but run, in the appropriate direction. Duck breast is superb, generous slices of rare meat and a pile of crisper, darker meat and skin, slightly smoky and peppery from the bacon. The nightly specials always include a couple of kinds of fish, perhaps yellowtail tuna with a porcini sauce, and frequently involve game, a challenge Rook meets with style. Venison, for instance, can be sauced any of a number of ways, using anything from dried cranberries to fresh figs. Smoked pork chops are so moist and smoky that they taste more like ham, arriving with what's described as Pennsylvania Dutch barbecue sauce.

First courses are another kind of agony. Potato pancakes? Smoked trout? Grilled chicken salad? Soup? Annie's is a fine soup house. The potato scores as one of the great comfort foods, especially when it's topped with real bacon crumbs and arrives piping hot. A sausage platter has a couple of sausages—not slices of sausage but whole, fat, link sausages like chorizo and salsiccia—a wedge of cheese like Tillamook, some grainy mustard, a small dish of homemade chutney, triangles of buttered toast and house-made pickled beets, asparagus, carrots and a garlic clove. A ploughman's lunch is updated with superb sausage, particularly the chorizo.

This is the sort of place whose green beans are actually haricot verts, and not the kind that were held in a warmer before they were served. Still bright green, they're crunchless and full of the flavor that beans are supposed to have. And why so many potatoes? Sehnert's Irishness is all over the restaurant as it is, and he insists this is just part of it. Three kinds of mashed Yukon golds (plain, garlic and horseradish) are more about the great taste of potatoes than they are about butter and cream. Garlic roast potatoes are crisp and delicious. But the showpiece is the gratin made with Amish blue cheese, so rich it could be a main course. It's a showstopper.

Lou Rook spent a year at The Trellis Restaurant in Williamsburg, Va., with chef Marcel Desaulniers, author of *Death by Chocolate*. It's no surprise that there's a chocolate du jour (maybe a chocolate hazelnut decadence with chocolate cake), and two kinds of chocolate mousse. But if you get that, or the apple pie, or the creme brulee, or the local fruit they've decided is fresh and fit to serve, you'll be missing one of the greatest St. Louis desserts. A four-inch square of bread pudding, sauced with sliced bananas and caramel, slightly crisp at the edges, slightly boozy, and incredibly rich and delicious. It's fabulous.

This is also a spot for vinophiles, with a splendid wine list of interesting wines from all over the world, and there are both good values and high prices that are worth it. Good notes, too, and a by-the-glass list with to up to twenty offerings.

Great place. One of the very best in the city. Too bad customers have to work so hard to eat there.

Anthony's Bar
Classic American Lunch

10 South Broadway
231-7007
Lunch Monday-Friday
Credit cards: All major
Wheelchair access: Good

It only uses a corner of the Equitable Building lobby, but Anthony's Bar, perhaps the classiest little room in the city, is a major lunchtime surprise. Unchanged since it originally opened as the bar for Anthony's Restaurant, it has the same classic style as the Grill Room of the Four Seasons in New York, with beautiful wood, vertical ribbons of light, and the gleam of highly polished crystal.

And service at Anthony's is every bit the equal of that at the New York landmark. Anthony's is a beloved child of Vince Bommarito and his flagship restaurant, Tony's, which is in the same building and where all the food is cooked. While Anthony's is far more casual than its parent, the genetic imprint is right there. There's always a pasta du jour, things like penne with pancetta and spinach in a marinara sauce or ditalini with red clam sauce. The fish of the day is a fixture, too, and there's a very good hamburger, and an even-better turkey sandwich carved from real turkey and heightened with peppered bacon. But maybe the most exciting thing on the menu is the soup.

This has to be the best $2.50 bowl of soup in town. It wouldn't know a can if one fell into the pot. The chicken noodle boasts an incredibly deep and hearty broth, the sort of flavor that comes from a lot of chicken and a lot of time. It only seems simpler than, say, the rich, dark and glorious cream of wild mushroom, because we all think we know chicken soup. One of the unsung glories of Tony's is its soups, and these are the same ones. And if you think it would be a good and money-saving idea to order and pay for the soup at lunch, and ask the staff to serve it when you return for dinner, well, others have tried.

Caesar salad is truly imperial. After good romaine is tossed with a proper Caesar dressing and freshly grated Parmigiana cheese, it's tossed one last time with a generous measure of tuna packed in olive oil. It's not a classic Caesar, but it's wonderful, and a furlong or two ahead of the grilled chicken ones.

The small lunch menu also includes hamburgers, fat guys with excellent beef. Our only complaint is that they lack the crispness of a classic flat-grilled burger. Sauteed onions are available, and they're a fine idea. Lunch dishes are about $6-$7, and many eat at the bar. Otherwise, potential diners have to wait in the lobby, but it's well worth it.

Arcelia's
Mexican Cuisine
2001 Park Avenue
231-9200
Lunch and Dinner, every day; Breakfast Saturday and Sunday
Credit cards: All major
Wheelchair access: Passable only to smoking area

We say with utter assurance that this is the only Mexican restaurant in the state that has a copy of *The Economist* hanging around. How the staid British magazine landed here we leave to more fertile imaginations. The customers are a mixed bag; blue-collar types, but looking around we also saw three generations of guys en route to a ball game, some nuns, and a group of after-work suits with loosened ties drinking from long-neck beer bottles. (We'll pin it on one of them if no one confesses.)

Arcelia's move from its former digs in lower Soulard has increased both seating capacity and popularity; the place is often jumping, especially on weekends. The decor in the lower back room with its white-trimmed paned windows goes beyond the sombrero cliches to some interesting Aztec murals on one wall.

Starters at Arcelia's have to include the guacamole, simple and creamy with flavorful chunks of avocado, tomato and onion. Chips are fresh and hot, and the salsa is fiery, heavy on garlic and pepper, but lacking fresh tomato. Another favorite appetizer—queso fundido, melted cheese with chorizo—is a happy, flavorful exception to our usual dark mutters about too much cheese on everything in town.

In addition, they feature two of our favorite soups, menudo and pozole ($4.25 and $4.75, respectively). Menudo is made from tripe, with a deep, rich broth full of Mexican oregano, brought to its peak with a squeeze of fresh lemon, and a handful of chopped onion thrown in if desired. Arcelia's serves theirs with or without hominy, a tad unusual. We—mainly the junior partner, the primary tripe lover—take ours with, thanks. Pozole is a similar broth, although not quite so rich as that from tripe, made with pork and cumin and oregano, and here sprinkled at your will with chopped cabbage as well as the onion. Good stuff, perfect for a dreary winter night. Or for a bleary Sunday morning—menudo is a traditional cure for a night's overindulgence.

There are make-your-own combination platters of any size you wish ($4.95 to $9.95) of tostadas, flautas, enchiladas, burritos, soft or hard tacos or tamales. You have your choice on most items of wheat or corn tortillas, and beef or chicken filling, although the tamales have a chopped pork filling, and a lovely corn flavor. The beef is ground, but well-seasoned. It's the chicken that charms, succulent and winning, truly finger-licking as the juice rolls out of the taco. Refried beans seem a tad tastier than most and the rice is ditto, not the dry, hard stuff that too often shows its face.

For the knife and fork set, there are a number of interesting entrees, some of which are familiar, like albondigas, or meatballs that come in a broth or with gravy ($7.25), and chicken mole ($6.95), and some of which are less common, like potato enchiladas ($6.95) or shrimp empanadas ($5.50). We tried a chile verde, a pork stew with tomatillos and green chiles in the gravy. The meat was very tender and the gravy tingly but not fiery, a nice piece of work. In a splendid moment, we noticed the tortillas, too. They were so fresh they smelled—well, wonderful—a happy smell rather like fresh-baked bread.

Dessert was a bunuelo ($3.25), flat rather than oblong, fried to crispy-chewy, sprinkled with cinnamon sugar, and served with ice cream, and some flan ($2.25), the latter as dense and firm as can be imagined, almost like a piece of candy. The caramel flavor was wonderful, sort of like eating a perfectly toasted marshmallow with a spoon.

Weekend breakfast involves chorizo and eggs, or chilaquiles, eggs scrambled with crispy bits of tortillas. Service is amiable and fairly quick. There are a few wines, but Arcelia's is for drinking beer or margaritas, which are nicely tangy, and far more flavorful than the kind pumped from a vat in the basement.

Babalu's
Sing a Spicy Calypso Song
8 1/2 South Euclid Avenue
367-7833
Lunch and Dinner Tuesday-Saturday; Dinner Thursday-Saturday
Credit cards: All major
Wheelchair access: Comfortable

For those old enough to remember Desi Arnaz, the name here is self-explanatory. For the others, well, Babalu was the name of a song, part of the Caribbean music he sang, predating Harry Belafonte and Top-40 calypso records. Arnaz was Cuban, but Babalu, the restaurant, is pan-Caribbean with hints of Brazil and Africa. The menu says Babalu is a spirit in the Santeria religion. It was news to us, but the story is relevant enough to be believable, and the restaurant is good enough that we'll believe almost any story, as long as they feed us.

The first hint of many good times ahead was that the pepper shakers contain red pepper, though a rather mild one. Specials of the day include a soup (mixed seafood with tomato, hard to pass up), an empanada (sweet potato, which sold out before we could order), and lemonade. Lemonade du jour? Indeed, and we sampled pineapple-guava. It was opaque, sweet-sour, fairly strong, quite good.

First courses are the expected—jerked pork skewers and chicken wings—and the unexpected—mussels steamed in chili, garlic, ginger and cilantro, and guacamole. The latter was a happy surprise, served with tostones, long ribbons of deep-fried plantain, the banana relative that's a staple starch in tropical New World cuisine. The tostones were crunchy, but without much flavor. The guacamole more than made up for it, though. Very chunky, with lime and green and red onions, a little tomato, some roasted garlic, and maybe just a little pinch of curry powder. It was an eminently successful combination, and very different from what most Mexican restaurants offer.

Shrimp and potato croquettes were accompanied by a cool curry sauce and some ginger puree, which made them even spicier. They weren't fiery hot, but an interesting demonstration of a different way to use curry. Black bean salad, a dab on the plate, displayed orange and cilantro, another surprise to the mouth that worked extremely well.

The traditional Cuban sandwich of ham, pork, Swiss cheese and dill pickles, press-grilled on a French roll, was rich and delicious. The pickles add a little sharpness to the mellow, slightly garlicky meats, and the press makes the roll crisp as a baguette, warm and tasty. Chicken is marinated in cumin and citrus, and with a mango mustard it becomes a sandwich. And it's always difficult to pass up a ropa vieja sandwich, the classic Cuban pot roast.

Another swell taste came from a grilled portobello mushroom topped with roasted green chiles and goat cheese, all tucked into a bun. The contents are so moist that they surreptitiously slide out during the eating, but the mess is worth it, with the mellow taste of the mushroom, the creamy cheese and the pleasant sharpness of the chiles. Both come with haystack fries, very long, very thin, and very crisp, seasoned slightly in the kitchen and mounded up very much like their namesake.

Dessert was a real serendipity. Someone at Babalu's had baked that morning, and the ginger cheesecake tart was not still warm, but you could tell it had been a half hour earlier. The crust was crisp, the filling rather pungent from the fresh ginger, and yet not overly rich.

This is a fine place for the eater who likes to explore the horizons, and a $12 horizon isn't far.

Balaban's
(Cafe Balaban, Balaban's Bistro 201)
New American

Cafe: 405 North Euclid Avenue, 361-8085
Bistro: 930 Kehrs Mill Road (south of Clayton Road), Ballwin, 391-9393.
Cafe: Lunch and Dinner, Tuesday-Saturday; Brunch on Sunday
Bistro: Dinner Tuesday-Saturday
Credit cards: All major
Wheelchair access: Passable

Balaban's is on its way to becoming a grand old St. Louis tradition. After all, Herb and Adalaide Balaban-Karp opened the original in 1972 and it became a stellar member of the class. It has survived evolution of ownership, neighborhood and, to a lesser degree, cuisine, and has become a consistently reliable, if sometimes noisy, source of pleasure to the community. Prices are high, with dinner about $30 per person without drinks, but it usually is a solid value.

The locations—in the Central West End and, more recently, in West County—are not identical, nor are the menus, but it's obvious they're siblings. Decor in the Central West End is traditional, the brick walls hung with immense train station-sized posters, often in French, some paying homage to St. Louis-born Josephine Baker. Similar, slightly smaller posters adorn the wall of the western outpost, located in an old dairy facility known as the Barn at Lucerne. The barn, if you stretch it a little, might have been in Normandy. (Why the interior designers chose to go contemporary in such a setting is beyond quick logic.)

If St. Louis lacks a first-rate seafood house, let the bivalve lover come here for fine oysters. Servers know the pedigree, and don't overhype the product. Pemaquids were described one night as "small, but other than that...." Small they were, and blissfully tasty, essence of ocean the way the best oysters are. The usual serving is with a gingery white vinegar sauce, no oil at all. It's hard to decide whether to use it or not, the oysters are so good. (The sauce would make a good diet salad dressing.) We also checked out the shrimp cocktail sauce; despite reports of it being seasoned with wasabi, the green horseradish often teamed with sushi, it tasted like a dense, horseradish-laden regular red cocktail sauce, nice enough but too heavy for these delicate oysters.

One of the traditional appetizers at both restaurants is a combination of several dishes, varying by whim of the chef but usually Asian-influenced. On Euclid, it arrives in a bento box containing small containers of each item. In the barn, it's arranged on a small stepladder-like easel, one of the better examples of the current trend to vertical food. The contents are nearly always winners, and a happy answer to folks who want a little of many tastes.

Chilled cucumber bisque has been on the menu from the beginning, like the Beef Wellington, and each deserves its place. There's some dill, and some lemon, and the soup is spectacular—light and rich at the same time, with wonderfully tart backtaste. Beef Wellington, an old-fashioned dish, involves a chunk of tenderloin surrounded by chopped mushrooms, wrapped in pastry dough. It's a splendid, classic dish, with one problem: It's almost impossible to get it rare because of the cooking technique. Many longtime customers won't eat anything else. Another winner is grilled salmon, glazed with a teriyaki-like sauce and carefully cooked.

Daily specials, some of which remain so for nearly a generation, are worth listening to— one night, for instance, they included tenderloin of lamb, duck breast with sour cherries and an individual potato gratin, and fresh sturgeon. Ligurian pasta, which is on both brunch (only at the cafe) and dinner menus, involves dried tomatoes, feta cheese and shrimp, and is another dish that has created long-term fans. Jerk chicken is far from the Third World, but remains spicy and highly reminiscent of its curry ancestors.

The brunch, by the way, can be extremely good, or deserving of returning to the kitchen. It all depends. Crab hash with poached eggs and a lime hollandaise, and lamb sausage with a delicious potato pancake, are now both gone, but knowing this place, may not be in permanent exile. Eggs Madison, with smoked salmon, and classic Benedicts, with Canadian bacon, are outstanding. The potatoes that accompany egg dishes are great, heavy with well-cooked onions and well-seasoned. Our only complaint is that the serving is too small. There are a lot of lunch items on the brunch menu, but there's always a muffin and a waffle of the day, and a frittata, too, but on at least one occasion, it was tough and had some of the smallest pieces of diced ham we'd ever seen. A garnish of honeydew and cantaloupe looked good, but the fruit had no flavor and was tough as a boot.

Dessert? Chocolate fritters lead the list—and probably would lead the city's dessert race, if there were such a thing. Yes. Listen to this: Chocolate truffles are dipped in a batter flavored with Bailey's Irish Cream and flash-fried. They emerge in almost Ping-Pong-ball size, smooth-crusted and brown and filled with melted chocolate. Be careful, it's sometimes hot as molten lava. If there's a must-have dish at Balaban's, this is it. There's also a creme brulee trio. Flavoring brulees is tricky—it's easy to have too much flavor and not enough brulee—but the cafe kitchen pulls it off flawlessly.

Service is generally very professional, though we hear the occasional complaint of cold shoulders to people who describe themselves as unknown to the restaurant or when eating alone at the Central West End location. The wine list is deep and excellent, a credit to Tom Flynn's knowledge, and it's usually fairly priced. A deeper by-the-glass list might add another worthy arrow to the quiver.

Bar Italia

Trattoria Italian

4656 Maryland Avenue
361-7010
Lunch and Dinner, Tuesday-Sunday
Credit cards: All major
Wheelchair access: Passable

It's difficult for us to believe Bar Italia is in its sixteenth year. At first, St. Louisans didn't seem to understand the then-cubbyhole restaurant. Strange salads (beans and tuna), strongly-flavored ice creams (intensely fruity gelato), and even stronger coffee (long before Seattle got wired on espresso) puzzled much of the clientele. No schmaltzy art on the walls, no tuxedoed waiters, not even pizza.... Whatever were the owners, two St. Louisans of Italian descent, thinking of?

They were thinking of Milano decor, food from all over Italy that went far beyond spaghetti, and the leisured tempo of a sunny table on a fine spring day. And somehow, thank goodness, we all caught on.

Now in the hands of Eritrea-born Mengesha Johannes (pronounce the "j" like a "y," in the Spanish style), who bought the place a while back and who, if anything, has lifted the skill level in the kitchen, it continues to please in so many ways. For a leisurely Saturday lunch or an after-movie snack, for un-clichéd pasta and singular desserts, or just for an afternoon of coffee and a book, this is the place to go.

First courses cover a broad range. The mussels are excellent, simply steamed with a little white wine and garlic and served with as much of the crispy-crusted bread as needed to mop up every bit of the juice. (They're also available as a main course.) Foolish to leave even a drop, of course, as good as this is. Caponata, the Sicilian-chilled eggplant salad with olives, capers and raisins, is a lovely savory-sweet dish that brings moans from customers when they've sold out. Like many dishes, caponata is made in as many styles as there are cooks. At Tony's, it's an entirely different dish, and Joe's mom's version is something else again. The calamari salad, with garbanzos or chickpeas and diced potatoes, is very Italian, the sort of cool-but-not-icy thing you'd find on an antipasto cart in Rome. Dressed lightly with lemon and oil, with fresh basil and a little tomato, it's tasty and satisfying.

Bar Italia may do the best green salad in town, winning for simplicity and flavor. It consists of romaine lettuce with a few other mixed leaves, dressed very lightly in oil and vinegar with a little lemon, and brightened by three olives of different types. Very simple, very elegant, well-chilled and tremendously satisfying. Alas, the Tuscan salad of beans and tuna is gone, except as the occasional summer special. Soups vary by the season, but are always reliable. They don't follow the Italian custom of not-very-hot, but if a server offers a pour of olive oil on the thicker soups, try it. Just a dribble provides the right seasoning.

There are more pastas on the menu than in days of yore, but they are delicious, with sauces that, like the salad dressing, never drown what's underneath. Perhaps the best is the penne with various mushrooms and garlic, emerging from the kitchen in an aromatic cloud that makes diners at nearby tables reconsider their orders. Fettuccine with an eggplant sauce is the vegetarian pasta, rich and tangy with tomatoes and olives, topped with fresh ricotta, even better to taste than to see. Risotto, available every Thursday, is at the whim of the kitchen. We marvel at the seafood—tiny bay scallops, big butterflied shrimp and tender calamari in their own juices and a little wine, sprinkled and teased with fresh basil, rosemary and parsley.

Veal scallopine is the only dish topped with cheese, other than a light sprinkling on the pasta. With the veal comes a bell pepper coulis, and the raisins and pine nuts that speak of Sicily. Slices of pork, almost scallopine, are sauteed with shiitake mushrooms and finished in a saffron sauce, indecently rich and yummy.

Fresh fish is available, with cooking depending on what the markets yield. Fat, soft-shell crabs were sauteed with a sauce of sambuca, the licorice-flavored liqueur, for an uncommon combination that worked well.

The wine list is lengthy, with all types of Italian wines, liqueurs, aperitifs, digestifs and the like. We have never been able to understand how Europeans not only drink, but enjoy, an alcoholic beverage like Cynar, made from artichokes. Many grappas, the fiery Italian liqueur distilled from the remains of crushed grapes (called "marc" in France), also are available

Bar Italia's desserts have always been something different. In Italy, of course, pastry and ice cream are snack food. At the end of a meal, most restaurants will serve nothing more than fruit. That authenticity, fortunately for us, has been dropped. The gelati are deeply colored, and taste of fruit rather than sugar.

Pastries are generally far less sweet than their American counterparts. Let us get past the bad part now: There's such a large variety that they have to wait in a refrigerated case, and the pastry gets soggy. Nevertheless, almost everything here is singular. Ann's favorite dessert is, of course, the lemon tart, a custard dense and intense with tart lemon flavor and topped with a narrow wedge of bittersweet chocolate, a fine combination. The new "sexy Jane" mascarpone cheesecake is fluffy rather than dense, with one of the few exciting bottom crusts we've found, and a veil of the bittersweet chocolate over the top, an outstanding version. There's zuccoto, a molded cake-and-cream dessert found in Florence and named for the city's Duomo, called the "zucco," or pumpkin, in slang. (Homesick Florentines are said to suffer from mal de zucco—or dome-sickness). This is pumpkin-shaped, not flavored. A blueberry torta was not too far from an American pie, except that it was only lightly sweetened, bringing the berry flavor forward, and with a little orange rind for contrast.

Good coffee, of course. The service hasn't changed much from when Ann first reviewed it and described it as "leisurely," although it becomes less leisurely on nights when it's jammed. But the overall tempo is very relaxed, just as it would be in Italy, and diners should be prepared to go with the flow. It's worth it, and still worth it even as prices have climbed—gently—through the years to a tab in the $20-$25 range.

Benedetto's
Italian Cuisine
10411 Clayton Road, Frontenac
432-8585
Dinner nightly
Credit cards: All major
Wheelchair access: Satisfactory

Benedetto Buzzetta is a member of a unique St. Louis restaurant club. He's one of a group of men who worked as waiters at Tony's, married sisters, and opened their own restaurants. Benedetto even named his first restaurant The Brother-in-Law's, and a successful operation it was.

In many respects, Benedetto's is an upscale Hill restaurant, picked up and moved to

Frontenac, deep inside Le Chateau Village, where it murmurs and buzzes, and then begins to rumble happily with the sound of people having a good time. Benedetto himself is a smooth, sophisticated host; warm without being overwhelming, helpful but not oppressive.

When diners are settled, the house provides a nice touch, bringing some bread with melted cheese and just a whiff of garlic, nice with a glass of cold white wine while reading and discussing the menu. The dining rooms, several middle-sized areas, are lit by chandeliers and decorated with the paintings that traditionally hang in St. Louis Italian restaurants. The dining room opens onto a terrace of sorts with an iron railing; outdoor dining for the meteorologically disadvantaged as it overlooks the atrium of the shopping center/office building. The facades resemble picturesque shops, but at night the area is very peaceful.

Salad is simple, mixed greens with some olive oil and wine vinegar, and a very light dusting of grated Parmesan. No balsamico, no cords of provel cheese, and much in the classic manner. We approve.

Toasted ravioli is on the appetizer list, but we sampled rigatoni Mediterrranea, choosing salmon (instead of lobster, the other choice) to go with the portobello and fresh tomatoes that sauce the pasta. The pasta was nicely al dente, with the earthy mushrooms pairing with the salmon in lovely fashion to create a rich, mouth-filling taste. This also is a good risotto house; the seafood risotto is one of the best in town, the rice blending perfectly with the seafood and the slight al dente texture a real plus.

We're not sure about the difference between veal involtini, veal spiedini and veal birds. Here, it's called involtini, and subtitled spiedini. The dish involves thin slices of veal layered with flavored bread crumbs, rolled and cooked in one of several ways. The bland-sounding bread crumbs are anything but, soaking up the meat juices and spreading the flavor, which included parsley and cubes of prosciutto. Baked and finished under the broiler, the result was a sort of Italian soul food, a dish an Italian would insist only his mother could prepare to this level of perfection.

Stuffed filet—usually with crabmeat—is a St. Louis tradition that goes back at least to Al Baker's, and Benedetto's version is excellent. The tender, high-quality beef was then sauced with a bit of Cognac, enough to offer a hint of the brandy, but not so much as to interfere with the delicate crab. Just the thing for the protein-deficient, and those in search of a dish to mark a special occasion.

The menu is laden with special-occasion dishes, rich and aromatic—artichokes and mushrooms are a favorite sauce for any meat entree, pasta comes with portobello mushrooms and mascarpone cheese, veal arrives in sherry, mushrooms, capers and bell peppers.

Steamed spinach is a delightful vegetable, and the wine list is lengthy, with good American and Italian entries and prices that are slightly high but not outlandish. Service is smooth and professional without being stiff, a reflection of the host, and dinner (appetizer, entree, dessert) will be about $30 per person.

Best Steak House
Budget Steaks

516 North Grand Boulevard
535-6033
Lunch and Dinner, every day
Cash only
Wheelchair access: Passable

There's no sense pretending the Best is haute cuisine. This is a steak house for working stiffs, a midtown veteran which preceded the large herd of budget steak houses like Ponderosa and Bonanza that populated the area in the late '60s and early '70s. The Best is almost a carbon copy of them, although better lit. With a menu hanging in front of a cafeteria-style line and a busy grill, choices are limited, but dozens of eating places, more pretentious and less of a value, have come and gone (mostly gone) in the Grand-Olive area while the Best has thrived.

Once, the neighborhood was home to the original Garavelli's, one of the best cafeterias of all time. Thompson's 24-hour cafeteria stood here, too, across the alley from the Fox, and served fine ham-and-egg sandwiches to weary newspaper reporters rolling home about 2 a.m.

The Best has steaks, hamburgers, gyros, pork chops and fried okra, cooked to order in what is basically an open kitchen. The steaks come from a whirling dervish of a fry cook who works the grill in a highly professional, expressionless style; an assistant deals with the fryer for potatoes and okra and such, an order for okra evoking a wide grin and a ringing endorsement. The okra was, alas, frozen, but the chunks were battered in cornmeal and were not greasy. They're not the Texas-fried okra we separately learned to appreciate—a little more crunch and a little cayenne, please—but they're not bad, and a perfectly reasonable introduction to the vegetable for okra-wary diners.

The steaks and chops are thin, but a rib-eye dinner for $6, and a porterhouse for twice that, won't guarantee a chunk of beef an inch thick. Still, the meat is tender and flavorful, and not overcooked. Cooking rare is difficult with cuts this thin, so don't expect red. Pink is manageable. The porterhouse was really a porterhouse, not some other cut in masquerade, and two pork chops were juicy. Several sizes of sirloins are available, too, and the Best is a bargain, with dinner $10-$15 per person for real meat.

The baked potatoes, by the way, are good examples of how even the best restaurants ought to be doing them—baked, not steamed, fluffy-creamy inside. They come with a dollop of butter or sour cream, and extra butter is available for a charge. There's also a thick slice of what's come to be known as Texas toast, but the dating crowd can relax because it's not garlic bread. The salad that accompanies dinner was a tired bagged mix, and easily the weakest part of the meal, with a ranch dressing that never saw a dude, much less a real, cowboy.

Desserts, even the baklava, are more of a gesture than anything else. The pastry was cardboard, and a chocolate cake had that no-chocolate flavor of cheap packaged cupcakes. Have a refill of iced tea, walk across the street to the Fox, and afford an orchestra seat with the savings.

Bevo Mill

German and American Cuisine

4749 Gravois
481-2626
Lunch Monday-Saturday, Dinner every day; Brunch on Sunday
Credit cards: All major
Wheelchair access: Satisfactory

Do mothers still point out to small children the huge, revolving arms of Bevo Mill? The building itself is the perfect example of good kitsch—a caricature so far around the curve that it comes back to be exactly what it spoofs. Inside, it's even more charming (surprised as we are to admit it). The large dining room's vaulted ceiling, chandeliers with tiny lamp shades and huge crenelated fireplace make it a showpiece of the good side of German-style baronial interiors, warmth softening grandeur to make it welcoming. The room evokes fantasies of a long table headed by a Jovian character tossing a turkey leg over his shoulder; its being home to multi-generational family groups celebrating birthdays or anniversaries is not difficult. In the entrance hall, look for the small gargoyles, each different, for a very old-St. Louis feeling, too.

The room has old-fashioned, ethnic soul; a patina of age and memories of nearly a century of laughter and joy. August A. Busch Sr., commissioned the building before World War I, and legend has it that he chose the spot because it was almost midway between the Pestalozzi Street brewery and his Grant's Farm residence. Anheuser-Busch still owns the property, and it clearly shows.

For several years, the food service has been provided by the Pat Hanon Group, and the kitchen work is barely satisfactory, even for dinners in the $20-$25 range. As a result, the restaurant bears a resemblance to the Muny Opera, both venerable St. Louis institutions, but neither qualifying for the title: Alone In Its Greatness.

In a place like this, as with almost all American restaurants that are special because of something visual—their view, their architecture—the odds are that the food will be secondary. It's an unhappy truth. When we opened the menu, however, we were pleased to see a good-sized list of German main courses, an area in which St. Louis is in short supply. German wine, too, but the list is undistinguished.

Among the appetizers, the sole German one features two kinds of sausage. One was finely ground pork or veal and rather knockwurst-ish, the other a coarser smoked bratwurst. Sliced into chunks and served in a sauce of grainy mustard and, of course, beer, they resembled fat mushroom caps. Moist and tangy, they were quite satisfactory.

A salad that could be described as miniature was mostly tired iceberg lettuce with some croutons, a shred of red cabbage and a few of carrot, piled high with Thousand Island dressing straight from the bottle. The salad is $1.50 extra with a dinner selection, not vastly expensive until you consider size and ingredients. The soup option gave a choice of the regular house soups, which included French onion, black bean (with mozzarella cheese, another St. Louis touch), and crawfish bisque. The bisque, at $3.50 extra, was thick as milk gravy and a beautiful terra-cotta color. Its taste had the slight bitterness that often shows when the roux or spices have been burned in the preparation. (Not one mudbug tail was in the soup, even as garnish—nothing, in fact, in the entire meal was garnished until dessert arrived.)

There's a generous menu of steaks, chops, veal liver and seafood available, but we went for the German specialties. After some debate, because the menu is full of things we favor (like pork and mushrooms and sour cream, sometimes in the same dish), we passed schnitzels and sauerbraten in favor of beef short ribs and hassenpfeffer.

Yes, that's rabbit, a fine-grained meat that is, indeed, not far from chicken in its taste and leanness. Hassenpfeffer was surely created to cook rabbits and hares that were brought in from a day's hunt; tough, rangy critters with busy lives that built up their muscles and requiring long, moist cooking to get them tender enough to eat. Today's rabbit is, like the hog, bred for lean, tender meat. Because it's so low in fat, it wants quick cooking. Here, two generous pieces came in a brown gravy, rather light on the pfeffer. The rabbit was stringy and tough on the outside; inside, it dissolved on the tongue as though meat tenderizer had been used.

Beef short ribs showed their characteristic flavor. They're a sort of he-man cut, good flavor being the reward for chewiness, fat, and often some gristle, and that's what this was. A rather lumpy gravy showed no evidence of the mushrooms mentioned on the menu. Both the ribs and rabbit had the same side dishes. The star was unquestionably the red cabbage, which was so crunchy it had to have been merely warmed briefly in the sweet, tangy sauce. Was that honey in it? The faint tang of caraway? Is there a little beet juice to continue the vivid Beaujolais-red color? Who knows, but the cabbage is outstanding. A potato pancake was long shreds, soft inside and crunchy or chewy outside, depending on which end you tried. It wasn't a Brooklyn pancake, but it might have come from someone's grandma in, say, Desloge. Definitely home style, complete with lots of black pepper. The mixed carrots and green beans fell completely flat, and the pebble-sized spaetzle might have come from the bank of an Ozark stream.

The server could have been a rookie. In his defense, we hope so. Our salad and soup were pushed aside when the entrees came, the check was offered as soon as the entrees were done, and he appeared completely clueless when he finally displayed the dessert tray.

Several of the desserts are done in-house, including strudel and a chocolate pie that night. We chose a bread pudding, which drew opposing views from us. It was pudding and cream, drenched in bourbon. The pudding itself was extremely dense and heavy, rather dry. Joe loved it; Ann found it low in flavor, except the bourbon and raisins. It's your call.

We hope the Bevo works on its kitchen. We think the service was an aberration. And we really would like to see this lovely old place stop using tacky plastic tablecloths. But where else can you hear background music like the Wedding March from *Lohengrin*, the Poet and Peasant overture, and other strident, tuneful German music that everyone will recognize from grade school ceremonials and old cartoons? And where else can you eat with gargoyles?

Big Chief Dakota Grill

Mainly Macho Meat

17352 Old Manchester Road, Wildwood
458-4383
Lunch and Dinner, Tuesday-Sunday
Credit cards: All major
Wheelchair access: Passable

The Route 66 nostalgia has a touch point in the Big Chief, even though the legendary highway never reached within several states of a Dakota, and the name is solely a reference to the home of a former owner. The motel cabins are gone, but the main building, dating from 1929, is in place, and clearly identifiable without being either disguised or over-enthusiastically restored.

There's some decorating enthusiasm inside, however, with lots of farm implements, old signs, Indian and cowboy mementos, and even an aged, brownish photograph labeled "Waiting for the Hanging."

True to the spirit of the Dakotas, a happy hunting ground for those inclined to the shooting sports, the Big Chief features a lot of exotic game and red meat. Elk and venison, pheasant and alligator make regular appearances on Fridays and Saturdays.

Interestingly, we had not realized how the once-popular frog legs had vanished from local menus. They're at Big Chief as an occasional special, but we have now been alerted to their absence, and we're glad we have all the way to the end of this book to note any others we see.

All week, however, ostrich tenderloin and bison burgers are menu regulars. Entrees are in the $10 to $20 range—including a salad, vegetable and starch—and some pastas, the ubiquitous boneless chicken breast, and shrimp. Mainly, though, this is a meat market, and we're not talking singles' bar. A one-pound pork chop? Salisbury steak made from bison? They're here.

One of the soups du jour was a garlic chicken broth, deeply tan and with a good balance of chicken and garlic. Fresh asparagus was a surprise guest that worked well. It might have been hotter, but it was soothing and flavorful. The house salad was iceberg with a little cheese and red onion. The server, a woman who paid close attention to what was needed, acknowledged that the Caesar dressing was low on anchovies. The house is a Parmesan peppercorn. Fresh, crisp croutons were nicely seasoned and generally perked up a mostly-forgettable dish.

The ostrich tenderloin is served as grilled medallions with a merlot and mushroom sauce ($19.90). Ostrich, of course, is stunningly lean by nature, and becomes Weejuns if it's overcooked. Ordered, and delivered, rare, it was absolutely tender, a mild-flavored meat that was aided by the sauce. Cholesterophobes can rest safely with this one, knowing their mouths and consciences will be satisfied. Not to let the virtue get out of hand, we took the Dakota fries with it, and of their kind, they were pretty good, fresh and crisp from that layer of potato starch they dust on things nowadays but without any other folderol. Three spears of grilled asparagus were properly al dente.

A porterhouse ($19.90) was ordered rare. It was too thin to get pinker than medium, and lacked the richness of really first class beef. Topped with a few mushrooms, some stir-fried onion slivers and lashings of minced garlic, it smelled better than it tasted, and the taste was better than average. The twice-baked potato was laced with chives and a few chunks of real bacon, dusted with something orange and run under a broiler. Not exciting but not offensive, either.

The desserts were cheesecake, carrot cake, something peanut buttered and chocolated, and a Kahlua chocolate mousse. The latter, which turned out to be a pie in a graham cracker crust was, alas, not very chocolate-y, and left the mouth feeling the sweet-nothing that frozen whipped toppings often give.

Some interesting wines are available by the glass or the bottle, and there's a large outdoor area for dining in the few truly good days St. Louis gets. However, the last couple of miles to Big Chief make for a nice, leafy ride that will be especially nice in the autumn. But hurry before the golf courses take over.

Big Sky Cafe

New American Cuisine

47 South Old Orchard Avenue, Webster Groves
962-5757
Dinner every night
Credit cards: All major
Wheelchair access: Difficult

Another sibling in the family that includes Remy's and the Blue Water Grill, Big Sky is a likable and popular restaurant, even more crowded on the nights when theater or opera is cooking at the Loretto-Hilton Center a few blocks away. Reservations always are a good idea; the alternative can be a lengthy wait.

It's an amusing place to wait, however, even though space can be cramped. The decor, with a variety of quotations inscribed on the walls, provides something to read and to talk about. The welcome is warm at all times, and they're honest about estimating waiting times.

The themes in Tim Mallett's restaurants are always loosely interpreted, the better to give his talented cooks room to play. The Big Sky is centered, more or less, on Western home cooking, with a fulcrum of mashed potatoes and gravy, both happily, heavily garlicked.

The presence of something like potatoes and gravy shouldn't mislead anyone; this is a thoroughly contemporary restaurant. Like Remy's and Blue Water, there are "small plates," both hot and cold, that run $3-$7. While they're designed mostly as an appetizer for two or three persons to nibble on, their use is limited only by diners' imaginations. "Large ovals," about $8-$17, offer more traditional entrees. The bread basket is a particular pleasure, especially the tangy cornbread, although the flavored butters sometimes clash with the breads.

Over the years, Blue Sky has built an admirable record, so a lackluster performance comes as a surprise. At a restaurant that usually provides strong flavors, it's surprising that the Caesar salad dressing seemed completely free of anchovies. The greens are crisp and fresh, but the salad section of the menu was anything but Caesarian. The popular tomato and onion salad sparkles with cucumber and Gorgonzola in the Big Sky version, and is served over focaccia that soaks up the juice.

Corn and shrimp chowder was so thick it stood up in the spoon, as well as vice versa, and while chowder is supposed to be a comfort food, this one was a bland, dull snoozer. A whole wheat tortilla with andouille sausage and potatoes, and more of the Gorgonzola cheese, was far more satisfying.

Main dishes always seem to include a pasta, perhaps black pepper fettuccine with sugar snap peas; artichoke hearts and asparagus tossed in a sweet red pepper sauce; some sort of roasted chicken; several choices of fish; and, often, succulent pork, like tenderloin slices in gravy seasoned with a rough mustard. Barbecued salmon was overcooked, though the tomato-cheese striping on the dish was a vivid flavor note.

In the spirit of family tables, there are "side bowls," generous servings of vegetables or starches to share around the table. Personal greed determines how many can share. These run $3-$4, and include the mashed potatoes. Even better, though, is the macaroni and cheese, dappled with pepper bacon and a little fresh sage and crowned with crunchy crumbs of their fabulous cornbread. A very adult version of nursery food, but quite irresistible.

Desserts range from homey to sophisticated. Look for some variation of creme brulee, ice cream, one or two chocolate desserts and the cobbler du jour. A blackberry and peach cobbler showed tasty fruit but missed on texture, with a gummy quality to the crust that could have been refrigerator-induced or undercooked.

The excellent wait staff, attuned to pre-curtain dining, delivers exactly what the customer needs in terms of time, knowledge and affability.

Blanche's
New American
33 North Sarah Street
652-9960
Dinner Wednesday-Sunday
Credit cards: MC, V
Wheelchair access: Comfortable

Blanche is not the proprietor of Blanche's. She's an elegant and friendly lady, but she seldom frequents the restaurant that bears her name. There are rules about these things. Blanche is one of Lynn Smith's two dogs—and Lynn is the boss, at least in the establishment she named and owns.

Blanche's is the current representative in a long line of Smith's St. Louis restaurants. She started with the City Cousin, bringing some delightful, semi-French cuisine (and pommes souffles that were the best ever served in the city), then operated the Other Cousin and Ginger's for a while, and finally served as a hostess at Culpeppers. Seven years ago, she opened Blanche's. (The business must be in her blood—she grew up in Detroit where her mother was the longtime hostess at the famed London Chop House there.)

Meals at Blanche's show some of Smith's imagination and experience in the business. She has a fine touch with herbs and spices, and knows how to make a guest feel welcome. The restaurant is dim, as opposed to dark, with a lovely tin ceiling, a feeling of space and a delightful patio whose greenery brings a pleasant aura of New Orleans only occasionally interrupted by the noises of Sarah Street.

The menu is modest, involving pork, fish and chicken with sauces that change daily. There are also a few memories from the City Cousin, such as the pepper steak and shrimp Westminster, stuffed with crabmeat and baked in a white Parmesan sauce. Very rich, very special.

Dinner, which will run $25-$30, begins with an old favorite appetizer, artichoke Tocco, with artichokes mixed with cream cheese and Parmesan cheese, then baked. It's a dip that makes one want to do a lot more than just dip in—swim in might be a better idea. Delicious stuffed mushrooms, a couple of small pizzas, and the ubiquitous chicken wings also are available. All tasty and cooked to order.

Blanche's is one of the rare restaurants with fried chicken on the menu (although only on Sundays, Wednesdays and Thursdays). But a real highlight, on all the time, is the Mediterranean vegetable pasta, with grilled fresh vegetables tossed on pasta that already has been dressed with olive oil and basil. The vegetables add a delicious flavor and texture to the pasta, and the combination really works. The grilled vegetables also are available without the pasta, as a dinner-sized salad atop greens.

Pasta topped with shrimp, mushrooms and broccoli is another winner, and a steak sandwich is served on French bread with spicy mayonnaise.

The wine list is small, but extremely adequate to keep company with the menu. Desserts, made in-house, are exemplary, especially Blanche's puff—vanilla ice cream in puff pastry with mango and blueberry sauces and a white chocolate garnish. Chocolate mousse in a brownie crust with chocolate and raspberry sauces is another rich delight, as is pecan pie with Kaluha and chocolate added. Desserts are rich enough for any meal, and probably too rich if the next stop is a visit to the Fox or the Sheldon or the Grandel Theatre or Powell Hall, none of which is very far away.

Blueberry Hill
Hamburgers, Bar/Diner Food
6504 Delmar Boulevard, University City
727-0880
Lunch and Dinner, Monday-Saturday
Credit cards: All major
Wheelchair access: Difficult

Make no mistake; food is not the focus at Blueberry Hill. But then again, what is the focus? Is it the mountain of toys from childhoods recently past that Joe Edwards has amassed? Or is it the posters and baseball cards on the walls, and Parcheesi and Scrabble and Ouija boards laminated into tabletops? Is it the music—the constant stream of good musicians who play gigs here? Or the staggering jukebox with two thousand tunes? Or could it be the dart board room or the corner window with periodic tableaux of holiday themes, Scenes From The Life of Elvis, and March tributes to Paddy O'Furniture? Whatever it is, it's charming without being cute, thank goodness.

Edwards and his wife, Linda, are among the leaders of the small, intense group that has kept the U. City Loop alive through difficult times (we'll touch on others as we get to their restaurants). Joe lived in the neighborhood when he first came to St. Louis in 1955, when it had restaurants, hardware stores, galleries, book stores, even a hotel and Mac Brown's gas station. Since then it has known good times and not-so-good ones, but those who kept fighting against decline and depression apparently have succeeded (but that's another story).

Chuck Berry and others still play at Blueberry Hill from time to time, and also at Cicero's (which used to share the block with Blueberry Hill and now has its own space a few blocks west). Edwards also owns the Tivoli, a movie house down the street, and is the man responsible for the stars of the Walk of Fame, which go to St. Louisans who have earned the tribute, not purchased it as they do in Hollywood.

The menu is essentially bar food with some additions like a daily special, a few vegetarian entrees and a couple of desserts. Consequently, it's an easy place to feed lunch to kids. We're never sure if they are as enchanted with the decor as adults think they ought to be—maybe they just see another kid's old, tired toys—but they tend to be well-behaved.

Still, it's essentially a place for relatively young adults and the street types who inhabit the Loop (though Clayton business types feed their pinball tastes here at lunch, and it's often used for father-son bonding on weekends). Service is, mostly, more professional than one would expect, with fast-moving servers who cover a lot of ground. This is, of course, a place that prides itself on its hamburgers. These are the fat, broiled kind, the standard being seven ounces of beef, with a 4 1/2-ounce size available for smaller jaws. For rare, try the big guy, so the kitchen has some control on the zone between raw and medium. Fries are ordinary, hot and well-drained, but not tasting of much but the grease in which they've been fried.

Lately, we've been hitting the jerk chicken sandwich, a boneless, skinless breast rubbed with Caribbean spices that make it sweet-hot, and then broiled. It comes with mango chutney, a good addition, adding up to one of the more passable chicken sandwiches in town. Hot dogs and the Reuben sandwich are outstanding, while roast beef and steak sandwiches and BLTs are serviceable.

The draft beer list is impressive, but we turn immediately, without passing Go (even if we're eating off the Monopoly board table), for the Woodpecker draft apple cider, the dry alcoholic English product that's so fine with food or to quaff while waiting. This is not an endorsement of the bottled Woodpecker (which is another bird entirely), but it is an endorsement of Blueberry Hill—maybe not a place to get a thrill, but fine for lunch.

Blue Water Grill
Seafood
2607 Hampton Avenue
645-0707
Lunch Monday-Friday, Dinner Monday-Saturday
Credit cards: All major
Wheelchair access: Passable

Location, location, location, say the real estate agents, but we've all seen excellent locations become disasters with one restaurant after another. If the opposite also is true, proof can be found in this almost-ramshackle little building just north of the Hampton Avenue-Watson Road division. David Slay, a meteor in the St. Louis dining firmament, transformed an old Dairy Queen into his first restaurant, La Veranda. When Slay went to Los Angeles, Tim Mallett took over and made the Blue Water Grill the cornerstone of his mini-empire, as it expanded to the Big Sky and Remy's.

Seafood has always been the strong suit at the Blue Water, where Mallett and then-chef Lisa Slay (David's sister, now at Remy's) first experimented with the small-plate, large-plate concept, an idea that makes sharing and experimenting easy to accomplish.

Today, however, the small plates also come in handy for the Monday special of tapas, a variety of Spanish dishes in appetizer sizes. Mention of barbecue also shows up from time to time on the chalkboard outside the door.

Attitude and service are pleasantly casual. Servers know the menu and the cooking styles well, and their wine list knowledge is like the River Jordan under Michael's boat—you know, deep and wide. The menu varies often, a necessary and worthy tactic, with seafood a specialty and touches of Asia, Mexico and the Caribbean along the way.

Small, crisp pizzas, often without tomatoes or cheese, but with such splendid toppings as smoked salmon and cream cheese or grilled vegetables and goat cheese, are regular appetizer items, and so are quesadillas with chicken or other fillings. Gumbo works well, too, as do roast pork carnitas. Salmon with pine nuts makes for an entree with nicely contrasting textures, and Mexican bouillabaisse, which adds Latin spices to the French-named seafood stew, is delicious. Amberjack, a type of tuna, is grilled to be rare, emphasizing its delicate flavors, and chicken stuffed with Gorgonzola cheese and crabmeat is another worthy entree. Potatoes show the same excellent imagination—au gratin with smoked Gouda cheese is our favorite, and mashed with chipotle peppers and chives a close second.

Breads are top-notch, too, especially the cornbread dotted with jalapeno peppers, and the wine selections are good. Among the wine offerings, a Firestone California gewurztraminer, with just a hint of sweetness, was a delicious partner to some of the spicier dishes. A full dinner will be in the $20-$30 range, and desserts like pumpkin-gingerbread pudding, raspberry-caramel flan, and white chocolate cappuccino and dark chocolate terrine are good reason to stretch the range a little.

Bobby's

New Orleans, with a Stop in Bora-Bora

7401 Manchester Avenue (at Sutton Avenue), Maplewood
644-3995
Lunch Tuesday-Friday, Dinner Tuesday-Saturday; Brunch on Sunday
Credit cards: MC, V
Wheelchair access: Satisfactory

The area's only Creole/Cajun/South Pacific restaurant gets a crowd that's eclectic enough to match the space that once was—honest to goodness—a former health club. This is the only restaurant of its style in the city. It's also one of the few places where you see business dinners, dates and family nights out (both Mom-worked-late and birthday-cake-laden) going on simultaneously.

With terrazzo floors and high ceilings "in fashionable downtown Maplewood," as the brunch menu says, there's a party going on tonight, and today, too, because Bobby's does lunch (and brunch on Sundays).

There's a bar on one side off the entrance, with the requisite televisions tuned to sports. But often the sound is turned off, because this seems to be turning into the sort of place where musicians show up to visit their buddies who are here for a gig. One visit produced a guy with his bouzouki, the Greek stringed instrument, and a well-known local professional musician who hauled out his horn after ordering dinner. Both sat in for a set or two, and the overall effect was quite fine.

On the other side is the dining room, which seems to be two stories tall, with French Quarter-painted facades, complete with balconies and some Spanish moss hanging in the corners. Add some Mardi Gras streamers, and the whole thing manages to come off as fun rather than sappy.

Food is primarily out of Louisiana, with things like red beans and rice, turtle soup, and oysters, either Bienville or Rockefeller. The Rockefellers are powerful with the scent of anise, and the spinach is rather more peppery than the Antoine's original. But they taste good. The red beans and rice were not quite piping hot, but the sausage was flavorful and the consistency properly creamy.

Main courses include the now-obligatory pasta (when did they pass the law that every restaurant in the country must serve it?), several fish, a fairly wide range of Big Easy food (jambalaya, etouffee, gumbo, barbecued shrimp), and two South Pacific dishes. Polasami basically is a spicy curry with coconut milk, and quite tasty, with a good amount of seafood. (It's also available with chicken or as a vegetarian entree.) Gado gado brings green beans, carrots, cauliflower and bean sprouts in a slightly spicy peanut sauce, topped with a sliced boiled egg, the general effect being faintly reminiscent of a pad Thai. A hot sauce is served on the side and makes a good addition. However, be warned—this is not a low fat dish. Like many dishes made with ground peanuts, oil tends to accumulate.

Chicken jambalaya was tasty, heavy on the pepper, and very comfort-foody, with a spicy pork sausage not quite like andouille. Entrees for dinner start at $6.95 and go up to $12.95, occasionally higher for specials.

Dessert was a bread pudding with a whiskey sauce that didn't hold up to the rest of the meal. The consistency was moist and tender, but someone had neglected to sweeten it. The peaches seemed to have been water-packed and the raisins lacked sweetness, too.

The wine list is modest, with a double-handful of wines by the glass, and prices are modest, too, though listing vintages would be a favor to wine drinkers. All in all, however, it's good to have Bob and Barbara Suberi back in town. Old-timers will remember Bobby's Creole, on Delmar Boulevard near Skinker Boulevard, where one of Joe's daughters hung out in the late 1960s, and then the move a block or two to the west, in the space where Andy Ayers operates Riddle's today. When the Suberis left town, they wandered the world, spending some time in the South Pacific, where they acquired a few recipes, too. Welcome home!

Breakaway Cafe
Basic American
8418 Natural Bridge, Bel-Nor
381-3554
7401 Pershing Ave., University City
Lunch Monday-Friday, Dinner Tuesday-Saturday
Credit cards: All major
Wheelchair access: Satisfactory

The basis of the New Orleans poor boy sandwich is roast beef, sliced very thin and served on a French or Italian roll. The trickiest part is the amount of gravy; enough to tenderize the beef and add succulent flavor to every bite, but not so much as to turn into a fountain when squeezed even lightly.

Proportions are perfect at the Breakaway Cafe, a little spot across the street from the University of Missouri-St. Louis and a real sleeper in the St. Louis restaurant race, if there is such a thing.

Paul Bandera's place, where Andy Ayers opened the first Riddle's, offers simple but stylish interior decoration, moderate prices and some imaginative menu and preparation ideas. Bandera's father, Paul Sr. (now retired and an occasional visitor), ran the family restaurant on West Pine Boulevard between Vandeventer Avenue and Sarah Street, and still reminisces about how his proximity to St. Louis University inspired the idea of pizza delivery to dormitory rooms.

Although we make a deduction for the absence of anchovies, pizza remains a major portion of the menu, as do pastas. And then there's chili-mac. Joe has tasted the combination in Cincinnati (where people have so little class they even boast about its presence in their diet), and he dislikes it strongly. We know that several St. Louis restaurants offer it, but this is the first time we've seen chili-mac under the pasta heading on a St. Louis menu. It's as if coexistence was good enough as far as it went, but now it's time for a full-blown takeover.

Pizzas are in nine- and twelve-inch sizes, and vegetarian toppings join the usual meats. Salads are excellent, and there's a wide range of sandwiches. Just don't forget the roast beef, because it's a sandwich that will whisk the diner away to New Orleans to let the good times roll.

And by now, under even a normal St. Louis time frame, the Breakaway's eclectic menu, with a few additions, will be in place at the corner of Pershing Avenue and Hanley Road, in the location that formerly held Black Tie Gourmet.

Bristol Bar & Grill
Seafood

11801 Olive Boulevard, Creve Coeur
567-0272
Lunch Monday-Friday, Dinner every night; Brunch on Sunday
Credit cards: All major
Wheelchair access: Satisfactory

For a restaurant that's been around more than fifteen years, the Bristol Bar & Grill must be doing something right. It continues to do a brisk business with full parking lots and plenty of traffic even late on a nasty Monday (though Mondays seem considerably less of a dining problem than they once were). Menus are printed daily so that the waxing and waning of the catch can be easily followed, without squinting at a chalkboard or listening to a lengthy recital of specials.

Fresh oysters from the Prince Georges Banks were cold and briny, arriving at the table with a well-horseradished red sauce and a half lemon on the side, at least one piece of crushed ice in each oyster. In addition, there was a lot of grit hanging around. Crab cakes took highest honors, with a big mass of lump crabmeat and minimal seasoning, designed only to elevate the taste of the meat, not demand attention by itself. They were absolutely platonic.

The standard lobster here is 1 1/4 pounds. The only other option is a tail, which comes from a giant crawfish and is what we consider sissy lobster, but even a small steamed lobster is a superb treat. Put on the bib and dig right in; eat the roe (the red stuff) and the tomalley (the green stuff) and fear nothing, the rewards are considerable. Catfish comes in a cornmeal crust, extremely moist and mildly crisp. But it needs seasoning, if only a little salt and pepper. Baked whitefish murmurs happily of garlic and dill with a bread-crumb topping. And shrimp are offered, at least sometimes, in a white wine and cream sauce; a simple, tasty style that calls for the highest quality of seafood.

The vegetable selection here is very interesting, and we praise a management that serves such things as leeks and celery, well-cooked and tasty. A mix of green beans, wax beans and strips of red bell pepper was lovely to look at, and were lightly steamed and still faintly crisp. Unfortunately, they, like the catfish, suffered from underseasoning.

The dessert tray presents mostly standards such as creme brulee, carrot cake and cheesecake. The chocoholic special layered a brownie-like cake, moist although a tad tough, with a generous amount of dense, slightly bitter chocolate mousse flavored with dark rum and cherry brandy, and some ganache on top. Sauced in raspberry puree, it was as good and as rich as it sounds.

The wine list offers about ten wines by the glass, including some sparkling wine, which isn't with the by-the-glass groupings, and an adequate selection by the bottle, though vintages are lacking.

At Sunday brunch, the star offering is a shrimp and crab stuffing, spicy and of excellent quality. Shrimp and immense crawfish are boiled, but with different seasonings, and both are winners. The paella seemed saffron-free, more like a Spanish rice with seafood.

Warm drop biscuits are passed around, in both plain and sweet styles, tender and very popular. Avoid the ham, which is of the pressed loaf variety. Hash brown potatoes with cheese on top are labeled "rosti," but this isn't the Swiss dish of that name.

Belgian waffles are made on the spot and feature a boffo strawberry sauce. Time was when it was necessary for the bread pudding from the dessert table, but these days, though, there's a swell rum anglaise for the bread pudding that takes the honors. The best of the crop on the dessert table was a deep chocolate mousse, not quite the same as the one in the layered dessert from dinner, and miniature key lime tarts.

Dinner will run about $25 per person; the brunch, a carry-your-own, all-you-can-eat affair, is about $10 less.

Broadway Oyster Bar
Casual Seafood
736 South Broadway
621-8811
Lunch and Dinner, Monday-Saturday
Credit cards: MC, V
Wheelchair access: Impossible, except for patio

The Broadway Oyster Bar must be very much like what existed many years ago in this part of downtown St. Louis, before most of it was demolished to make way for the Arch and the Jefferson Memorial. An ancient brick building with irregular floors, it boasts a tiny working fireplace and, in the winter, drafts so severe that there's a real need for the quilt that hangs inside the front door. The interior is dark, and so authentic a saloon that it would win praise for both its appearance and its age. (As one of downtown's oldest buildings, it dates to the 1820s or so, when it was built as an inn.)

Having gone through numerous changes of ownership since the days of Bob Burkhardt, it continues to offer live music and a menu of New Orleans-style seafood that sometimes come very close to the real thing.

Oysters are often, but not invariably, very good here. In New Orleans, of course, there is no such thing as out of season for oysters (although it's acknowledged that they're not at their peak in the summer months, spending their energy on making love rather than getting fat). Nevertheless, some of the best summer oysters we've ever had from the Gulf showed up at the Broadway. Not very big, but briny and crisp. For some reason, this is referred to as "sweet" in oyster-speak. Rockefellers here are not topped with cheese, thank goodness, a heresy carried by some places to people who've never had the real thing. Crawfish can also be very good for those willing to get their hands messy. We've learned to suck the heads like real "yats," as New Orleanians call themselves, because the succulent crawfish fat usually stays there when you break them open. Appetizers, including steamed shrimp and oysters on the shell, are priced from $2.50 to $7.50.

Speaking of oysters, they decorate two very different sandwiches here. Fried oysters, as they're called on the menu, come on a split baguette with tartar sauce. Very few deep-fried oysters are worth the calories, we think, because heat and breading overwhelm the delicate taste of the bivalve. When you throw in a loaf of French bread and any trimmings, there's not much room for oyster flavor, even in New Orleans. That brings us to the other oyster sandwich, called a "grinder," the Massachusetts-Connecticut name for the submarine-poor boy-hero. Whole oysters are sauteed with garlic and green onions and a little pepper, mixed with a smidgen of butter and the oyster liquor, and stuffed into a baguette. It's not quite as good as it once was— fewer oysters, for one thing, and some orange liquid called grinder sauce—but it soaks up lots of oyster juice, making a mess and a very happy diner. We like it a lot.

In addition to usual (burgers) and unusual (veggie grinders) sandwiches, look for New

Orleans trademarks like jambalaya, gumbo and so on. For some reason, barbecued shrimp have squash chunks in the dish. But we're particularly enamored of the red beans and rice, so flavorful that two or three beans flavor a whole spoonful of rice. We suspect the ham cooked with the beans is the Louisiana-spicy stuff, which is one reason it's so good. Entrees and sandwiches are $4.50 to $8.50.

Bread pudding here seems to vary with the cooks, so we can't give an accurate reading. But the sweet potato pecan pie left Joe moaning. Good crust that hadn't been refrigerated, a filling of sweet potatoes and nutmeg and not much extra sweetening, with crisp pecans on top and whipped cream (aerosol, alas) haloed around it. It sang.

Maybe not the place to take your elderly aunt, unless she's always had a wide Bohemian streak. Then she'll love it.

Bruno's Little Italy
Italian Cuisine
5901 Southwest Avenue
781-5988
Dinner Tuesday-Saturday
Credit cards: All major
Wheelchair access: Satisfactory

When Bruno's Little Italy opened in a storefront on Hampton Avenue in 1978, it caused a great deal of commotion. The food was outstanding, the wine list was intelligent and wide-ranging. It did land-rush business. Eventually Mario and Giovanna Bruno left their storefront to move to the periphery of the Hill. She'd always run the kitchen, and after the death of her husband, she took the full responsibility of both business and family.

It couldn't have been easy, but she has succeeded in the restaurant and, to judge from the fine little fellow that her daughter and son-in-law (both of whom work the front of the house) have produced, she's done well with the family, too. The baby, who also hangs out on Southwest Avenue, is the subject of conversation from the regulars. And, like the food, he draws oohs and aahs.

While dishes here often seem echoes of standards at many St. Louis Italian restaurants, most of Mrs. Bruno's cuisine offers variations on a theme rather than mere echoes. The menu, from which one may construct dinner for around $25, is particularly heavy in seafood.

To illustrate both echo and variation, one may have an eggplant appetizer as a traditional Parmigiana, or as eggplant regitana, in a white wine and garlic sauce. There's toasted ravioli— we enjoyed watching St. Louis grandparents introduce a new generation to it one night—and a soup made of dried porcini mushrooms, their duskiness mellowed with cream. We sampled roasted peppers, cut into thin strips, marinated in a little olive oil and garlic, topped with dices of Parmesan. The cheese, firm and slightly salty, offered a good texture contrast to the silky peppers. Strikingly handsome mussel soup sported six immense green-lip mussels in a broth accented, but not masked, by cream. Opalescent strands of onion arched slightly above the soup. The first spoonful was faint, even disappointing, but a stir and the liquid realigned itself somehow to turn into mussel magic. Not too heavy or too salty, a little sweetness from the onions to offset the brininess of the shellfish—very satisfying.

All entrees but pastas come with a salad, a small, sprightly mound that manages to overcome a little sugar in its dressing with some red onion, a few squares of cheese and some herbs. The lettuce is fresh, not overdressed, not brown—but next time we may ask for it dressed with the juices from the roasted peppers.

It was tempting, but the Eggplant Fan overcame the urge for rigatoni alla Norma, an eggplant and tomato sauce. Bruno's also offers osso bucco, chicken with crab, asparagus and cheese, or a steak with green peppers and mushrooms. Ann, whose favorite pastas all have seafood sauces, was in heaven with fusilli fra diavolo, corkscrew pasta with a spicy and quite chunky tomato sauce full of small shrimp and larger pieces of calamari. Almost shockingly al dente, the fusilli were a good match for the seafood textures. Squid, in tidy scrolls, may have been cooked a few minutes too long, but the shrimp were perfect. It was a St. Louis diavolo, not very hot but nicely garlicky, and the dish arrived with a bowl of red pepper flakes for as-needed zapping.

Spaghetti with a simple meat sauce also was carefully cooked, and significant for tasting extremely meaty without seeming to contain much. No small achievement, to be sure, and we hold it as an example for alumni of the Gotta-Have-Meat-Dammit school, or "The physical presence isn't always necessary for pleasure."

In another seafood scene, a dish, simply called calamari scampi, pairs large butterflied shrimp and more calamari in another, very different, chunky tomato sauce. This was sweeter, with the taste of basil noticeable but not overwhelming. The shrimp and calamari were both carefully cooked, and eminently pleasurable.

While the dessert list may look mundane, cannoli and tiramisu are anything but ordinary. Cannoli shells are crispy, not pre-filled, and the filling particularly creamy and tasty. Tiramisu is traditional, not terribly sweet, packed with espresso flavor and light enough that the eater feels indulged rather than stuffed.

The wine list is as strong and elegant as ever, and Mario would be pleased to look at it now. It's still expensive, but there are some good values to go with the high-priced classics.

And if one wishes to be very good to oneself, a final note is Mrs. Bruno's homemade lemoncello. Unlike the deathly sweet and often fake-tasting alcoholic drink that spent years in well-deserved obscurity (and now hot stuff in Italy and New York), this is smooth, dry, full of the scent and taste of lemon peel, but none of the bitterness given by the white pith. It's a charming, homey touch to an excellent meal.

Busch's Grove
Traditional American Cuisine
9160 Clayton Road, Ladue
993-0011
Lunch and Dinner, Tuesday-Saturday
Credit cards: All major
Wheelchair access: Comfortable

Busch's Grove, first of all, is unrelated to the Pestalozzi Street Busch guys. It's a hangout for the folks who arrive late and sit in the front seats at the Muny Opera or the Fox Theatre, offering safe, reassuring food in a safe, reassuring setting. The decor was Ralph Lauren when Ralph was still selling ties.

Its most distinctive feature is probably the screened cabins in the fenced-in area behind the restaurant. Screens are nice, especially for those of us who are considered by mosquitos as the equivalent of Dom Perignon, but the view is pretty much of the fence (with nice pink geraniums hanging every dozen feet or so) or of the other cabins. The air circulation problem is supposedly solved by ceiling fans.

Our service was good, but we were known by sight to the house. Over the years, however, we have had many reports of unknowns receiving extremely chilly service. The dress code has relaxed, apparently, with polo shirts without jackets being seen even at dinner in the dining room.

The menu, generally a bastion of things like shrimp cocktail, spinach salad and prime rib, does wander into a few newer areas. Toasted ravioli, to our surprise, is on the appetizer list, and so are chicken wings. Chicken livers are a possible entree, along with chicken DéJon (as they spell it out here), catfish broiled with Cajun spice and trout piccata. First courses run $3-$9, entrees $15-$24 and up for specials. Whiskey is expensive, but wines are less vigorously marked up. The list is short, but we had a lovely Sancerre at a modest price.

Vichyssoise is the classic Franco-American cold potato and leek soup. This version was bland, with a strange, slightly viscous texture, and was either near room temperature or somewhat cool (depending on where one dipped the spoon), presumably a result of microwave defrosting. Baby back ribs were baked, we think, no smokiness being detected, but were meaty, not greasy, crispy at the edges, cut in individual ribs and served with a couple of lemon wedges and a wet cloth napkin, a nicely hospitable touch. The sauce was standard, but the end result was quite nice for baked barbecue.

A Caesar salad had packaged croutons and powdered Parmesan, but the romaine was fresh and cold. Despite promises on the menu, it wasn't tossed with the dressing, which did show evidence of anchovies somewhere in it, and perhaps garlic powder, too.

In a restaurant as traditional as this one, the fried chicken, if it's offered, should be good enough to beat the drive-through stuff. We're glad to report that Busch's Groves' chicken certainly does. Four crisply battered pieces, well-seasoned, arrived quiveringly hot. When it had cooled enough to bite into it, the chicken was moist and tender and full of flavor, a real winner. An order of crab legs arrived with the legs split open for ease in eating, although a seafood fork would have helped. They showed a little evidence of drying out, but mostly were tender and sweet. Side dishes are potato or a variation of the seasonal vegetable medley (zucchini, carrots, green beans and broccoli, always in season) that everyone in town seems to serve. The potatoes are baked in foil or cottage fries, which actually seem to be made from scratch. Rounds of potato are deep-fried and carefully drained to be almost as crisp and certainly as greaseless as good French fries.

Desserts may come from either in-house or from outside suppliers (we have some good ones out there these days). We tried a devil's food cake that arrived with miniature chocolate chips paving the outside; tender and slightly bittersweet, it was a good end to an American dinner.

Cafe Campagnard
Contemporary French Country Bistro
403 Lafayette Center (Manchester Road at Baxter Road), Manchester
256-3949
Dinner Monday-Saturday
Credit cards: All major
Wheelchair access: Passable

The repetition of the word "cafe" may be a little confusing, but we'll tour this West County shopping center, home of Cafe Campagnard, very slowly. The cafe is the offspring of some alumni of Cafe Provencal, in the location that used to be Cafe Renee.

Okay? Got it? Pop quiz later.

The DNA trail of Cafe Provencal shows in the style of both meal and menu at Campagnard. The menu, which changes frequently, encourages diners to mix and match in fixed-price, three-course meals that are about $25 a person. The light, warm room feels very California French and meals are highly satisfactory, heightened by a good, moderately priced— exclusively French— wine list.

A duck confit arrived with a salad that carried a particularly fine vinaigrette, plus toasted hazelnuts, dabs of fennel-scented onions and some beets. The dried codfish and potato fritters were fluffy and tasted of fish that had been well enough soaked to remove any unwelcome salt. Some is expected, but this had almost none. Its ratatouille garnish surprised the eye with corn as a prominent ingredient.

Grilled tuna wrapped in thin slices of eggplant with Israeli couscous led the way among entrees. No one asked about rareness; it came slightly pink in the middle. The pearl couscous was too lightly spiced to stand up to the tuna, despite a red-pepper coulis. A lamb steak, rare as requested, if slightly chewy, came with a spoonful of minced fresh tarragon in a liquid base. Almost an herb paste, it was pungent and green and very good, and presumably a substitute for the advertised vinaigrette. Briefly steamed escarole and artichokes in a ratatouille-like sauce were the sides.

Dessert was a triple chocolate tart, over a caramel lattice on the plate. Layers of graham cracker crust, dark chocolate ganache, milk chocolate mousse and whipped cream caused mixed reviews. One of us thought it very good, the other felt it was unremarkable. Creme brulee with honey and rosewater was a baked version, overcooked to the point where the crust was—pardon the expression—burnt.

Cafe Campagnard feels a little more formal in service and general atmosphere than its Clayton forebear, and despite a few shortcomings, it is good enough to raise the ante for restaurant food and ambience in West County.

Cafe de France
French Cuisine
410 Olive Street
231-2204
Lunch Monday-Friday, Dinner Monday-Saturday
Credit cards: All major
Wheelchair access: Passable

The classic story is told by restaurant and food writer Patricia Wells. An American in Paris is stopped on the street by another American visitor who says, "Can you help us? With all these restaurants, how do you tell which ones are French? You know—the kind that serve souffles."

Cafe de France is the kind of French restaurant that serves souffles. That's not a disparaging remark. Far from it. Classic French cuisine is orgasmically good. We harbor a deep and abiding belief in it.

Marcel and Monique Keraval's establishment has had its ups and downs since he and the late Jean-Claude Guillossou brought haute cuisine dining to St. Louis, first together and then separately. It has remained a pillar of downtown through good times and bad, serving lobster bisque, foie gras, quail and other classics both by the book and in Marcel's painstaking adaptations. We've had some marvelous meals there, and some that fell short in several places.

Currently, Cafe de France seems to be a mixed bag. It's a pleasure to see young couples dining here, some being carefully steered through the menu, which has an early/late bird special, a prix fixe of varying length, and an ala carte section. In addition, one may order ala carte any item from the special or prix fixe. The waiters can be very gentle with newcomers, explaining dishes and how they'll taste. When taking an order, however, the wording from the waiter might leave the impression that the salad and the sorbet, for example, are included in the price of an entree. They certainly are not, a fact which can cause pain when the check arrives. It's bad form.

The wine list is elegant and excellent, and even more expensive than dinner. Great Bordeaux and Burgundy varieties are on hand, along with some top California labels.

Appetizers run $4-$10.50, higher for some specials. Keraval makes the pates here, and they can be glorious, from rough country loaves to silky goose liver. Several variations of salmon, smoked, marinated or fresh, compete with crab cakes short on lump crabmeat, shiitake mushrooms, composed or tossed salads, and several delicious soups. They always include lobster bisque and turtle with a generous tot of sherry, but they often seem heavily salted. The quality is high, with fine, long-simmered stocks, but a lighter hand with salt would be welcome. A special of two slices of foie gras served in a blackberry demiglace was memorable, although there was the faint taste of scorching in part of the sauce.

Sliced Roma tomatoes with thin slices of feta cheese and random crescents of red onion were lightly and tastily dressed with a whisper of vinaigrette. Given the availability of good olives these days, the use of tasteless California black olives was a surprise to the point of shock. A salad of fresh mixed greens was more vigorously seasoned, with a heavier hand with vinegar than expected. There's some argument that bitter greens can take it, but the contrarians, including us, vote for oil to soften the bitterness.

This may be one of the few places in town offering an intermezzo of made-in-house sorbet before the main course. Raspberry was sweet-sharp, perhaps with a little cassis to push the flavor. Lemon turned out not to be sorbet, but that's quibbling. It had quite a few ice crystals in it, but that's quibbling, too. It was almost a frozen lemon mousse, with cream and candied lemon peel bits, luscious and thrilling to the tongue.

Entrees (up from $18) might be things like lobster thermidor, pheasant, duckling, lamb, or several variations of veal. Marcel also likes game, and it's often on the list of specials, including things like the ultra-lean ostrich, which he handles well. Chateaubriand with bearnaise sauce and a rack of lamb with rosemary and ginger are available only for two.

Beef Wellington, puff pastry around mushrooms and pate and beef tenderloin, is showy and tricky and another classic. The tricky part is getting the beef and the pastry both properly cooked, and the diner who prefers blood-rare beef should plan on compromise. It's a great, old-fashioned dish, full of rich aromas, great textures and serious taste. Keraval gets the meat as rare as we've seen it, and the pastry is perfect, flavored with the pate and the mushrooms and the meat.

Poached Dover sole, chosen over sauteed or grilled versions, is a thin, delicate fish that's easy to overcook; it was boned at the table and served with a simple browned butter sauce and a lemon half. It was silky, not overcooked, and not cold after all that boning, the sauce managing to be both rich and subtle at the same time. Tiny haricot verts, or string beans, crunchy and garlicky, baby carrots whose small ones were sweet and soft and the larger ones were neither, and a crumbly polenta were the sides. Polenta is hardly what one expects here, but it was full of the sweetness of corn and the characteristic texture that made it a good foil for the fish.

Marcel Keraval would probably be happiest, we suspect, if he did nothing but make desserts all day and all night, too. They have long been his strong suit. Complicated constructions of chocolate cake and mousse, creme brulee, tarte tatin and eclairs pop up on the dessert tray. For a long time Cafe de France was known for its souffles. There's no mention of them on the menu, and we have reports that requests are strongly discouraged. Since they take a long time to prepare and must be served right from the stove, they need to be ordered early. We did.

The longer we eat out, the stranger it is to us that souffles have fallen into disfavor. A small souffle is no richer than a single serving of creme brulee. It's airy and extravagant, the fluff sitting much more lightly on the stomach than many of its newer rivals. Traditional Grand Marnier is special, but raspberry is spectacular.

It's always an unpleasant surprise to find the restrooms here so ill-lit and ill-equipped, given the amount of care that goes into the kitchen and the front of the house. Any interior designer worth his lampshades would trade a consultation for a half-dozen souffles.

Cafe Istanbul
Turkish Cuisine
600 East Lockwood Road, Webster Groves
961-7479
Dinner Monday-Sunday
Credit cards: All major
Wheelchair access: Satisfactory

Cafe Istanbul, offering the tastes of Turkey, is another step toward cuisine maturity in St. Louis, the opportunity for us in River City to share the world's flavors.

A recent arrival on the Big Bend-Lockwood curve, in a small strip mall, Cafe Istanbul inherits a space that has been home to several restaurants, and it offers a number of dishes that look familiar in description, if not in name. At the same time, the fact that the food represents a different ethnic group, and brings different flavors and textures, may be slightly disconcerting at first.

Or it could be different colors. The hummus ($3.50), for example, is a salmon pink, tinged from a puree of roasted peppers. The peppers' fit in the recipe is as smooth as the dip itself, which also benefits from a few green olives that are tasted but unseen. This hummus is a thick slather rather than a dripping dip, nicely suited to a knife.

Other first courses include a homemade yogurt with cucumbers ($2), vaguely reminiscent of the Indian raita but seasoned instead with garlic and dill, a refreshing dish that would help a light summer lunch with the accompanying pita. There's a black-eyed pea dish ($2.50) that puts the Dixie versions to shame, a heavily garlicked salad to convert the pea-resistant.

Some of the first courses also appear on the dinner plates, like a grated carrot salad that's dressed simply with balsamic vinegar and oil. The balsamico is a great match for the sweet carrot, and the two really swing. Another repeater is a potato salad with chopped tomatoes and peppers. Again with a vinaigrette, it's a homey-feeling dish like Mom would make.

A lentil soup accompanies all the dinners. It's a small portion, designed to tease the appetite rather than appease it, and it's a distinctively un-dense soup. The seasoning notes are primarily mint and black pepper, giving the tongue cool and heat simultaneously. The soup is vegetarian, but the seasonings carry the stock very nicely without any need for meat. Cafe Istanbul also serves it sufficiently hot, a touch the high-priced joints often seem to overlook. The soup, too, is available separately.

This is eggplant heaven, with two eggplant appetizers and at least two appearances as major ingredients in entrees. We tried the stuffed eggplant in its stuffed-with-meat version ($9.50). The vegetarian one, very traditional, is called imam baldi, or "the priest fainted." Unlike the Italian pasta known as strozzoprieti, or "priest stranglers," in this case the priest fainted because the eggplant was so good. We'll let others consider the theological ramifications. Joe is a great fan of eggplant in almost any incarnation—fried, chopped, chilled, heated; it absorbs garlic and olive oil and other great flavors, and it's one of the great Mediterranean vegetables.

Not surprisingly, this is a site for kebabs, coming as chicken ($10.50) and beef, both solid ($11.50) and ground ($9.50). The beef chunks were a good grade of beef that had been marinated to increase their tenderness and flavor. They arrived pink inside, a generous portion, resting on a cinnamon-scented pilaf with the occasional pine nut. The ground beef kebabs had nothing to be ashamed of either. Crusty on the outside, lean and moist with parsley and a light dose of the garlic, they were outstanding.

Lamb chops ($12.50) arrived as thin loin chops, six or seven to a serving, having been marinated in something similar to that used for the beef kebabs. They were slightly pink inside, and remarkably tender. The plate, like the others, not only held the pilaf, carrots and potato salad but a grilled tomato half, particularly good with lamb, and a grilled Anaheim pepper, one of the mildest of the so-called hot peppers. By avoiding the seeds and membrane which tend to cluster near the top of the pepper, even the cautious can manage it.

Baklava is a good balance of crisp and syrup-saturated, cut in small squares so the guest needn't try to penetrate the layers of phyllo dough and walnuts to manage it. It was a fine version. The other house dessert is rice pudding. The senior partner is not a rice pudding fancier. The Istanbul's version is baked, but the custard is thin and flowing, and the pudding is topped, if you wish, with cinnamon and ground walnuts. Wish. We promise you, it's an ambrosial combination that lifts it above the mundane stuff. Even the reluctant one was charmed.

The wine list is short, and a little perfunctory. But Istanbul also has fruit juices unlike anything that Dole ever saw. Our favorite is sour cherry, just pungent enough to stand up to the food.

Remarkably, the cost for all this runs about $20 for an appetizer, dinner that includes soup, and dessert.

The Istanbul is run by Gultan Ilhan and her brother, Ismail. She is raising two children, teaching part-time and completing a Ph.D. She says she opened the place on an impulse. We hope she keeps it open, and that she again serves lunch, which she did when she first opened in the late spring of 1998.

Cafe Manhattan
American Diner
511 South Hanley Road, Clayton
863-5695
7641 Wydown Boulevard, Clayton
863-9050
9992 Lin-Ferry Drive
849-4143
Lunch and Dinner, daily
Credit cards: All major
Wheelchair access: Passable

"There must be lots of good little neighborhood places," some readers say. "Why don't we hear about some?"

In the case of Cafe Manhattan, and similar, good little neighborhood places around the city, the reason is simple: Fans don't share their spots with outside-the-neighborhood folks. And most people prefer to eat close to home; if they wander, it's for something ethnic, or something more upscale at times of celebration.

Cafe Manhattan now has three locations, two a half-block apart in semi-residential Clayton, and a third in south county. The original, on Hanley Road, where Wydown Boulevard ends, has been a favorite for many years, offering pizza and sandwiches when the urge is strong not to cook and eat at home, and not to dress much for going out. Manhattan Express, around the corner on Wydown Boulevard, has a similar menu, and though it lacks a grill and deep fryer, it has the advantage, some would say, of a few outside tables.

The cafe is glass brick, and black and white, and red and chrome—can you sense we're getting ready to say "diner"? There's plenty of Coca-Cola memorabilia, but there's no feeling of walking into a franchise nostalgia joint. Customers are relaxed and extremely casual when it comes to dress—two guys in cutoffs and baseball caps sit down just for a beer (imported, thanks), many run in to pick up carry-out orders, a family finishes a pizza. Food has the same casual aura as the clothing, with heavy, diner-style china, comfortably clunky coffee mugs and large portions. Sandwiches are overstuffed. Lunch or dinner comes to about $15.

Bowls of chili and chicken noodle soup made for excellent starters, the soup heavy with short, fat noodles, very tidy-looking but home-y tasting. Chili might offend the purist, because it carries lots of tomatoes. But it was meaty and well-seasoned (fairly spicy, if you're faint of heart) and piping hot, one of the best restaurant chilis we've had in a long time.

Bacon, lettuce and tomato is a winning sandwich, with crisp bacon and lots of juicy tomatoes (juiciest in July and August). Pizza has a choice of three styles of crusts and lots of toppings, and comes in three sizes. Burgers are fat and juicy. Meat loaf sandwiches have been a favorite of Joe's since he carried them, still redolent of garlic, in his high school lunch. Cafe Manhattan's was fat and tasty, and a joy to eat.

A classic St. Louis sandwich—braunschweiger and onion—met the '90s with the addition of lettuce, tomato and a "special sauce." Do we see creeping McDonaldism? The sauce turned out to be Thousand Island-ish, and helped the braunschweiger. Fries were hand cut, fresh and hot, and malt vinegar is available on the side, which is exceedingly proper if you belong to the English fish-and-chips school of seasoning.

Good, informative service, a full liquor license and moderate prices, and while it isn't Manhattan, it's reminiscent of several Long Island diners.

Cafe Mira

Modern American

12 North Meramec Avenue, Clayton
721-7801
Dinner Monday-Saturday
Credit cards: All major
Wheelchair access: Difficult

One of the earliest entries in what became the Great Clayton Restaurant Race of 1998 was Cafe Mira. On the site of the former Cafe Zoe, Mike Johnson, who trained in New Orleans, and his merry band have sprinted away from the starting line and begun working magic on food.

Inside, the decor has changed only a little, although it s sometimes difficult to see through the crowds that cluster here. Mira was discovered fairly rapidly, and its popularity is deserved. Three courses will average about $35 per person without beverage or tip, a tab that hasn't seemed to slow the calls seeking reservations.

A deft hand with spicing and a soaring imagination are obvious in the meals at Mira. A spinach salad was lifted from cliche by bits of andouille sausage and spiced pecans, along with a particularly smooth vinaigrette. Sweet and spicy Thai calamari and rock shrimp, sauteed and then topped with a tangy dressing, were barely chewy to bring the optimum texture. As far as flavor, they seemed peppery and sweet at the same time, a full range. Even stranger, the same dressing seemed to bring different flavors from items like the rock shrimp and the calamari. Other first courses are things like a tart of portobello mushrooms with goat cheese and roasted peppers, and gravlax, or salmon cured in-house with Asian slaw and wasabi sauce.

Among entrees, the cooking can be as simple as a roast free-range chicken with roasted garlic potatoes or grilled salmon accompanied by applewood-smoked bacon. And Johnson can get more complex, too. Additional Asian spicing showed up in a pork tenderloin in red curry sauce. It sat on perfectly cooked jasmine rice with julienne of vegetables and chopped peanuts, full of fascination without blowing the lid off from heat. Tuna cooked medium rare became a Mediterranean dish with couscous, roasted tomatoes, leeks, spiced black olives and a few strands of red pepper, zucchini and yellow squash that trailed across the top. The spicing showed a little saffron and a surprising amount of black pepper that brought its emphasis late in each mouthful, delicious and fascinating. Veal chops sometimes wear morel mushrooms and truffle oil and watercress, a good accompaniment for the tasty juices.

A bread pudding described as chocolate showed chocolate only as a topping, but it also bore caramel, caramelized banana slices and a glorious roasted banana ice cream. It was a marvelous, serious grown-up treat, not to be wasted merely on good children who eat every bite.

Wine here is a serious subject, with a fairly expensive list, but this is a restaurant for splurging. Some good buys are tucked in here and there. Cafe Mira also carries the Bert Grant wheat beer, and both pear and apple cider. Service is smooth and polished without being condescending.

Cafe Napoli
Italian Cuisine
7754 Forsyth Boulevard, Clayton
863-5731
Lunch Monday-Friday, Dinner Monday-Saturday
Credit cards: AE, MC, V
Wheelchair access: Satisfactory

In the food world, there's a lot of discussion about the origins of cioppino. There are those who claim it's a California invention, born of the San Francisco fishermen who gave the world Fisherman's Wharf and Joe DiMaggio. There's also the argument that it really is Italian, from Liguria, where Italy abuts the French Riviera, and that it might be related to bouillabaisse. But it's hard to imagine a community on the Mediterranean where fish stews and soups haven't been part of the cuisine for centuries. Consequently, we won't argue the appearance of cioppino at Cafe Napoli.

Naples surely would be willing to claim credit for the wondrous dish that Tony Pietoso created. A diner with any sense should be staking a claim, too, for a cup or bowl of the thick, spicy, seafood-laden soup that makes grown men (and women) moan. "When available," says the menu. That means, like many traditional dishes, you have to have the right ingredients or it doesn't fly. It also means the stuff dashes out of the kitchen, and more than one diner has been disappointed. Your best chance is on a Friday, or perhaps a Saturday. This is a tomato-based soup, not the creamy ones of Northern latitudes, pungent with basil, a little oregano (we think) and red pepper. There's a little pop at the end of a mouthful, enough to linger and make a person eat slowly, the way they do in Naples.

The large menu has fifteen kinds of pasta all priced as first courses, as well as the usual chicken, fish, veal and beef. Premature decision-making is not a good idea, as there's always a large number of specials illustrated by plastic-wrapped pieces of raw material.

First courses are mostly fairly traditional like bruschetta, toasted slices of bread, either with roasted peppers or tomatoes, both cheesed and put under the broiler, and calamari, either in a tomato sauce or fried. First courses average just under $5, and a full dinner, without wine, is about $25. We like the eggplant Parmesan, a generous serving of tender eggplant with a tomato sauce that manages to enhance rather than smother the eggplant taste. Carciofi alla piccata is marinated artichoke hearts, which can be enhanced by the addition of anchovies.

The house salad is lettuce and onions under a non-sweet, quite good vinaigrette that doesn't have sugar, although we're partial to Napoli's tomato salad, which comes with red onions (mozzarella is on hand for those who prefer it).

There's always a veal chop special prepared various ways. It's an enormous hunk of meat for veal, usually stuffed with something tasty like mushrooms or crab, with a compatible sauce. This is excellent veal, imaginatively prepared and always alluring. Liver is agrodolce, sweet-and-sour, rather than the usual Venezia, or strips of fried liver and fried onions. Napoli's onions have been cooked almost to a marmalade to enhance their sweetness, and then a little balsamic vinegar is added to balance it out. They manage to get the liver cooked to medium rare here, too, not easy with half-inch slices, but it adds up to an outstanding dish. Pasta Ischia, a special, came with sea scallops, garlic, white wine, and fresh tomato, deeply tasting of the sweet scallop juices with a little tang from the tomato, exciting and satisfying to eat. Seafood in general is respectfully treated in this house, as witnessed by the fact that five of the fifteen pastas involve fish or shellfish.

Beef? How about a fillet with eggplant and cheese in a tomato sauce, or medallions in Marsala with fresh mushrooms and green peppers? Or maybe a simple chicken cacciatore or broiled shrimp with olive oil, lemon and capers?

Desserts are mostly ice cream, with a tiramisu that's pretty fair. Creme brulee is well-browned, unlike some around town, but the custard isn't as eggy as we'd like.

The wine list is strong in first-rate, reasonably priced reds, especially those from Italy. We sampled a Rubesco from the Lungarotti family, a blend of sangiovese and canaiolo that was excellent with rich sauces and with beef and veal.

Always a worthy experience, and at realistic prices, too.

Cafe Natasha
Persian Cuisine
6623 Delmar Boulevard, University City
727-0419
Dinner every day
Credit cards: All major
Wheelchair access: Passable

There are no Persian rugs at Cafe Natasha, but the kitchen provides other sorts of magic carpets, including the kind you ride in your head and heart to wonderful new things. Those things can—and we say should—include food, and Cafe Natasha delivers them so well that it's worth taking the Karastan out of the garage and riding it over to the U. City Loop.

A small, tidy establishment, this is a husband-and-wife operation that has settled here after an exhausting time running a downtown restaurant, too. First courses are completely vegetarian, and range from the very simple—like pita with feta cheese, parsley, cilantro, radishes and green onions as toppings for nibbling—to kookoo, a delicious, dense, baked egg-spinach dish with more parsley and cilantro, plus lots of spices and some walnuts. A few slices arrive as an appetizer; a larger serving works as a main course.

Homemade yogurt also comes in different styles. Try it as a thick dip ($3.50), moistened with olive oil, atop the pita, or a slightly thinner version ($3) with dill, mint, cucumber and green onion, again for dipping, or soup ($2.75) with raisins and walnuts. All these arrive with pita wedges in the bread basket. We also liked the peppery olives ($2) and the eggplant dip ($3.50), a vague relative of baba ghanoush.

Main courses come with a choice of osh or a garden salad. Osh is a lentil soup with barley and mung beans, thick and delicious and spicy. The salad consists of iceberg lettuce with the usual brief touches of garnish, plus some homemade dressings. We chose a yogurt Italian, creamy and interesting, and perhaps with a little cinnamon to leave the faint impression of sweetness.

We talk a lot about lamb. It's a particular favorite of ours, and Natasha is a great place for beginners. Chops ($13.50) are not big thick cuts but four or five small, rather thin loin chops that are marinated and then grilled. The marinade, which is mysterious but not strange-tasting—we almost have to think there's soy sauce in it, incongruous as that may be—leaves the chops tasting nicely meaty and altogether winning. It's a great dish to tempt the cowardly eater, and we commend it. Beef kebabs are coarsely ground and well-seasoned ($9.50), or strips that have been marinated ($10.50). Both choices are very lean and surprisingly tender. Alongside is basmati rice, fragrant and well-cooked. The shaker on each table contains sumac, a slightly sour flavoring found in parts of Asia and the Middle East. It goes on the rice, adding some nice flavors. There's also a chicken kebab, a fish dish and several for vegetarians.

Desserts are homemade, led by an apple pie full of cinnamon and cloves and slightly warmed. Delicious. The cream cheese pie is similar to cheesecake but creamy rather than fluffy, and particularly pretty. We keep meaning to try the faludeh, the noodle dessert, but we always get distracted.

Service is concerned and careful, there's a nice little wine list, and mint tea or Turkish coffee. This is a place that pays attention to iced tea, by the way. None of that instant stuff here. It's clear and strong without being bitter. Just don't spill it on the rug.

Cafe Provencal
American-Accented French Bistro
40 North Central Avenue, Clayton
Wine Bar, 34 North Central Avenue, Clayton
725-2755
427 South Kirkwood Road, Kirkwood
822-5440
Dinner every night at one place or the other in Clayton
Dinner Tuesday-Saturday in Kirkwood
Credit cards: All major
Wheelchair access: Comfortable (Kirkwood), Difficult (Clayton)

Cafe Provencal has been—literally—jamming them in at its Clayton location for several years. So when its Kirkwood sibling opened in 1998, it left us feeling slightly guilty because it solved the few problems we had with the Clayton site. There's lots of room and the tables are well-spaced in Kirkwood; in Clayton, tables are close in a small brick-walled room. In Kirkwood, chairs are large and comfortable; Clayton uses escapees from an ice cream parlor. But while the menu is not always the same, the food is superior in both spots. And it looks good, too. A friend recently off a fancy cruise said that the Provencal-Kirkwood plate looked as lovely as the ones on the ship.

The basic premise is simple. There's a fixed-price meal offering three or four courses from a list of appetizers, soups, salads, entrees and desserts, although courses also are priced separately. Most, but not all, of the food is French influenced, which leaves a menu with first courses of pate, escargot or seafood ravioli, Caesar salads or salades Nicoise, and desserts like creme brulee or blueberry cheesecake.

Prices are modest, too. The three-course meal is $18, the four-course, $22, in Kirkwood. In Clayton, where rents are higher, the price is $20 and $24, respectively.

Eddie Neill, the owner and premier Francophile, makes great pates. Both the spreadable kind and the meat loaf kind are savory and full of deep, complex flavors that leave the mouth smiling and wanting more. A smoked salmon appetizer arrives with a couple of slices wrapped around a small serving of crab mousse, curry and lemon mayonnaise, a deviled egg and a flaming red crayfish, plus onion, capers and chopped cucumber, usual accompaniments to salmon. Green salads are reliable, with good greens, a light vinaigrette, and perhaps a dusting of cheese or a few nuts for accents.

Neill often has unusual entrees, fish like skate, meat like rabbit, very authentic, although we keep hoping for tripes Nicoise. With the understanding that they aren't for everyone, there's usually only one oddity at a time on the menu, leaving plenty of other choices. The menu changes almost daily, so just watch the windows for current attractions.

This is a good house for roast pork, lean and tender, and sauced in various ways, with Marsala wine, or garlic and rosemary. Roast chicken is full of herbs rubbed into the skin and roasted to a near-definitive crispness. In summer, there are main courses like a salad Nicoise—good greens, the usual accompaniments of egg, tomato, green beans, tiny potatoes and anchovy, the heretical use of grilled fresh tuna (in France, it's always canned), and a tasty and sparingly-used vinaigrette. A grilled rib-eye steak is served with a green peppercorn sauce, juicy meat well complemented by the accent. Sea bass, a mild fish, comes in a thick chunk carefully broiled, and served with a sweet red pepper sauce to bring up the volume a little. Everything comes with potatoes or another appropriate starch, and a few vegetables. The plates seem less crowded in Kirkwood, which we also like.

Desserts are done in-house, and there's always at least one chocolate choice, although something called a chocolate tart turned out to be a thin, brownie-like square with powdered sugar sprinkled over it and slices of sweet, ripe peach that garnished it. It was wonderful, tender and chocolaty. Fruit tarts are good, although they sometimes suffer from refrigeration. And creme brulee here is very reliable.

This is a serious wine house, with interesting French wines at very charming prices. It's a place for superior Sancerres, a far better alternative to Chardonnay, and excellent rosés from Provence or the Cote d'Azur. Rhone Valley wines display hearty reds. Many wines are imported by Kermit Lynch, whose name on a bottle usually speaks to both quality and value. Diners who only speak American wines are encouraged to ask questions from the staff, generally knowledgeable or willing to find an associate who is. The staff is affable, able to move food quickly for parties with a time limit, and in tune with the food they're ready to serve you.

Cardwell's at The Plaza
Modern American Cuisine

94 Plaza Frontenac (Lindbergh Boulevard and Clayton Road), Frontenac
997-8885
Lunch and Dinner, every day
Credit cards: All major
Wheelchair access: Comfortable

The recent separation of the two Cardwell's has been virtually undetectable to the palate, we think. The newer site, next door to Neiman-Marcus, has kept Bill Cardwell himself. He's a major and positive influence on his kitchen, and he has have been a major and positive influence on St. Louis cuisine over the past decade.

It's difficult to realize this is a mall restaurant from its decor. There's a retail counter for both fancy foods, to use the grocery trade name for things like gourmet mustards and imported olive oils, and store products to go, like soups, on the mall side. The bar/counter area is always active with people eating or drinking and schmoozing a little. There's a comfortable area with chairs and slightly-higher-than-usual cocktail tables nearby, always a classy touch.

In the dining room, more than a little California influence is evident in color, accessories and roominess. It even manages to soften the occasional outbursts of noise and laughter from the bar area. It's a warm, handsome room, with tables well-spaced and five small private or semi-private dining areas. Our only quibble is the plastic cloth table coverings in the main room, which seem to detract from the general level of tastefulness. The private rooms, in contrast, have white tablecloths. The sliding-glass hazard is lessened by constant use of paper cocktail napkins but a tall glass of iced tea on a sticky-hot day makes them shred quickly. In a house that has entrees topping out near $20 and some wines over $100, it's incongruous.

The restaurant uses its wood-burning oven well, making pizza, roasting chicken, and smoking ribs and shrimp. Cardwell's approach has seemingly been to begin with American food and then venture into other ethnic directions. Fried chicken wing joints and potato skins might be joined on the appetizer list by a platter of stuffed grape leaves, caponata, and couscous salad. Guacamole, if it's available, is extremely good, made to order, served with three colors of freshly fried tortilla chips, carefully seasoned and served with half a lime for extra zip. Soups, too, flourish here, whether they're St. Louis' beloved French onion or a cold roasted tomato soup with a few chiles thrown in for fun.

Smoked shrimp are available as a first course or as an entree, depending on the vagaries of fate. We recommend them without reservation. They're moist and smoky and huge, full of flavor without any need for doo-dad sauces. Fish here often end up in a mixed stew from any point on the globe that has a shoreline and a distinctive flavor. The Thai version is excellent, with clams, mussels and shrimp plus other fish in a lime and curry broth with vegetables and rice noodles. Another version sets shrimp, clams, salmon and grouper in a tomato-based broth full of saffron and basil and punctuated with carrots and a few peas. Mediterranean, for sure, maybe somewhere just east of Nice. Pizza and pasta are always around in varying versions. The roast chicken, massaged with olive oil, garlic, lemon and herbs, lolls on a bed of mashed potatoes only mildly garlicky but sporting as garnish a half-dozen slightly browned roasted cloves, grabbed happily by the senior partner.

Chef Dave Owens, it should be noted, is a vegetarian. Instead of a diminution in the quality or quantity of meat entrees, the result has been an increase in vegetarian and even vegan dishes here, each marked on the menu. And who could resist a portobello mushroom stuffed with spinach, ricotta and bel paese cheese and roasted in that oven, with an arugula-fennel salad nearby? On the other hand, featured in a cookbook called *Burger Meisters*, was Bill Cardwell's burger topped with bleu and cheddar cheeses, apple-smoked bacon and spiced tomato relish. It's obviously not vital to taste everything coming out of the kitchen,

Desserts are good, made in-house, although arm-wrestling may be required to claim the last piece of peach pie or chocolate-banana tart with roasted banana ice cream. Twin creme brulees of lemon and key lime were surprisingly tart, and provided a good surprise.

The wine list, too, is solid, with good values at the lower end of the price list and some bottles to dream of at the high end. Cardwell's makes an effort to find inexpensive good wine, and it has obviously worked. The list covers the world and the markup is modest. Crackerjack service finishes the evening on a high note.

Meals with restaurateurs can be spectacular experiences, and we had one with Bill and Rich some years ago when we all were at a food conference in New Orleans. A tiny dive named Uglesich's, well off the New Orleans' restaurant path, was the target for the day, and the meal was glorious. We never think of New Orleans, or of them, without murmuring a silent thanks.

Cardwell's of Clayton
New American Cuisine
8100 Maryland Avenue, Clayton
726-5055
Lunch and Dinner, Monday-Saturday
Credit cards: All major
Wheelchair access: Satisfactory

When the Cardwell restaurant siblings divided early in 1998, everything went so smoothly that most people didn't hear about it. Rich Gorczyca now is in charge of the Clayton restaurant and Bill Cardwell is at Plaza Frontenac, but if either restaurant has suffered any pangs in food or service, it's hardly noticeable.

Cardwell's was probably the first of the Clayton restaurant cluster to succeed through the '90s and lead the exponential growth that hit the county seat in the middle of the decade. Other restaurants had done well in Clayton, but they were traditional American, St. Louis Italian or classic French. New American cooking had struggled, as had other white-tablecloth spots.

Then Rich Gorczyca, in front of the house, and Bill Cardwell, running the kitchen, came from Gilbert-Robinson, and suddenly New American food made sense to Claytonians, both day-timers and full-timers. Their cooking was a take on the familiar but put together differently, dazzling combinations that made a vivid impression.

The restaurant, and its food, are very San Francisco in many respects. Dark wood, white walls, mostly tile floors, a noisy bar, French doors open to the patio on nice days. Some of the artwork is due for a change, as the '80s-style prints that still hang in many doctors' waiting rooms are now cliches. And—small complaint—the menu covers are tattered, an odd thing to be overlooked in a house that generally doesn't miss a thing.

The bar is one of the places where young professional Clayton gathers to drink and socialize, and the uproar can be overwhelming, especially near the front door, where the tile floor helps the roar along. On the other hand, it makes for interesting people-watching and eavesdropping. Try to keep a straight face.

All this is secondary to the food. Not surprisingly, the menu shifts rapidly, and as with all similar restaurants, the food you ate last summer may be gone long before winter arrives. Prices put it at the lower end of the upper echelon, but represent good value. First courses run $5-$10, and entrees $12-$25.

A lot of thought goes into the soups. Summer brings gazpacho made from roasted local tomatoes, the smokiness giving a new twist to what's now an American standard. It was a twist in the right direction, too, the flavors full and well-balanced with just a touch of heat from the peppers. A stellar soup. Another was poblano pepper and sweet corn, so dense and rich it could have been a vegetarian chili. Spicier than the gazpacho, it layered cumin and probably a little garlic with the roasted peppers and sweet, slightly crunchy corn morsels.

The house salad comes with walnut oil and roasted garlic vinegar or Nauvoo blue cheese dressing, and there's always at least one other salad available. Carpaccio is made with smoked peppered sirloin, draped around a crispy cup of browned cheese that holds a small, anise-accented arugula and fennel salad. A drizzle of truffle oil adds an additional layer of flavor.

Lamb is crusted with mustard, herbs and bread crumbs with a potato gratin alongside. Duck is nearly always here, perhaps with ginger and kumquat sauce over a quickly roasted breast. A slab of halibut sounds bland. But when it's served over lemony pasta with tomatoes, mushrooms, asparagus, artichoke hearts and basil, it becomes thrillingly good. And the food here, we might add, always arrives hot. It's not just the usual "Be careful, these plates are hot" heat—the food itself arrives absolutely hot from the stove, not held under warming lights until someone delivers it.

Pork chops with a tamarind glaze were only mildly flavored, but a sweet-hot mango chutney was full of zing. The fat Israeli couscous alongside was curry-flavored, an amusing cultural juxtaposition that worked well. We'd have been happier if the chops were a little more moist, but loin chops can be tricky.

When it comes to dessert, Cardwell's uses the thrill-a-spoonful Quezel sorbets of Ron Ryan, who makes sorbets and ice creams far above the ordinary. There also are fancy desserts, like chocolate silk pie, a dense, dense mousse set on a crunchy hazelnut crust, and splendid items like cobblers made with good local fruit.

The wine list is a fine one, with judicious pricing and interesting bottles from California, France, Italy and even Missouri. Good values here, and a winning selection by the glass.

Carl's Drive Inn

Burgers and Root Beer
9033 Manchester Road, Brentwood
961-9652
Lunch and Dinner, Monday-Saturday
Cash only
Wheelchair access: Impossible

There may be a better flat-grilled hamburger in St. Louis and environs, but we've yet to find it. These are not the fat burgers that emerge from kitchens like O'Connell's. They're thin, and seared within an inch of their lives to emerge hot and slightly crusty around the edges. The first bite is one of the classic St. Louis eating experiences. The buns are nearly as hot as the hamburgers, and the grill is no more than ten feet away from any diner. Owner Frank Cunetto knows the importance of delivering this kind of food immediately. The lunchtime and afternoon crowds attest to his wisdom.

The burgers come as singles, doubles, or triples, and of course, there's cheese, too. Carl's also does a curly-q hot dog, cut almost through into smaller segments so that it curls as it grills and can fit, with its browned sides, onto a round bun. The standard foot-long is available for the more traditional types or the chili dog fancier.

All this comes with French fries or onion rings, which don't quite live up to the magnificence of the meat. On the other hand, the chili and tamales are good, and the winter-only soups are exciting, led by a surprisingly fiery, and outstanding, chicken and white bean.

Adding to the happy difficulty in ordering is the beverage question. Frank makes his own root beer, which comes, of course, out of a barrel and into huge frosted mugs. And it's good. But the almost-unsung competitor is the chocolate shake. We're not fans of the milk shake that's so thick you eat it with a spoon. That's a dessert, not a beverage. But this is nicely slurpy, just thin enough to drink through a straw without dislodging your teeth. Root beer floats are excellent, too.

The only serious drawback to Carl's is that sleepiness follows a blow-out meal. Better have a designated driver.

Only the eat-till-you-die types can spend more than $10 on a meal here.

Carriage House at DeMenil Mansion
Modern American Food
3352 DeMenil Place
771-5829
Lunch Tuesday-Friday, Dinner Thursday-Friday
Credit cards: AE, MC, V
Wheelchair access: Difficult

Not often do we find a place where the food is as good as the view. But Greg Mosberger, who by now must surely be tired of the constant link that describes him as having been a chef for Richard Perry (we promise this is the last time we will mention it), has put his high-quality food in a charming setting.

It also is difficult to avoid using the word "tearoom" in conjunction with the Carriage House. It mainly provides lunch, it's in a beautiful garden setting marred only by the noise of traffic from I-55, and there's an air of people having a good time at the table. Service is eager, pleasant, and polite without being at all formal. And prices are reasonable. Soups and other first courses are $2.95-$5.95, salads $3.25 to $7.50, sandwiches about $6. There also are main courses from $4.95 to $11.95. At dinner, only the entree prices go up, to average $14.

Appetizers pay tribute to local products with fried green tomatoes, crisp in a batter that's spiked with basil. A little chunky (ripe) tomato sauce is served with them, but the point is the crunchy tomato, great fun and not quite what Grandma cooked. There's also a pretzel from Gus' that's stuffed with beer bratwurst and served in slices with a dip of country mustard and another of candied carrots. There's also a beggar's purse, phyllo dough wrapped around crabmeat, a couple of pizzas and onion soup.

Cobb salad serves as an entree, especially at lunch. A large soup bowl with a layer of high-quality mixed greens is topped with stripes of sliced grilled chicken, avocado, hard-cooked egg, real bacon and blue cheese crumbles. The vinaigrette is citrus-scented, and poured lightly enough that the ingredients don't get soggy, making for a nice crisp meal with lots of different tastes and textures.

We passed up bison burgers and stuffed baked potatoes, even a roll of lavosh (sort of a large Lebanese soft tortilla) stuffed with smoked turkey, cheese, and a garlic mayonnaise, and finally settled on cold beef tenderloin. It turned out to be a wise decision. The beef was just a little below room temperature, fork-tender, slightly rare, very juicy and with a dark brown exterior that gave added taste. A few pieces of roasted potato rode along, as well as tiny, tangy French cornichon pickles and some marinated olives and whole-grain toast triangles. It was close to superb.

Dessert is mostly made in-house, and the customers benefit. There's always a Ted Drewes sundae available, but the baked goods draw the eye, and also induce some neck-craning from nearby tables when the tray is brought around. A flourless chocolate cake scented with amaretto and topped with fresh raspberries is one possibility. Pie with seasonal produce is always a good idea—blackberry came in a crust so flaky it had survived refrigeration, no small task. And a combination of baklava, strudel and cassata cake brought phyllo dough, ricotta, nuts and some fruit together in an innovative grouping.

At night, the menu is slightly different, with seven entrees and no sandwiches. Honey-smoked pork tenderloin and huckleberry sauce is tempting, and so is salmon glazed with chinese mustard. For a whiff of nostalgia, the strawberry shrimp from, yes, the old Richard Perry, are the first appetizer on the menu.

Don't get the idea that this is a ladies-who-lunch place, although there are some. There seem to be a fair number of business folk, mostly male, and a few couples smiling warmly at each other.

Casa Gallardo Grill
Nuevo Tex-Mex
St. Louis Galleria, Brentwood Boulevard at Clayton Road, Richmond Heights
727-2223
Lunch and Dinner, every day
Credit cards: All major
Wheelchair access: Comfortable

It looks as though the Casa Gallardo Grill is back in the saddle again. When it first opened, it was really exciting food. Not only was it good, but it was new to our palates. Now, chipotle chiles and mango salsa are on menus and grocery shelves all over town. And as mango madness spread, the food sagged at the Grill. We're happy to report that things are looking up again.

Even without innocent, almost-accidental entertainment, the food is good. The tortilla press, which looks as if it were rescued from the neighborhood dry cleaner, is great fun. See the tortillas tossed onto a rotating grill. Watch them bubble up and flip over, then go to an insulated dish. The effect is mesmerizing, and having the contraption next to the front desk must cause traffic jams. Decor is Reagan-era southwestern, now beginning to look dated. But service is deft, and very snappy at lunch time.

Diners are first greeted with a container of the tortillas they saw, two kinds of salsa, both good and both quite spicy, and a scoop of honey butter, all quite easy to fill up on because the menu takes some reading time.

The general idea is rethought favorites, so the quesadilla is mesquite grilled chicken, for instance. Salad dressings are serrano-grape vinaigrette or creamy cilantro with pumpkin seeds. There are spring rolls and calamari, as well as roast chicken and fajitas.

Guacamole ($6.95, average for appetizers) is prepared tableside, another floor show, with three avocado halves scooped into a metate, diced and tossed with onion and seasonings. "Mild, medium or hot?" asked the waiter. We chose hot, but even that was far from wild. We were slow, however, and forgot to tell the waiter to skip the cheese they sprinkle atop the guac, which seems to overwhelm the avocado. We put a little salsa on top, and it was a winner—the dark red, redolent of chipotle peppers, seems to work best. The guacamole blends all required tastes, and seems to add some more at the same time. It's delicious, and in perfect balance.

Pasta and salads? Yes, as well as the expected combination platters of enchiladas, burritos and tacos. Entrees range from $7.25 to $13.95. Two soft tacos come stuffed with large chunks of steak in one, carnitas of pork in the other, and slaw in both. The pork was particularly good, arriving juicy and interestingly spiced. The sides were New Mexico beans, a soupy mixture of varieties, and a sweet corn cake, a scoop of something much like a warm, very moist cornbread, very good indeed.

Texas toothpicks are a rack of pork ribs, steamed and then baked with a tamarind sauce, tangy and sweet-hot. The very moist meat fell off the bones, but the grease has melted away, leaving an immense pile of savory meat that must be eaten with a knife and fork, and were too steam-cooked to satisfy Joe. Real mashed potatoes, enriched with serrano chiles, sit alongside.

Desserts are mostly made in-house, cheesecake and sopapillas and mango flan, among other things. The wine list is a passing polite gesture, but there's a margarita menu, whose server insists they're all hand-shaken. A request for a plain one, please, brought a tart, sharp drink that tasted good. So did everything else.

Charcoal House
Steaks and Chops
9855 Manchester Road, Warson Woods
968-4842
Lunch Monday-Friday, Dinner Monday-Saturday
Credit cards: All major
Wheelchair access: Impossible

Dinner at the Charcoal House is visiting a world where nothing can go wrong. The venerable wood frame building is snug and traditional, full of quietly chatting groups from prosperous Gen Xers on up—way up. Garb is informal, tidy sport shirts to coats and ties, and there's an air of politeness. Service reflects that. It is well-oiled and smooth, stylish as veteran servers can make it, and the menu avoids surprises. As Holly Golightly said of Tiffany's, "Nothing bad could ever happen to you in there." Or at least not much. There's an air of security and permanence.

The menu is traditional, too, steaks and chops and, as a bow to the cholesterol-challenged, a few fish dishes. Now in the fifth decade of its existence, with brothers Steve and George Angelos in charge, the Charcoal House remains in the ice (or iceberg) age when it comes to salads, which basically are a polite gesture in the direction of nutrition before The Main Event. Shrimp cocktail, ordered to re-create a retro experience, involved four immense shrimp hung over the edge of a cup of red cocktail sauce. The sauce was pungent with a good hit of horseradish, but the shrimp were soft and flabby, lacking flavor. In addition, surgery had been performed near the large end of two of them, with a piece removed to leave the smaller section drooping properly over the lip of the cup.

Visiting the Charcoal House is a beef experience, like a filet mignon draped with a few mushrooms, or Steak by George, where delicious, lightly-battered onion rings replace the mushrooms. It was a superior piece of meat, tender and easy to cut and flavorful, a characteristic filets occasionally avoid. Even a young diner's carving skills were up to the chore. The porterhouse, a 20-ounce cut, was even finer, handsome and a perfect knockout in flavor and tenderness. It remained so the next day, too, when it served as a most proper lunch. The porterhouse is the best of all possible steaks, and also the most expensive, but the Charcoal House also has sirloins and a first-rate beef brochette, with green peppers, onions, mushrooms and other things tucked between chunks of beef.

Baked potatoes were large, fluffy, properly baked and ready for the butter or sour cream that awaited them. Among the many nice things about the Charcoal House is that diners can dress potatoes the way they wish, even if the dress is out of fashion. A request for broiled salmon with lemon garlic butter and the hash brown potatoes, drew the question, "Do you want onion with those?" from the waitress. A brilliant question, and one that should be answered with a firm yes. The salmon was also retro, and cooked to a degree of doneness well past the usual standards of this decade. Maybe not hard and tasteless, but certainly several stops past medium. The potatoes were in a small casserole, shredded with lots of onion. But the dish had been more than slightly underdone and then put under a broiler to brown, a disappointing version. The wine list is shorter than it should be, but a few proper bottles can be found.

A carrot cake with white chocolate icing was a slight switch on the usual cream cheese, and it was extremely sweet, but tasty. Everybody does a chocolate suicide cake these days (and many of them probably come from the same oven somewhere in this area), but it's a delicious dessert, and excellent here, too. And the retro extended to the days of drinks called tumbleweeds (and other regional names). Kahlua, vanilla ice cream, a blender. Forget the seafood and the hash browns. This is a meat house and a first-rate one, it's awfully good meat. Dinner will usually be $20 to $25 per person for appetizer, entree and dessert, and it's well worth it.

Charlie Gitto's on The Hill
Italian
5226 Shaw Avenue
772-8898
Dinner, every day
Credit cards: AE, DC, MC, V
Wheelchair access: Satisfactory

What a surprise to visit this sports celebrity hangout and find good news at every course. The front room is dark and subdued-cozy, older and much more elegant than its downtown sibling, with rich wood booths, pleasant darkness. While the menu initially looks much like the St. Louis standard Italian, a second look (and an ear to the specials) begins to give hints that something good is afoot. Risotto comes in a choice of appetizer or entree sizes, chicken or seafood. Pasta avoids a lot of the cliches, such as a Bolognese sauce on a chunkier pasta. The clams in an oil-and-garlic sauce are fresh ones, not from a jar. Yes, there's toasted ravioli, but there's fritto misto, too.

The seafood risotto appetizer boasted shrimp, salmon and scallops in rice that was creamy and still slightly firm to the chew. The broth was more than just canned clam juice, and the spicing showed a hint of red pepper that shoved other flavors to the fore. Cioppino, the famous Italian seafood stew, was a tomato broth with various kinds of shellfish and fish piled decoratively in mid-bowl. Carrots and orchiette (shell-like) pasta also were hanging around, our first sight of them in cioppino. But the broth was sharp with lemon and saffron, and the kitchen avoided overcooking the seafood.

Veal Nunzio was medallions sauteed with cheese over them (what is it about cheese-on-meat in St. Louis Italian restaurants?), topped with fine lump crabmeat and a lemon butter sauce. Veal is tender, crabmeat ditto, and sauce quite fine. Lamb chops came with a tasty green peppercorn-red currant glaze, three fat chops sitting on an Italian nonna's version of a potato pancake, and sauteed leeks glistening as the vegetable. The sides with the veal were less satisfactory. Green beans and carrots were hot, garlicky and very crunchy—too crunchy—and boiled new potatoes were cold.

The large menu offers plenty of tasty choices, and a satisfactory wine list, with plenty of good Italian offerings, but it's light on by-the-glass selections.

Dessert was tiramisu, airy and not too sweet but with discernible booze, and a couple of cannoli. These are what you always hope cannoli will be but rarely get. The shells—fresh, tender and crisp—are filled to order with a simple ricotta that combines to create Italian soul food.

Service is professional without being either frosty or overfamiliar, and dinner will be in the $25-$30 range per person. Gitto's is a Hill veteran, and its success is deserved.

Chef Hsu's Hunan Star
Chinese
13239 Manchester Road, Des Peres
822-8750
Lunch and Dinner, every day
Credit cards: All major
Wheelchair access: Passable

Tom Hsu may be the finest Chinese chef to work St. Louis since the late DuBois Chen ruled the range at Trader Vic's, but Hsu can be a frustrating soul to follow around. Joe has been eating Hsu's food since this lean chef with a piercing gaze and a Fu Manchu mustache started cooking in the area. And every good review of Joe's was followed by two things—an increase in business and a sale of the restaurant.

Hsu would then leave town for a few months, return, and repeat the program. After a while, Joe got smart and stopped eating at—and writing about—Hsu's restaurants.

Things seem calmer today. Hsu has been at his current address for four years, a record for permanence in St. Louis, and his cooking shows more skill, more style, more command of his talent at every meal. We dined there during the summer, a day after he had prepared a Vietnamese wedding feast for two hundred and twenty guests. The restaurant was half-full, Hsu looked exhausted, and the meal was magnificent. Dishes ranged from mild—almost sweet— stir-fried shrimp with a variety of vegetables, to tangy tea-barbecued chicken, to spicy squid and shrimp in a jalapeno pepper-and-black bean sauce. With a less careful chef, the latter dish could have been a blazer. Too often, when Chinese restaurants use dried red chile peppers for heat, the peppers are tossed in, seeds and all, and the result can be just too much. But Hsu knows that when the seeds are removed from the jalapeno, and the pepper is cooked, the fire is lessened considerably. There's still a pop, but both the taste and the heat of the peppers can be enjoyed in the dish, and not pushed to the side.

Hsu shows a superb balance in his cooking, and he will adjust spices to the taste of the diner, but both sides have to speak the same language. We prefer the term, "Indian medium," in Indian spots, which is plenty hot for most Americans, and we often ask for "somewhere between seven and eight on a scale of ten," in Chinese restaurants. Of course, when Billy Wilder wrote, "some like it hot," he was referring to us. We suggest starting on the low side and increasing the heat, because it's impossible to go the other way. Most Chinese restaurants have hot oil. Ask for it, use it sparingly, and if you like it, buy some at Jay's or another Asian grocery store and add a little to the scrambled eggs on Sunday mornings at home.

The black bean sauce is spectacular, and Joe's friend, Herb (referred to for years as the Old China Hand), will eat it with clams every single day. It is that good, but we like more variety. Hsu's hot and sour soup tingles all the way home, and his cold noodles with sesame sauce is a fine appetizer. The vegetarian dishes are exciting, such as the dry sauteed string beans, which come with or without meat. Eggplant with garlic sauce is another winner, and if the Chinese eggplants are available, we think they're better than those used in Italian cooking. The Asian variety is smaller and a lighter violet, often striped with white, and is prettier and firmer when cooked.

Hsu's dumplings are satisfactory, but we prefer his shrimp toast or scallion pancake, along with his barbecued pork.

Service is quick and good, and the location is bright. Beer and tea are our drinks of choice here, and there's usually fresh pineapple for dessert, always at the peak of sweetness.

By the time this book is on the street, Tom Hsu may have packed up his knives and woks and mustache and moved to another kitchen. We hope not, because he's a spectacular chef, and we have agreed that if we ever get married again, we'll call him to prepare the wedding feast.

Chuy Arzola's Tex-Mex Restaurant
Fajita Central

6405 Clayton Avenue
644-4430
Lunch and Dinner, every day
Credit cards: DSC, MC, V
Wheelchair access: Passable

There was a time when the crowds were so thick at Chuy's that parking in the nearby blocks became warfare. The trendy folks have bolted to other, newer spots, but Chuy's goes on, feeding a loyal crowd that wouldn't think of committing fajita adultery.

Fajitas are the dish that made this Dogtown spot famous.

There also are the usual combination plates ($7-$10) with burritos, enchiladas, chalupas, tacos and so on, and a recent excursion into the enchiladas proved pleasant (and under $8), although the filling is ground beef rather than the shredded that we prefer. Hey, it's Tex-Mex, and that's usually what arrives. The refried beans here are particularly tasty, too.

The fajitas, sizzling fiercly, are served for two ($17), for one ($9), as a plate ($8.50), in a salad ($7.50) or on nachos ($9). Beef or chicken come with lots of grilled onions and peppers, lettuce, cheese, sour cream, a nice lumpy guacamole, and a fresh and notable pico de gallo with jalapenos that give it a good pop. Flour tortillas, of course, to wrap the diner's choice of meat and toppings—watch that shirt, buddy.

Lots of families here with little kids getting their jaws around a miniature version of the fajita roll. There's a high noise level, rushed service on busy nights, and forgettable margaritas, but fajitas alone are making Chuy's an institution.

Cicero's

Pop Italian and American Diner

6691 Delmar Boulevard, University City
862-0009
Lunch and Dinner, every day
Credit cards: All major
Wheelchair access: Satisfactory

Didja hear the one about the McDonald's that was serving a McLox? Actually, it"s true—although it was spelled McLaks when we saw it at a harborside MickeyD's in Oslo, Norway. "Laks" is salmon in Norwegian (and in several other Northern European languages), and it was a burger, maybe more like a croquette, made from ground salmon.

We go into this to explain that once again St. Louis is at the forefront of international trends. We found a salmon burger at Cicero's. It was our first visit there, we admit with a slight blush. But it's a bargain, with satisfactory food in huge portions for modest prices (like many of the spots in the multi-tabled U. City Loop).

For one thing, and no small thing it is, the pizza (from $5.95) is really good. The thin crust is good, but chewy rather than cracker-crisp, and the latter is a quality that always makes us think the crust is premade. The sauce is moist enough that the cheese, which is mozzarella, not provel, tries to slide off. Eminently satisfactory, as Nero Wolfe, the gourmet detective, would have said.

An order of spaghetti and meatballs ($10.20) brought pasta that was slightly al dente and sauce with a strong flavor of basil. The meatballs were tender and could never have a second career as golf balls, like some we've tried. Not bad at all.

And the salmon burger ($5.95)? Well, it was a salmon patty, well spiced with black peppers and quite good, although it was unfortunately dry when placed on a whole wheat bun. It took a lot of mayonnaise, tomato and lettuce to wet it down. (It'd be great with a couple of eggs over easy—but that's another review.) Nevertheless, a valiant effort.

A huge and very interesting beer list, many on draft, and also some on-draft Woodpecker dry cider, a favorite of both of us. Some interesting wines as well. They also offer chocolate Pepsi. We'll think about it tomorrow. At Tara.

Desserts are in a large case in the dining room, and you're encouraged to go up and inspect them. We had some lemon cake ($2.95) and a brownie. The lemon cake tasted like what Mom used to make, vividly yellow and moist, with a tart lemon frosting that made us wish for the chance to lick the bowl.

Cicero's is loud and casual, and considering those major hurdles in an obstacle race, service is extremely deft.

Citizen Kane's Steak House
Steaks

133 West Clinton Place, Kirkwood
965-9005
Dinner only, every day
Credit cards: All major
Wheelchair access: Passable

Citizen Kane's seems to be one of those places people either vigorously like or don't want much to do with. In an old house with the resultant series of small rooms and enclosed porches, movie photos and a sled on the porch give the theme to owner Frank Kane's brainchild. Aside from the photos, the decor is unremarkable, and the menu makes it clear that things are kept very simple here.

Appetizers are all traditional American, like shrimp cocktail and onion rings, and are in the $4-$8 range. Sauteed mushrooms are large white button mushrooms, and come with a wine-bolstered garlic-butter broth, simple but good. Main courses include soup or salad plus a side dish, and go from a $16.95 "Daily Inquirer Special," to a $23.25 New York strip. Interestingly, while menu items do not indicate weights, the waitress related weights of all the specials, including fish.

The Rosebud Salad contains none. Fortunately. It's romaine with a little red onion and some cheese. The vinaigrette dressing is sweet. A house dressing is a Mayfair, "with a very light anchovy base." When we looked mournful at the word "light," the waitress suggested some anchovies on top, a good compromise and a good result. The soup was an Anglo-Saxon version of egg drop soup, chicken broth with nicely julienned vegetables and bits of egg, pleasant and hot enough.

The rib eye or Delmonico steak was almost an inch-and-a-half thick, and was a perfect rare. Rib eyes aren't lean steaks, but that contributes to their flavor, and this was a very good one. Across from us, a couple ordered well-done filets mignons. They didn't arrive burnt, and were clearly cooked through. In some restaurants, well-done steaks are charred to death out of what seems to be sheer retribution on the part of the kitchen. We think well-done is a mistake, but restaurant customers deserve edible meals. The Kane's wine list is slender, but moderately priced, with some by-the-glass selections as well.

The pork chop was unavailable, alas, so we had some tilapia with the bearnaise sauce discussed on the menu. It was properly cooked, if unexciting, and the sauce had enough tarragon, but carried a metallic taste as though it had lemon pith or had suffered some chemical reaction. For those who don't care for red meat, there's a chicken pasta and shrimp scampi over pasta. The boardinghouse potatoes were not sauteed, although the accompanying onions and peppers were—the potatoes appeared to have been deep-fried. A vegetable du jour was Mexican-style corn, niblets with peppers and tomatoes and a little pungent seasoning. Kane's gets points for trying to do something different, and this was certainly a step in the right direction, maybe not a five-star dish, but interesting and worth eating.

Carrot cake is made in-house. It's dense, rather unsweet but full of the classic flavor, topped with a soft, creamy frosting. The combination works very nicely, calmly and without high drama, like two long-time lovers strolling hand in hand through the grocery store.

And we liked the polite service, too.

Colorado

New American Cowboy

3761 Laclede Avenue
652-3044
Lunch Monday-Friday, Dinner every night
Credit cards: AE, MC, V
Wheelchair access: Satisfactory

Colorado has come into its own. It opened as a second operation of Lee Redel and John Rice after the success of Redel's, but after Redel's closed, Rice moved the Redel collection of antique table radios and, it seems, a great deal of its momentum. It's ideally situated for dinner before events in the Grand Center area.

The decor is amusingly close to the knotty-pine world of what tourist Colorado really was like in the Fifties, with old advertisements, postcards and posters. The back room, quite dark, isn't used much unless Colorado gets really busy.

The menu covers a broad range of tastes from sirloin steak to Thai noodles, with excursions into enchiladas and pizzas. Several dishes are reminiscent of Redel's, and there are plans to revive the fried chicken and salmon cakes. The latter, though, are going to be spicier, we understand. Rice is fond of vigorous spicing, and makes his own hot sauce with chipotle chiles and the incendiary habanero.

Appetizers run from $3 to $10, but some of them are large enough for a main course, like a half-pound of grilled shrimp on a bed of citrus salsa or a fresh tuna salad. We had a bowl of chicken noodle soup that had barely survived an encounter with the kitchen salt box, but an order of Thai noodles was large and well-seasoned with a peanut sauce, chicken strips and lots of green onions.

Entrees run $8-$15, with the top end for a large, fully-loaded vegetable pizza. Interestingly, bread costs fifty cents extra except with pasta. A trout special was a boneless fish stuffed with green onions and capers, wrapped with a strip of serious bacon, a fine combination. Mashed potatoes seasoned with basil and sun-dried tomatoes were uncommonly good. The vegetable medley (excuse us, but couldn't we get a Cole Porter medley instead?) was the all-too-common zucchini and yellow squash punched up with red bell pepper and some jalapeno. Enough with the squashes, world, can't we come up with more interesting vegetables? The jalapeno did help, however.

Flank steak fajitas were only three strips of beef for two large flour tortillas. It was excellent beef, accompanied by sauteed mixed peppers, including chipotles and perhaps a jalapeno, a few mushrooms and some garlic. A good version, certainly, but heavy on the vegetables. A number of menu items carry the heart-healthy symbol, and perhaps that sense of virtue has led the kitchen to cut back on meat.

Interestingly, the mixed berry cobbler was made with a batter rather than a pie crust. The result was more of a pudding cake than what Midwesterners would expect from the word cobbler, but it was moist and tangy, with blueberries taking first place in the berry count.

Affable, considerate service, but sometimes the kitchen or the dining room staff lose the rhythm and entrees appear two bites into the appetizers without anyone seeming surprised except the customer.

Cravings
Buttercream Central

8149 Big Bend Boulevard
961-3534
Lunch Tuesday-Saturday, Dinner Friday-Saturday
Credit cards: MC, V
Wheelchair access: Satisfactory

One of the more interesting lunch menus shows up at Tim Brennan's restaurant, Cravings, which serves as the public side of his business. The other side involves catering to order, primarily spectacular cakes for special occasions.

We're very fond of the turkey sandwich, smoked turkey piled high and dressed with a cranberry relish, but not at all reminiscent of Thanksgiving (probably because of the smokiness). Curried chicken salad holds chunks of white meat, and a curry-green dressing with notes of garlic and ginger perks it up even more. Sliced almonds and the occasional raisin provide intermittent surprises to the mouth. There's tuna with a tapenade of sun-dried tomatoes and black olives, and a BLT as well, all served on wheatberry, a tender French or a Portuguese egg bread, pale yellow from the yolks and slightly sweet. All come with a side dish and average $6.

Non-sandwich items, from $5 to $9, lean heavily toward the vegetarian, with salads, focaccia pizza, spanokopita and zucchini Umbria (like ratatouille but without eggplant), and tarts made with mushrooms in a rich, buttery, crumbly pastry crust. Other fillings include cheddar cheese with scallions and tomato with goat cheese.

No visit to Cravings is possible, however, without dessert. Big glass jars of fat cookies line the counter, labeled to entice the wary as well as the unwary. The lighted case greeting arrivals is filled with Brennan's James Beard Award-winning work, including a hazelnut zuccotto, which is a sort of mousse in a cake, and a lime blueberry bombe.

We, however, are partial to the lemon cake with a blueberry-and-cream filling, which combines two of our favorite fruits, and the chocolate cake with cranberry filling. For those who grasp the wonder of chocolate and raspberries, this is a highly desirable next step in chocolate appreciation, the chocolate mellowing the cranberry's slight bitterness with a result that leaves aficionados groaning. Desserts are mostly under $5. Some good wines are available by the glass, and service is by folks who have (mostly) studied the menu offerings very closely indeed.

Crazy Fish

Modern American

15 North Meramec Avenue, Clayton
726-2111
16125 Chesterfield Village Parkway, Chesterfield
532-9300
Lunch and Dinner, every day; Brunch in Clayton, Sunday
Credit cards: All major
Wheelchair access: Satisfactory

Zany names, once confined to rock groups and race horses, are now so common that when Crazy Fish opened five years ago, not everyone realized this was a restaurant that meant to specialize in piscatorial pleasures. Despite the name, entrees are almost evenly split between fish and meat, and there are some vegetarian dishes, too.

The flashy, colorful restaurant in the area we've named the Clayton Rectangle has been so successful that proprietor Chris LaRocca has expanded to a second, larger location with a similar menu. The new West County spot will keep its sandwiches on the menu later in the evening and have a few more pizza choices. LaRocca also has opened a handful of fast food operations, some in a wrap mode and others dealing in quick Mexican meals.

The most significant piece of equipment at Crazy Fish is the wood-burning oven, used to roast vegetables as well as meat, fish and pizzas. Who would have thought a smoky Vidalia onion might be wilted into a poppy-seed vinaigrette and tossed with spinach and feta cheese? The dressing is honey-sweetened, a dab much for our taste, but still a fascinating piece of work.

An appetizer platter brought slices of toasted bread, a huge head of roasted garlic, very mild and quite caramelized, a tapenade with olives and balsamico (no anchovies), a spread made from sun-dried tomatoes that was surprisingly sunny-tasting, bright and perky and not at all chewy, and a round of goat cheese rolled in fresh herbs and some black sesame seeds. A successful combination of goodies, and a particularly good choice for grownups who want an excuse to play with their food.

A silky-tender, extremely rare chunk of yellowfin tuna was sliced and piled on top of an orzo (rice-sized and -shaped pasta) salad with generous slivers of red onion, fennel and cucumber. The tuna was crusted with pepper and filled with wonderful flavor. It outshone the salad, which was much more subtle.

Bison meat loaf is a signature dish, the grilled triangles of meat, piled around a mound of mashed potatoes and remaining moist. Crazy Fish usually has several kinds of mashed potatoes on hand, so ask. (The Yukon golds are the simplest, a little garlicky but not overwhelming.) An Asian-glazed turkey dish was a grilled slab of breast, a delicious mango and pineapple salsa and half a Thai sausage, which was loose and crumbly but moist and full of tastes like cilantro and lemon grass. The turkey breast wasn't overdone, and the combination was exciting. It came with guajillo chile mashed potatoes so orange in color that the mouth expected the flavor of sweet potatoes. They, too, were fresh and full of flavor without being more than mild to medium in their spiciness.

Pork dishes receive special care, and the daily fish specials, with a fine, varied, imaginative group of sauces coming from the kitchen of Dave Rook, are usually outstanding.

Desserts are mostly made in-house, and they're good. A tulip of white and dark chocolate, for example, was filled with sliced berries, a white chocolate hazelnut mousse and lots of whipped cream.

The wine list is large and well-chosen, with many by the glass. On one evening, seven different chardonnays were available. Servers are zippy and knowledgeable, and able to keep a straight face when they describe carrots, yellow squash and green beans as seasonal vegetables. (We didn't ask which season.)

Crazy Fish does a good sit-down brunch, too, with a menu that ranges from warm banana nut bread to huevos rancheros. Lots of lunch items, plus things like blueberry and white chocolate griddle cakes. We particularly like the spicy house potatoes.

The Crossings
New American Cuisine
7823 Forsyth Boulevard, Clayton
721-7375
Lunch Tuesday-Friday, Dinner Monday-Saturday
Credit cards: All major
Wheelchair access: Passable

To those who say that modern American cooking is all alike, we give you the Crossing, singing bright, true high notes in the Clayton choir. Among the fine entries in the class of '98, The Crossings blends traditional Midwest flavors with ingredients and combinations that could have come only from New York's finest restaurants (where Cary McDowell and Jim Fiala spent time in the kitchens of the Gotham and Daniel).

The restaurant is bright and clean, working on two dining levels with a staff that moves crisply and has an intelligent understanding of the menu.

An opening amuse-gulee was described as an onion souffle, but it was both more and less; with sweet Vidalia-style onions like an onion tart, and the delicate flavor of an onion quiche with its cream and eggs.

Similarly, the beets turned into a salad of the red vegetable, roasted and diced into tiny chunks, then formed into a cylinder with superior goat cheese in the middle, like the filling of a sandwich, all topped with a light vinaigrette dressing. The combination is exciting, with a slight tang, and superior to either field greens or traditional greens. The Crossings also offers rich, hearty soups, like a mushroom that was rich and musky, yet soft and clean of finish on the palate. Pacific Coast oysters, served with a dipping sauce of shallots and vinegar, show that the Crossing knows how to pick shellfish and has a good supplier.

Pasta, almost al dente even with an egg-noodle tagliatelle, also is superior. The tagliatelle, with a couple of greens including arugula, was delightful, though it yielded top honors to linguine with small, tender, superb mussels whose flavor and aroma flooded the dish. Missouri trout, cooked with bacon and sage, was as good as any we've had, and the tuna, rare and sprinkled with pepper, also was a winner. Vegetables like roasted mushrooms and potatoes worked perfectly. Roast duck is served three ways, each better than the one before—rare, delicate breast slices, woodsy shreds in a choucroute style and grilled liver, rare and sweet, the next best thing to a foie gras. Roast veal, simple and succulent, is almost an afterthought in this company, but it's terrific.

So are desserts—tangy, flavorful, chilled rhubarb soup with enough strawberries to make it taste like strawberry-rhubarb pie. Creme brulee is heavy on fresh ginger, and those who don't like the spice should stay away, but chocolate cake, dense and dark, is delicious, and perfectly accompanied by vanilla ice cream that still displays bean bits.

The area we've named the Clayton Rectangle (as easy to get lost in as the Bermuda Triangle but with tastier food) keeps getting better as restaurateurs push one another to new heights of flavor sensations, and The Crossings need not stand aside for anyone in this august company. A glorious meal.

Crown Candy Kitchen

Classic American Soda Fountain
1401 St. Louis Avenue
621-9650
Lunch and Dinner, every day
Cash Only
Wheelchair access: None

Self-indulgence by its very nature is a highly personal thing. Some folks think the height of irresponsible fun is an evening on one of the gambling boats. For others, it's a visit to a spa or a day of skydiving. We'd go for a night at the Plaza Hotel or a visit to Crown Candy Kitchen.

Actually, the food's better at Crown Candy. Eloise and room service notwithstanding, the Plaza doesn't have the innate sense of just how a bacon, lettuce and tomato sandwich should arrive—the toast and bacon still warm, the lettuce cold and the tomato bursting with juice and flavor. Crown Candy does. They pack the sandwich with lots of bacon that's just short of shatteringly crisp, the way it should be and the reason why it isn't called a lettuce, tomato and bacon sandwich.

This is a family place, of course. Children need to grow up knowing about jukeboxes and ice cream sodas and malted milks, just as they should know about long division and Newton's laws and that "i comes before e except after c." Given the menu, it's amazing that the adults don't act more like kids than they do. Courthouse regulars talk touchdowns instead of torts, media people catch their breath and daydream a little while they wait.

They don't have to wait long, either, which is another good reason it's child-friendly. The waitresses move rapidly, and the soda master shows grace in motion as he makes the old fountain equipment purr and the malt containers gleam. The master, part of the family that has been running Crown Candy since 1913, is too old and we need his skills too much to call him a jerk.

Several menu boards—ranging from ancient to merely dated—function as menus, and there's a paper one available, without prices. It's quite difficult, however, to spend much more than a sawbuck for lunch. It isn't mandatory to order a sandwich or soup with or before the ice cream, but the salty-crunchy foods are a good contrast to sweet-smooth treats. Joe's father was a fan of thick pretzels with an ice cream soda, and he claimed that the salt and the sweet made both taste better. He was right.

This is a hamburger-free zone, a world where commendable grilled cheese, tuna salad and chili serve as alternatives to the BLT. Sandwiches come with potato chips and a couple of pickle slices, just as they once did at drugstore soda fountains.

Malts here are real malts, not shakes, unless you specify. They don't come bulging out of a machine either, but are made to order with ice cream, milk, malt powder and a wide range of flavors. Many insist on banana, straight from the ripening heap in a big glass bowl on the counter. For sodas, sundaes and their kin, the same mix-and match rules apply. Joe, for instance, is a fan of chocolate sodas with coffee ice cream. The caramel here is actually butterscotch, by the way. In another nomenclature clarification, Newports are sundaes with whipped cream, pecans and a cherry.

One of the unsung heroes of the menu is the hot fudge banana split; chocolate and banana make a killer combo. This is a great place for coffee ice cream, too, but either black walnut or butter pecan might also do well. Oreo, we found, is overkill. However, we wish all the ice cream was a little richer.

Crown Candy refers to itself as Chocoholics Local #1, and other possibilities are chocolate ice cream with marshmallow sauce, with pineapple or, for chocolate-covered strawberry fans, strawberries? Or there's hot fudge over black cherry ice cream.

Some people fret about the neighborhood, which is north of downtown. But it isn't a problem. Quite frankly, we've never been to Crown Candy when there wasn't at least one police car parked in front and someone checking meters. Some police do doughnuts; the smart ones, like ours, do Crown Candy.

Culpeppers
Hamburgers, Sandwiches, Soups
300 North Euclid Avenue
361-2828
12316 Olive Boulevard, Creve Coeur
469-3888
312 South Kirkwood Road, Kirkwood
821-7322
Lunch and Dinner, every day
Credit cards: All major
Wheelchair access: Satisfactory

The northeast corner of Euclid and Maryland Aveues is the center of the Central West End, and Culpeppers, at the center of the center, has become a neighborhood landmark as a place to hang out, and for a long time, also as a place for some excellent bar food, though the reputation is fading.

In some areas, like soups and many sandwiches (the classic BLT stands out), it can be said that Culpeppers defined bar food. And, of course, the restaurant introduced Buffalo-style hot chicken wings to the city. Lunch, even at 10 p.m., is about $15.

Culpeppers had gained fame many generations ago as a pizza pioneer when it opened at the end of Prohibition in 1933. It also became one of the favorite hangouts of the late *Globe-Democrat* gossip columnist, Bob Goddard. When it closed in 1971, it became the Whitfield Gallery, Kerr-Oberbeck, and a short-lived bar-restaurant called Ginger's, named after Ginger Rogers and operated by Lynn Smith. Herb Glazier, a veteran of the peak years of Gaslight Square (when he and Sam Deitsch operated the Opera House), reopened Culpeppers under its original name in October 1977, in partnership with his fiancee, Mary McCabe, creator of spectacular soups and dispenser of terrible jokes.

It was a saloon and a hamburger joint, they said, but near-miracles came from the tiny kitchen, and good, strong drink over the bar from a corps of expert bartenders led by Jack Rinaldi. Sports and television were not on the agenda, but conversation, good music and a giant jukebox were. Until Glazier and McCabe sold out in the '90s, Culpeppers offered solid food, French fries that were thick and crisp, spicy gazpacho and the best ceviche in town in the summer. Now there are two county branches of Culpeppers, but the aura is not the same. Smaller staffs and portions and soups from mixes make it seem as though the bottom line has become the most important thing.

Cunetto's House of Pasta
Pasta Is Primary; other Italian dishes, too

5453 Magnolia Avenue
781-1135
Lunch Monday-Friday, Dinner Monday-Saturday
Credit cards: All major
Wheelchair access: Impossible

The first thing a would-be Cunetto's customer needs to know is their no-reservation policy. The second thing is to arrive extremely hungry. This is no place to visit for a little snack.

Cunetto's is one of St. Louis' favorite restaurants. Crowds have come here for years. It always does well in restaurant surveys. For years, its charm eluded us, and we mostly stayed away. Things seem to have changed, though. There's even a no cholesterol, low salt section on the back of the menu.

It's a pleasant, residential-looking dining room with mirrors paned and draped like windows, and a homey selection of artwork that includes everything from photos to J. M. W. Turner prints. The servers are clearly pros, pleasant folks who know their menu and move quickly.

A dish of cracked olives ($3.10) is offered as a first course, a pleasant temptation while studying the rest of the very large menu. These are seedless, crushed slightly and marinated in a wine vinegar and brine mixture with celery and onion, nice to finish off the drink half-done in the bar when summoned to a table. The fried eggplant ($4.25) is startlingly good, an immense pile of narrow sticks, crisp with light breading, exquisitely drained, a dish to convert the eggplant-uninitiated. It comes with a dish of red meat sauce, thick and lumpy and slightly sweet with tomato, but the crunchy sticks are just fine solo.

Pasta fagiole ($3.50), still occasionally pronounced as "pastafazool," is a bean soup thickened with small pasta. In Tuscany, the land of the bean-eaters, smoked meat is a rarity, and the soup is almost thick enough to stand a spoon in. Cunetto's has some ham, and is not quite as dense, but other than that, it's superb, the best we've found. It's an outstanding version, rich with herbs and broth, full of ditalini and good tastes.

The house salad ($3.50) is chopped iceberg and romaine with lots of toss-ins—green onion, a little pimento, the occasional crouton, some bacon bits, and a creamy anchovy-based dressing. Like another pre-dressed house salad in another well-known St. Louis pasta place, it's very heavy on the dressing. However, it offers a nice variety of textures and tastes. The small salad is probably two cups of eating material, so be prepared.

Those generous servings are beloved of St. Louisans, who seem intent on getting their money's worth no matter what their income bracket. In all parts of the price spectrum, restaurateurs report that St. Louisans demand large servings, even if they don't eat them. And no one who leaves Cunetto's seems to go empty-handed. The pasta servings are immense. An order of linguini with red clam sauce ($9.50) produced what seemed about a quart of pasta and sauce. Especially sauce. The pasta was not overcooked—the menu says all pasta is cooked to order, and we suspect it's so—and the sauce, a tomato sauce with a generous amount of clams and garlic and red pepper, was delicious. But there was so much it puddled in the bottom of the bowl, an unnecessary amount. That much sauce should not be necessary to provide sufficient flavor, and it makes for messy eating.

We also had macaroni with olive oil, garlic and anchovies ($7.75), a lovely reminder that macaroni wasn't always the stuff in the Kraft box. The long, thick tubes swirled in the simple, aromatic sauce studded with bits of anchovy. It, too, was al dente, very much the peasant food. We are researching the anchovy gene, by the way, as it seems to be present in our family. It was demonstrated when a grandchild asked for, and got, a serving of linguini alla Pavarotti ($7.75 for adults), a portion of pasta with a tomato and anchovy sauce fit for a Luciano-sized child. The menu talks about red pepper, too, but this was mild, not nearly as pungent as the clam sauce, and just nicely fishy, the anchovy having dissolved, as it often can, with the cooking.

Thinking about dessert when a tow truck has been called to carry home the leftovers is probably foolish, and the dessert menu is simple: cheesecake ($2.50), ice cream ($2), including spumoni and tartufo ($2.75), cannoli ($2.75) and tiramisu ($4.50). The tiramisu had just disappeared, and the last tartufo, a chocolate-covered ice cream, fled to another table just after we had ordered it. So we had a cannoli, with a crisp but rather thick shell and an unremarkable filling, and tried the spumoni, which was, well, spumoni.

Cunetto's is full of good surprises, but they've gotta curb that guy who ladles out the sauces and dressings.

Da Nang
Vietnamese Cuisine
3216 S. Grand Boulevard
664-6702
Lunch and Dinner, Tuesday-Sunday
Credit cards: All major
Wheelchair access: Passable

Between the two of us, there are decades of restaurant-reviewing experience. But, as we strolled on South Grand Boulevard, we experienced a first—a customer rushed out of Da Nang in mid-meal to stop us and urge us to eat there. Proprietors, yes, have done this, but never a customer.

Coincidentally, we were on our way to Da Nang that night, so after we finished our initial errand (which was looking at a new place about to open), we returned.

It's a classic South Grand restaurant caught early in its history, the storefront with minimal decor and plenty of speakers of the home language. In the front window sits a large pot of lemon grass looking reassuringly like an ordinary house plant. Other clientele are graduate-school types and a few non-Asian locals.

Rather than the various rolls we often get for first courses in Vietnamese restaurants, we opted for pork ribs ($6.95) and chicken salad ($4.95). The latter, also known as goi ga, held shredded chicken and cabbage seasoned with mint, onion, cilantro and a light, non-oily dressing. The flavors were perky and the texture crunchy-chewy. It had been freshly made with a generous amount of chicken. The cabbage supplied more crunch than taste.

Suon noung ruou, the marinated and broiled pork ribs, were described as "flambed at your table." After a little ignition difficulty, we were treated to flames surrounding bright green lettuce, which formed the bed for the ribs. Interestingly, the lettuce wilted very little in the process. The spare ribs were accompanied by another thin but very meaty cut, in what was a lot like a teriyaki marinade but less sweet. They were chewy but not tough, and not overwhelmingly salty.

De xao gung hanh, ginger lamb ($8.50), showed off green onions and a reasonable amount of ginger in a stir-fry. The lamb was satisfactory in quality, but gray and a little short on quantity. The stars were the vegetables, and the sauce that rode nicely on the sticky rice that accompanied the course. A ga xao xa ot, lemon grass chicken ($6.50), was full of good tastes with the sweetness of sauteed onion, although the lemon grass didn't predominate. It was starred as being a spicy dish, but was far from hot.

Da Nang's menu features many vegetarian dishes, as well as other intriguing things like clay pot combos, the ubiquitous noodles, and pho, the classic Vietnamese meal-in-a-bowl soup. As best we can tell, it's pronounced "fuh." There's a fair amount of cultural overlap, with kung pao platters and sate sauces and curries. We're not sure how much of this is an attempt to appeal to a wider audience, or how much is from cultural influences that have rippled through Vietnam over the centuries.

To Da Nang's credit, the menu promises "natural and authentic" food, and is careful about identifying imitation crabmeat and explaining that the food is made to order, so service may be slow. (It was, but not excruciatingly so.)

Dessert was fried bananas, slices of fruit in what was much like a tempura batter. Despite the syrup atop it, it was only mildly sweet, and quite charming. Finish the meal with Vietnamese coffee, the thick drip stuff with ice. Da Nang's version is particularly leisurely as it drips slowly, and we had plenty of time to reflect on how glad we are it's 1998, not 1968, in Da Nang.

Delmar Restaurant & Lounge
Modern American
6235 Delmar Boulevard, University City
725-6565
Dinner every night
Credit cards: All major
Wheelchair access: Passable

"Lounge" is just the right word to describe the decor at this restaurant, which once was occupied by Painted Plates and then the Grateful Grill. Jerry Garcia rotates in his grave, however, at what's going down here.

The Delmar makes you think of a movie from the early '50s with Doris Day playing a singer in her pre-virgin days. It's red and black leatherette and chrome, and a polished tile floor that's just waiting for someone to take a sweetie for a spin. The music is eclectic, but we're sure the twenty-somethings we saw quietly conversing at the bar—a proper demeanor, to be sure—consider it middle-aged stuff. We heard music from the '40s, '60s and '70s, and something that seemed to have been recorded by a Russian group speaking English.

It looks great. Service was rather rattled, however, several items missing from the menu unacknowledged until ordered or even received by the kitchen. One glass of zinfandel was misidentified, another declared MIA and then rediscovered. They have about eight wines by the glass, and one of the pear ciders we're getting so attached to. Without drinks, the tab should run about $22 a head.

An appetizer of grilled polenta tasted more as if it had been fried, but it was nicely corny, and the mushroom ragout that topped it was well-seasoned and tasty. The smoked chicken was inconsistent; one mouthful dry and smoke-free, another moist and flavorful. Falafel was rather bland, but a well-spiced, chunky tomato coulis brought it up to speed. There are also several pizzas and some pastas, which can come as an entree or appetizer, always a good choice for a diner, and especially good here, when the kitchen stays open late enough to be an after-event destination.

Hoisin-glazed salmon came on a bed of cellophane rice noodles, piping hot and moist but not rare. The crispy noodles offered the proper base for the tangy hoisin seasoning. On the other hand, apricot-glazed pork loin missed the mark embarrassingly, with flavorless, tough meat. Once in a while there's pork that the best butcher in town could not identify as tough, and we allow for that, but this was dry and overcooked with an apathetic, listless glaze. On the other hand, the accompanying potato gratin almost made up for things. Potatoes, sliced paper-thin with lots of black pepper, seemed to have almost no cream in them, but they were downright seductive. Among the other entrees are lamb chops with a sauce of stout and roasted vegetable cakes.

Espresso pound cake is the Delmar's version of what's essentially a tiramisu, and a pretty darned good one it is, too. Topped with a chocolate ganache and with lots of coffee and a little alcohol in there, it's nice and moist with a good range of flavors. A winning bet.

This place has a late-night menu from 11 p.m. until 2 a.m., and a 3 a.m. liquor license. Even though things were rocky, we're hoping they make it. Late night places need encouragement because they're one of the marks of a genuine metropolis.

Dierdorf & Hart's
Steaks and Chops
701 Market Street
421-1772
323 West Port Plaza, Maryland Heights
878-1801
Lunch Monday-Friday, Dinner every night
Credit cards: All major
Wheelchair access: Satisfactory

The most lasting legacy of the late, lamented St. Louis Football Cardinals is this pair of strong, solid steak houses owned by a pair of former Big Red standouts—offensive tackle Dan Dierdorf, now in the Hall of Fame and a Monday night ABC commentator, and Jim Hart, a tough, strong-armed quarterback who never got the recognition and credit he deserved, and now is athletic director of his alma mater, Southern Illinois University.

Strictly a steak-and-chop house, this dark wood, large-booth operation is not quite in the league with such national standouts as Morton's and Ruth's Chris, though its prices are such that it should be. It stars large portions and very sharp knives, with three sizes of filet mignon, two of sirloin and a bone-in T-bone cut that involves the less succulent half of the porterhouse. All the beef is tasty, tender and properly cooked.

The menu is displayed on a tray (a la other steak houses and Al's) and discussed by the server. But the tray is overcrowded, and on our visit, the lamb chops shown were fatty and so poorly trimmed as to dissuade us from the order. A veal chop, the second choice, was tender and pleasant, but with little flavor.

The baked potatoes, apparently Yukon gold, are fat and delicious, and steam pours forth when they're opened. The same potato also is served "smashed," or coarsely mashed, with something tangy like blue cheese or horseradish. Potato chips are like those served at Llywelyn's, and even non-fans of vegetables find it difficult to resist the creamed spinach. Salads are Caesar, green and tomato-onion.

The feel of the place is such that one orders the traditional steak house appetizers like shrimp cocktail (six large, not very tasty ones, for $9) or escargot, the latter swimming and simmering in garlic butter and just right for one who loves garlic butter and doesn't care—or know—about escargot. Oysters on the half-shell are usually very good.

The wine list is more than adequate, but on the expensive side, and not nearly as complete and attractive as it was when the restaurant first opened. Service is smooth and professional, and when dessert time arrives, there are some special ones from the Sugaree Baking Co., including a superior chocolate-chip banana cake with dark chocolate icing.

Dierdorf & Hart left its Union Station location in the summer of 1998, and moved lock, stock and sirloin to the old Premio space at 701 Market Street. It looks like a good move for numerous reasons: The downtown room is smaller and probably less expensive; there's less unnecessary space for a bar; and the Market Street home is closer to Busch Stadium, the Convention Center and the Ugly Dome, and to the downtown hotels frequented by the convention-and-business traveler.

It's rather sad, however, that Union Station, which helped throw dirt on a feeble downtown, is now facing a similar fate while downtown clambers back into the sunlight.

Dominic's
Italian Cuisine
5101 Wilson Avenue
771-1632
Dinner Monday-Saturday
Credit cards: All major
Wheelchair access: Impossible

This is the original Dominic's, plopped on a quiet corner of the Hill. Under the watchful eye of valet parkers, Lincolns and Mercedeses sit comfortably near the hydrant at the front door. It's indicative of the crowd, especially on weekends, and the most prestigious auto is closest to rescue in case of fire. Inside, it's oil paintings and chandeliers and guerdons, just what one would expect at a high-ticket St. Louis Italian restaurant, where dinner is in the range of $30 per person before drinks or wine.

The patrons often sound as if they're dining at their own country club. It's a dressy crowd, although a coat- and tie-less chap strolled in with two very attractive women and was seated without elevated eyebrows, at least from the staff.

Dominic Galati himself, smooth, elegant and reserved, usually oversees things. While he's very hands-on, helping with the plating, talking about special items in the kitchen, he's not a schmoozer. Restaurants are serious business and few know it better than Dominic, who goes back more than thirty years, when he succeeded Andreino at the location. In those days, Dominic and his wife, Jackie, lived upstairs over the store, and her mother did much of the cooking.

Like other top-drawer St. Louis restaurants, much attention is paid to customers. This is a serious kitchen, even though the menu looks rather standard. Meat is of the highest quality, seasoning is careful but not boring, and little hints of innovation can be found, both on the menu and on the plate.

For example, roasted sweet peppers with anchovies is three large slabs of roasted pepper, two red and a yellow. Still a little crunchy, they're each topped with an anchovy fillet and served with a round of mozzarella that tastes so fresh it's like eating the sweetest milk there ever was. Simple, very much like what you'd find in a restaurant in Italy, and full of good tastes. There are standards like shrimp cocktail and smoked salmon here, as well as fried calamari and prosciutto with melon. Salads are dressed tableside, of course.

A special entree is the shrimp vino blanco, shrimp cooked in white wine, garlic and lemon juice, big hefty guys that taste absolutely regal in the sharp, succulent sauce. With it is capellini in a red sauce that tastes like an arrabiata, fresh tomato with some basil but also a hefty pinch of red pepper, not fiery but pungent and mouth-filling.

Pasta here is theoretically available only as a first course, and that includes risotto, a Milanese with porcini, another uncommon combo. We're beginning to think a lot of people believe they ought to order some kind of solid meat at our town's fine collection of Italian restaurants, and pass the pastas as just another side dish. They shouldn't. Especially with the current dietary emphasis on more carbohydrates and less protein, pasta fits right in with, say, fettuccine with pesto or ravioli with ricotta and a Bolognese sauce. Dieticians despair, however, over goodies like fettuccine Alfredo and spaghettini carbonara.

It's difficult choosing an entree here. Zuppa di pesce (fish soup)? Veal with artichokes and wild mushrooms in a cream sauce? Halibut with white wine and garlic? Fish of the day? A tenderloin Siciliana was two slices of grilled meat, rare as ordered, a few garlicky bread crumbs, an unannounced sprinkle of cheese (we can never escape it), and a sauce that seemed to be a sort of Italian bordelaise, brown, slightly sharp, picking up the meat juices and browned bits and using them in an excellent execution. Osso bucco, the veal shank, was a four-inch-diameter chunk of meat, with an oyster fork provided to help dig out the marrow. The meat itself was wonderfully rich and succulent, so tender that another five minutes on the heat would have left it in shreds. The sauce was tomato based, with bay leaf and garlic and a little wine. Ann is the osso bucco lover, and this one was eminently satisfactory. It's usually served on the risotto Milanese, but she decided on something else, and got chunky gnocchi, thick dense shells to go with the rich sauce. Next time she'll probably go for penne or rigatoni, since the gnocchi were a little too dense, but it was her choice, not the kitchen's.

Dessert is traditional, too, except for some special ice cream drinks, one banana flavored and another with praline and nocello, or walnut, liqueurs. We went for tiramisu, individual dishes rather than squares, rather adult and un-sweet, although not heavily alcoholic, with a good balance of ladyfingers, mascarpone and the grated chocolate that was layered over the top.

A superb, if extremely pricey wine list sees plenty of action with this crowd. Service is quite deft, with waiters who seem to have been at it since the restaurant began.

Dominic's Trattoria
Italian Cuisine
200 South Brentwood Boulevard, Clayton
863-4567
Lunch Monday-Friday, Dinner Monday-Saturday
Credit cards: All major
Wheelchair access: Comfortable

This quiet, somewhat elegant dining room overlooks the skating rink and swimming pool in Clayton's Shaw Park. A sibling of Dominic's on the Hill, the restaurant has Clayton prices of about $25 a person to match the decor which, fortunately, does not include the Italian Restaurant School of Painting.

We've enjoyed excellent soups like lobster bisque and chicken broth with tiny orzo pastas in the past, so we trudged in other directions. Carpaccio was a bit too heavy on the shredded Parmesan, but had a lemon aioli sauce that was wonderfully tangy atop beef that was paper-thin and obviously freshly sliced. A grilled portobello mushroom and sweet pepper dish with a piccata sauce was full of the vegetal tastes and aromas that Italian cooking does best, and the mushroom grilled up beautifully. Salads include a green bean salad, not a usual item on St. Louis menus.

This is a particularly good pasta place. If there are pappardelle noodles with duck sauce, rise from a sickbed to get some. Seafood risotto fell a little short; the rice did not receive the long, constant stirring that brings forth a creamy liquid to hold the grains together. The result still was far better than many because of a little tomato and a lot of seafood broth (and some chicken broth, they acknowledged), along with a real duke's mixture of seafood, both shellfish and soft fish, a great flavor, pushed along with a little red pepper. The other dish was sausage with escarole and white beans, very paisan-ish, the fennel-aided sausage providing a fine background to the beans, which weren't overcooked.

Dessert includes Jackie's Dessert, which is a cassata cake with a lengthy history of excellence. The triple chocolate cake was cold, and rather dry, and would have been better at room temperature, but the texture was good, and so was the quality of chocolate. Decent but not great coffee, complete but rather dear wine list, and attentive service from all hands.

Duff's
American Cuisine
392 North Euclid Avenue
361-0522
Lunch and Dinner, Tuesday-Sunday; Brunch Saturday-Sunday
Credit cards: All major
Wheelchair access: Difficult

We long have held that Duff's—sterling member of the famous Class of '72, a year a number of fine St. Louis restaurants arrived—is the place to take folks whose eating habits we don't know. Conservative or fearful eaters can get a steak or a hamburger and a salad without running into anything too alarming on their plates, and more adventurous eaters will feel quite at home. The city mice among our friends find it comfortably hip; the country mice find it exotic but non-threatening, and all enjoy the tales of when it stood in for a Greenwich Village bar in White Palace.

Gossipy lunches, dinners with Bach on a guitar, poetry readings of varying quality and rainy winter nights with Christmas lights glittering on the pavement, are twined through our memories, both separately and together. We've always been well-fed here, sometimes extravagantly so. Karen Duffy and Tim Kirby, from the old days, are still running things, and Jim Voss is in the kitchen more now that the Grateful Dead is defunct (although the kitchen runs so smoothly our tastes could rarely tell if he was on or off the road).

Duff's menu is international eclectic, with things like a comfy mishmash of smoked salmon quesadillas, or crawfish cakes, or Thai peanut noodles. And those are mere samples of the appetizers. Samosas made with phyllo dough are vegetarian, filled with curried potatoes and peas, crispy and somewhat messy to eat, but delicious whether you use the mango raita as a sauce or just slurp it up on its own. The savory and very unctuous pate, coarse-ground rather than spreadable, comes with real cornichons, onion marmalade and mustard, to pile on the toast in various combinations.

Pepper steak seems to be the one constant on the menu, and it's always reliable, never embarrassing the host whose conservative guest chooses it. Duck breast, served rare and swathed in a tart cherry sauce, rode on sweet potato and wild rice pancakes, a dish we still dream of. Such pleasures come and go as the menu encounters seasonal evolution and, like almost everyone else, we window-shop the menu when we're in the neighborhood to see what's cooking. There's always a pasta dish and a vegetarian entree, perhaps a giant burrito with black beans and grilled vegetables with an innovative salsa like avocado-tomatillo. The ethnicity continues with spicy Jamaican chicken with black beans, plantains and some mango, and a platter of hummus, couscous salad and spanokopita.

Desserts are strong on fresh fruit, with cobblers and tarts featuring the ripest of the season under simple, elegant crusts. St. Louis Shrapnel ice cream may have made its debut here, but that was a long time ago, and the bear claw long has been a favorite dessert item, with or without ice cream.

Appetizers are $3-$8, main courses $11-$20, and dinner always has been one of the city's best dining bargains. The wine list is deep and wide-ranging, and offers some of the best values in town. Kirby knows his wine, and his list always is priced toward a clientele that loves wine, but remains on a beer budget. Once upon a time service was occasionally dazed, but that's long past.

Another thing that seems to be past is the collection of graffiti. Once, it was the best in town. Times change and we all grow up, at least a little, but we never seem to outgrow the meals at Duff's and, thankfully, they don't change.

Duke's
American Food
601 North Grand Boulevard
531-0111
Dinner before events at Grand Center (Fox, Powell Hall; call about others)
Credit cards: All major
Wheelchair access: Satisfactory

The closest restaurant to the stages and concerts of Grand Center, Duke's has to be congratulated for its persistence. Despite reviews that have been tepid at best, it's stayed open. And every night a performance is scheduled in Grand Center, it feeds a pre-show crowd, the pink and black decor glowing through big steamy windows facing Grand Boulevard.

The place is only open on performance nights, so call beforehand. The phone is answered by a machine, instructing you to leave your reservation request of which night, smoking preference and number of people. Interestingly, the recording doesn't ask for a phone number. Is Duke's never overbooked?

The menu is titled by months, so we presume it changes slightly. It is short and fairly simple, listing pastas, steaks, a chicken breast. Add four appetizers (including toasted ravioli) and the side dishes, which already come with the entrees, and the dessert list. The wine list, like many, doesn't list vintages. It's also short, including about five wines by the glass, but it's moderately priced. A full dinner of appetizer, entree and dessert is usually less than $25 a person.

A sirloin strip steak was surprisingly good, with some steamed new potatoes alongside. It was sufficiently tender and cooked as requested. At $18.95, it's the most expensive entree on the menu. Whipped sweet potatoes with pecans were downright yummy.

A triple chocolate cake is called Chocolate Loving Spoonful Cake. Neither the singing group nor the Doughboy ever produced one of these. It was a moist layering of chocolate ganache and brownie-dense cake layers, killer rich with a good bitter edge to the chocolate and not a trace of the slightly burnt taste that can whack your expectations.

The servers are loquacious but agile and—obviously—used to getting people to curtains in time. But why didn't someone sweep the dining room floor before dinner?

Dvin Restaurant
Russian, Armenian, Greek Cuisine
8143 Big Bend Boulevard, Webster Groves
968-4000
Lunch and Dinner, Monday-Saturday
Credit cards: All major
Wheelchair access: Satisfactory

Just as Big Bend Boulevard makes its big bend to the west, and spins off Lockwood Boulevard in front of Webster University, a half dozen restaurants have opened to almost take the place of the late, lamented Webster Grill. There's a hamburger joint, a pizza joint and a bagel joint, and restaurants representing China, Turkey, Buttercream and Football.

There's also Dvin, which briefly touches on Grecian food, and offers strong samples of freshly made, tasty cuisine from Eastern Europe and Russia.

There's a streak of hominess in interior decor running from Mittel Europa eastward into the former Soviet Union that stubbornly tries to warm up even the most barren of settings. It nearly always succeeds, too. This boxy storefront wears artificial greenery, lots of photographs and other wall art, and plastic lace tablecloths. The tableware, even the glasses, sport floral designs.

First courses top out about $4, sandwiches at $6 and entrees at $9.75, but many are considerably less. An appetizer might be hummus, or a kidney bean and fried onion dish the menu describes as a variant of hummus. Juicy, sweet-roasted peppers benefit from cottage cheese with the tiniest of curds and a splendid olive oil marinade. The diner who equates borscht with the bright creamy pink of beets has a surprise coming. Dvin's borscht is heavy with tomato and cabbage in a liquid filled with a jumble of vegetables, and coming closer to sweet on the sweet-sour balance.

Goulash, pelmeny dumplings and chicken Kiev appear as main courses. Vegetarians can have a pilaf, or eggplant or vegetable sandwiches. Stuffed cabbage shows nicely-flavored ground beef and excellent cabbage in a sauce redolent of tomatoes and bay leaf. Lamb strung on a skewer turns out to be lean, full of flavor and very tender from a marinade that leaves a tart, slightly peppery tang to the meat. The usual vegetable medley is stretched by mixing in fried potatoes and onions, a definite improvement.

Dvin brings a new approach to blintzes, using large blini, or buckwheat pancakes, to make chicken blintzes, with the meat spiced delicately and intriguing to the mouth. Dvin also uses blini for blintzes, stuffed with smoked salmon and with the traditional cheese.

Two desserts, baklava and napoleons, are sliced in diamonds so precisely they look like something served at Disneyland. The dense baklava, heavy with the taste of honey, lacks crunch. The napoleon got mixed reviews; Ann said it was soggy and lacked flavor, Joe liked it.

Despite its desserts, Dvin presents interesting and often delicious food.

El Maguey
Mexican Cuisine

7014 Chippewa Avenue
832-3632
14559 Manchester Road, Manchester
230-5733
135 Concord Plaza, Mehlville
843-8265
13377 Olive Boulevard, Chesterfield
878-5988
1151 Duchesne Street, St. Charles
949-8848
65 Centre Point, St. Charles
939-2060
Lunch and Dinner, every day
Credit cards: All major
Wheelchair access: Varies by location

We've listed only six St. Louis area addresses for this mini-chain of Mexican restaurants. Another half-dozen stretch from Independence, Mo., to Mobile, Ala., with a stop in Paducah, Ky. (unfortunately, no Memphis and no Natchez). We found El Maguey late one night in Sedalia. Nine o'clock is late for Sedalia, and even the fact that the State Fair was in progress didn't seem to keep local restaurateurs from getting a good night's sleep, apparently so that they could awaken in time to milk the cows.

However, that visit, in 1997, changed us from skeptics to believers, with tasty taco fillings that went beyond hamburger, and interesting dinners like chile colorado and carnitas. We didn't realize they also were in St. Louis. We had a lot to learn.

A return visit to the Chippewa site left us considerably less enthusiastic. The menu covers the usual Mexican standards, tostadas to tamales, and more unusual things like the chile colorado, a sort of beef stew, and chilaquiles, fat corn tortillas stuffed with chicken. There are several vegetarian dinners, too. Everyone should escape with a check that's about $12 a person before beverage, tax and tip.

Margaritas were bland and watery. The salsa on the table comes in small decanters, a bright red of pureed tomatoes, and mild to moderately hot. Chips were definitely warm, and whisked out of the kitchen to a crowd of hungry families. Guacamole was fresh and slightly chunky, with good spicing and no evidence of abuse by mayonnaise. A dollop of guacamole and a touch of hot sauce made the chips work well. Little else did.

Chili with beans arrived with the entrees; however, it was not chili but hamburger mixed with refried beans, then heated with some tomato sauce. Our guess is that there was none in the house that night, so a few things were broken up and tossed into the microwave. It was not chili that a respectable restaurant—especially a Mexican restaurant—would serve. Enchiladas, from corn tortillas, were beef, chicken and cheese, rather bland, with immense amounts of shredded lettuce, a sliced Roma tomato and a little sour cream. The special fajitas lacked the beef ribs, chorizo sausage and carne asada the menu had promised, offering only beef, chicken or shrimp with first-rate grilled onions and green bell peppers, heated until they showed charred edges here and there. The meat lacked salt. In fact, it lacked any flavor beyond the meat itself.

Refried beans were dense and fairly flavorful, but rice was underseasoned and dry. We had hoped to try a dessert, but the check was placed on the table and until we pulled out a credit card to pay it, no one stopped by our table again.

Lots of people obviously like El Maguey; we saw several parties greeted as though they were regulars. And there are reports that each El Maguey is individual in its style of preparation. But this one needs a lot of work—and to say a St. Louis restaurant needs work to reach the standards set in Sedalia, well, it's certainly saying something.

Farotto's Pizzeria
Pizza and Pasta
9525 Manchester Boulevard, Rock Hill
962-0048
Lunch and Dinner, every day
Credit cards: All major
Wheelchair access: Passable

Use the left-hand door at Farotto's—the one closest to the carry-out counter—and the aroma of ovens at work rises in waves. It's powerful, and it's right, because this is the way a pizza place should smell. It's also the way it should look, with smiling people in white uniforms tossing dough, sliding pizzas into the inferno, removing them with care. Piles of boxes, waiting to be filled, add to the effect.

Joe has been a fan of Farotto's for a long time, since the days when the tiny carryout area was all there was, along with a pair of tables for two and a bench where pizza-waitees got hungrier while the old magazines got older and time ticked by with agonizing slowness (much the way it does on Christmas Eve). Today, it's far larger, which shows how far good pizza dough can expand.

We think pizza is darn near perfect at Farotto's, and we know the magazines are a lot newer. The crust is thin and crisp as a cracker. The only drawback is that the thinness of the crust militates against too many toppings, which can create more weight than the crust can support.

At last count, there were sixteen available toppings, half of them vegetables, and there's a vegetable special of onions, mushrooms, black olives and broccoli, which Joe prefers to call "the vegetable that dare not speak its name." Another special, of sausage, onion, anchovies and mushrooms, is available as well, but neither "special" is a bargain. The basic pizza is $6.95 for twelve inches, $8.95 for fourteen; with individual ingredients at $1.20 each for small, $1.50 for large. Simple arithmetic will show no financial advantage in ordering a special as opposed to adding ingredients one at a time.

Pizza preference, for ingredients or for toppings, is extremely individual, and often defended at an all-out volume. It's a battle we won't fight, however. As a matter of fact, we're divided on cheese preference—Ann for provel, Joe for mozzarella—though we find room for compromise on toppings.

The menu also includes pastas of various types, and standard sauces and fillings. Salads also are standard, mostly iceberg lettuce with provel cheese and a choice among dressings, including a house special of vinegar and oil that is on the sweet side. It's puzzling why Italian dressings, which should involve vinegar, olive oil and garlic, are showing up with added sweetness at so many restaurants. We wish the chefs would go back to basics.

A cup of onion soup, with a good melted-cheese topping, is tasty, and a side order of meatballs in tomato sauce made for an excellent appetizer with some crusty, crunchy bread. Tony Bommarito designed the wine list, a modest one with good values and several Italian offerings by the glass. The Rock Hill spot also is a bargain, with dinner mostly under a sawbuck, though too many pizza toppings will break that barrier.

Fast Eddie's Bon-Air

Meat 'n' Beer

1530 East 4th Street, Alton, Ill.
(618) 462-5532
Lunch (but see below), and Dinner every day
Cash only
Wheelchair access: Satisfactory

Lunch at Fast Eddie's Bon-Air doesn't begin until 1 p.m. Monday through Thursday. We think the reason for this is that it would lower productivity in the entire city of Alton and surrounding areas by at least 40 percent. On Friday, Saturday and Sunday, lunch begins at 11 a.m. By 2:30 p.m. on a Friday, the place, which seats 380 persons, is almost full. Few show any intention of leaving.

What is this joint, anyway? Basically, it's a bar that also sells food. Fast Eddie's claims they haven't raised prices on the food in ten years, and we believe it.

Walking in, there's a large bar in a room where the walls are almost invisible because they're hidden by stacks of beer cases. It reminds Joe of a place on Mackinac Island, where it was explained to him that the full beer cases were necessary to hold up the roof under the weight of winter snow and to keep the heat in. By the time enough beer had been drunk to pose a threat to security, the weather was beginning to turn warm. That was the bartender's story and he's been sticking to it.

On the far side of the bar is a counter where customers place orders and pick them up. Waitresses bring drinks to the tables, which stretch out into several adjoining rooms, about as far as the eye can see.

Everything is cooked from scratch on the grills, so almost everyone gets some shrimp to eat while they're waiting. At a quarter a shrimp, which means $3 a dozen, these are astoundingly large and consistently well-cooked, with a red sauce that has lots of horseradish. The rest of the menu is an 8-ounce hamburger (99 cents) that puts the drive-through joints to shame; a really excellent bratwurst (69 cents); pork kebab seasoned with a little seasoning salt ($1.29); steak-on-a-stick, tenderloin that's tender and with a slow-rising burn in the marinade ($1.99); and chicken, which turns out to be the big joints of wings lined up on skewers and looking like a chorus line ($1.49). French fries are 99 cents, and since they are cooking constantly, they are fresher and better than most around town.

Lots of TV sets turned to sports, and one of the oldies radio stations on the speaker system starts the entertainment. At night there are well-known local bands. But maybe the best fun is people-watching. The dress code here would probably be "tank tops optional." T-shirts and caps from everywhere, and other interesting chapeaux. A minority of folks isn't wearing jeans—the early-bird-special crowd who realize this is A Serious Deal, and are happy to put up with the noise to eat this well for so little money.

And they are eating well. The food is fresh, well-cooked, and tasty. This is, in the phrase of Tim and Nina Zagat, "a Grade A bang for the buck."

The Adam's Mark—Faust's

American Gourmet Cuisine, Modern and Traditional

315 Chestnut Street (Adam's Mark Hotel)
342-4690 for reservations
Lunch and Dinner, every day
Credit cards: All major
Wheelchair access: Comfortable

Tony Faust was the first legendary St. Louis restaurateur. At the turn of the last century, his restaurant stood not far from the Adam's Mark Hotel, which named its main dining room in his honor. Those were the days of trenchermen like Diamond Jim Brady, and gargantuan portions of food created from the finest raw material across the nation spoke loads about what St. Louisans—yea, all Americans—demanded. It was big and luxurious and indulgent, and fast trains came from everywhere to bring the freshest and the finest to Tony Faust's.

Sounds pretty much like what Faust's does now. No longer, however, is a starched collar or a corset mandatory for dining. Hotel restaurants don't have tight dress codes these days, so a polo shirt and a pair of shorts can be seen next to Brooks Brothers or even Armani's finest.

While service is attentive and careful, there is no sign of an intimidating air, though the menu may cause some at the sight of entrees averaging about $28. That's intimidating enough to many.

The menu changes slightly through the year, but some items remain constant. Lobster bisque, for instance, is a perennial, terra-cotta colored and subtle in its flavoring rather than a rowdy show of crustacean power. The house salad wears a Dijon vinaigrette, some scattered berries and a mild goat cheese, sufficiently exotic to be interesting but hardly intimidating.

Despite its name, a tuna tower doesn't qualify as vertical food, rising only a little more than two inches above the plate. Slices of tuna carpaccio with dribbles of wasabi cream and a curry-flavored oil serve as a base for more uncooked tuna, this time diced and molded into a cylinder topped with a buttery yet bouncy avocado salsa. It's a fine dish for sushi lovers, full of interesting tastes. A lobster appetizer of half a tail and one claw, each shelled, introduced three separate salsas, one mango, one tomato and the same avocado. All were elegant.

Although Faust's does seafood very well, it also shows a fine hand with duck, and there's always one kind or another on the menu. A recent example sported a glaze with sun-dried cherries, a pineapple sauce spiked with rum and a few stir-fried green onions over a generous serving of wild rice. The duck was delicious, lean and cooked in the traditional way, rather than the rare slices of breast that have populated dinner plates the last twenty years or so. It arrived moist but well done. The same wild rice works as a base for another festive meat, a rack of lamb crusted with pecans, and there's roast chicken with a goat cheese stuffing spiked with spinach and peppers.

Steamed lobster, available up to three pounds at certain times of the year, sat in a ring of carrots and asparagus that would fit inside soda straws. Nestled here and there were a few inch-wide pattypan squash. The crustacean lay on a small mound of very good mashed potatoes, in case, we suppose, any leftover clarified butter needed to be used up. Her (it was a female, with its delicious red roe) tail and claws had been shelled, the knuckles gone into never-never land. It was as sweet a lobster as we've ever had. Besides the clarified butter, there was a Champagne citrus beurre blanc sauce, interesting enough, but unnecessary. We think that lobster deserves to be eaten in elegant simplicity. Even butter, which accents its sweetness, covers up the brininess. Cold lobster can take a little homemade mayonnaise hearty with lemon, but that's as far as we will go.

Desserts travel on a display rack not unlike a Victorian plant holder. There's always something desperately, deeply chocolate, always some fresh berries, always the creme brulee with beautiful texture. Beyond that, the kitchen begins to vamp. We ended up with a cookie-cake-custard-fruit tart, which looked gorgeous, but, as with so many fruit tarts, the pleasure was more with the eye than the mouth.

This is a very serious wine room, but the wine director and sommelier, Robert Kabel, is thrilled to deal with anyone who just wants a good glass of wine. To that end, there are fifteen wines by the glass and several half-bottles, a short wine card and a bigger, considerably more extensive wine list. Kabel is one of the smartest wine guys in town, and tracks down all kinds of fascinating labels. He knows wine, and he will talk about it with anyone who is interested. The result rarely is the most expensive bottle, but always one the drinker will enjoy, and learn from.

Our main quibble is the decor. While chairs are extremely comfortable, a detail some places overlook, the room doesn't do the food justice. Bits of porcelain are in cabinets and on a shelf, there are some open beams and stone, but it all seems cobbled together. The room just doesn't feel nearly as exciting as it could. Some tables have views of the Arch, but even at dusk, those windows, facing east, were covered. And the restrooms are standard hotel lobby, a poor match for a restaurant that provides elegant meals at top-drawer prices. Giving a plastic wrapped rose to female guests at the end of the evening doesn't make up for paper towels and tight quarters.

The Adam's Mark—Chestnut's
Standard Coffee Shop
Brunch on Sunday

There is nothing quite like the sight of a guy in T-shirt and shorts skillfully samba-ing across a crowded room with a plateful of chocolate cake and cream puffs. This enduring image, which really captures Chestnut's, has stuck with Ann ever since she first visited, not long after it opened. Casual attire; this is a hotel lobby, after all, with people here for conventions and ball games joining locals. Live music—not too loud—and more calories than a Third World nation may eat in a single day.

This probably is St. Louis' favorite brunch place—we suggest reservations—and it's quite good. For one thing, they choose items that can stand up to a buffet table, something that is, amazingly, overlooked too often at brunches. For another, the selection, as well as the quantity, is immense.

There's an omelet station, of course, but there's also a pasta station, where a brief consultation between chef and guest can put together any of a wide range of possibilities. Sushi of fair quality, cold seafood, oysters Rockefeller and cold shrimp co-exist with salmon, of course. For a while, there was an employee doling the salmon out slice by slice, insisting that it be "prepared," meaning put on a bagel with cream cheese and a choice of toppings. The faint implication was out of tune with the rest of the service here, and we're glad it ceased.

Breads are prepared in-house and can be extremely good. Breakfast items mostly take second place to those for lunch, with a carving station for roast beef and a long line of chafing dishes which star roast duck, a first for brunch in our experience. The rich duck is hard to dry out, and manages the Sunday experience with great aplomb. Several stir-fries are available in woks big enough to use as body armor, although the vegetables become soft after standing.

Dessert here has always looked better than it tasted, especially the chocolate products. It's somewhat less so now, but it could still use work.

The tab is $21.95 per person, including some sparkling wine from New York State.

Favazza's
Italian Cuisine
5201 Southwest Avenue
772-4454
Lunch and Dinner, Monday-Saturday
Credit cards: All major
Wheelchair Access: Passable

When Joe first arrived in St. Louis, Favazza's stood just a couple of blocks east of the *Globe-Democrat* (now *Post-Dispatch*) building on Twelfth Street (now Tucker Boulevard) and Franklin Avenue (now Martin Luther King Drive). Like the Typo Bar and the Press Box and Kopperman's, it was the closest place to eat and drink, practically across the street. A few blocks farther, sometimes a factor in selection in that spring of 1955, were the Bismarck, Rose's, Dunie's and Thompson's Cafeteria.

In those days, the area east of Twelfth Street was very different. Franklin Avenue, busy with auto traffic, service cars and streetcars, ran right into the Veterans' Bridge and led to the sins of East St. Louis, where the action was just beginning when Missouri was closing down at midnight on Saturday nights. Today, Martin Luther King Drive ends just east of Tucker Boulevard while Cole Street, then a narrow, old-fashioned city street, is now a wide, bustling boulevard that leads to the Ugly Dome and the bridge via a mass of ill-designed, confusing highways.

Cole also was the main drag of a small Italian enclave; people lived in shotgun houses, shopped at the Italo-American Import Co. and similar spots in the neighborhood, and sat on their front stoops to talk and watch the world go by.

Favazza was, and still is, the name of the owning family. It means "flea," in Italian, and that's what the restaurant and its owners were, and still are, called. Big, elderly, clunky pinball machines—without flippers, no less—once stood inside the front door, odds numbers flashing continually, tilt mechanism set to frustrate newspaper types who expected to make an easy killing.

All gone, or almost so. Names, and even directions, have changed. The *Globe-Democrat* doesn't exist, and with the exception of what is now the *Post-Dispatch* building, most of everything else in that area has been flattened for new, ugly structures where no one lives or loves. Favazza's has moved to the Hill, re-establishing its Italian roots out there. The restaurants and bars—and personality—of the old neighborhood and the old days are gone.

And lo these forty-plus years later, the menu at Favazza's and the cooking style are much the way they were downtown. Hearty portions of well-cooked, standard Italian fare. Not much to indicate great imagination or the desire to be innovative, but the Hill grew to its fame on Southern Italian cooking, and the family has joined in.

Toasted ravioli—of course—leads the appetizer list, but it's pleasantly soft, as if it were freshly made, and the meat filling is nicely spiced, and the sauce succeeds, too. There are times when familiarity is what is needed. Lots of basil in the sauces, and a firm hand with garlic.

Fried eggplant is a longtime favorite, as long as the batter isn't thicker than the eggplant slice, and Favazza's works. Veal Parmigiano, breaded and topped with cheese, is tender and flavorful. Entrees include salad and vegetable or pasta, and all are under $20. Add an appetizer and a glass of wine, and the bill will remain under $25 per person.

When there is company from out of town, and they want to know what the food on the Hill was like when Yogi Berra and Joe Garagiola were kids, this is the place to take them. And it often feels like dinner in an Italian home.

The Feasting Fox, Al Smith's Restaurant

South St. Louis Eclectic

4200 South Grand Boulevard
352-3500
Lunch and Dinner, Tuesday-Sunday
Credit cards: All major
Wheelchair access: Difficult

If there's a restaurant in St. Louis more capable of giving people déjà vu than this one, we can't think of it. The landmark Al Smith's restaurant was on the verge of being demolished when the Luepkers rescued it. A visitor would swear nothing had changed since—oh, 1958 or so. They salvaged madly from many now-gone restaurants, taking booths from the Nantucket Cove on West Pine Boulevard, and chandeliers and molding from the Top of the 230 in Clayton. Even the chairs came from Famous-Barr's tea rooms, and a large piece of stained glass had lived in the Webster Grill. The overall effect is so perfect, it's enough to make Ann haul out a Mamie Eisenhower hat for Sunday brunch. Prices are a trifle more modern, around $20 a head.

The ravioli appetizer here is poached, not fried. There's also a spinach and mushroom fricassee, grilled eggplant salad and onion rings. The sausage sampler offers four different kinds of pig, including garlicky bratwurst and peppery Polish sausage. Sausage in phyllo dough was too dry, but a juicy, nicely flavored chunk of what appeared to be a knackwurst saved the day with delicious meat, flavored by tiny, tangy mustard seeds. The German black bean soup was thick and tasty with lots of chopped ham and minced onions that had been resting in a vinaigrette, one of the better black bean soups around. A house salad, however, left us wincing, with brown iceberg lettuce and a mushy tomato. The house dressing was Dijon and horseradish, okay enough, but not sufficient to redeem the lettuce.

Most main courses here are traditional, with fried chicken, fried shrimp, and steaks, but there are some newer ideas like salmon au poivre and Black Forest sweet and sour pork. A stuffed pork chop came with a filling of aromatics, including fresh sage, not an easy herb to manage, but carried off without allowing the sage to overwhelm the other ingredients. The pork chop was moist and flavorful, just slightly pink at the bone. On the other hand, pork loin Normandy (the night seemed to morph into a pork producers' commercial) was devoid of any snap. The sauce had no discernible taste (a similar-looking one on the chop seemed a little livelier) except for the occasional currant or rare apple slice. Sauerkraut was finely shredded and rather mild. Horseradish potatoes looked much like duchesse potatoes, piped and run under a broiler, and were very snappy, both in appearance and flavor.

But leave room for the apple strudel. Crisp pastry and dense, but not leaden, filling sat in a lovely creme anglaise, flavorful but not heavy.

In the heart of south St. Louis, Al Smith's Feasting Fox is a perfect spot to show off the delicacies of the area, but does not. Bread is ordinary, soft, white instead of sharp, dark pumpernickel or seed-sharpened rye. Mustard is from Mr. Gray instead of something special from any of the dozens of local and regional purveyors. Draft beer is merely a couple choices from the local giant and one from Killian's when so many of today's craft brewers go unrepresented; a wine list that is barely adequate. Much room for improvement to make this a showplace again.

Fio's La Fourchette
Contemporary, with a Swiss-French Accent

7515 Forsyth Boulevard, Clayton
863-6866
Dinner Tuesday-Saturday
Credit cards: All major
Wheelchair access: Impossible

In many ways, this top-drawer St. Louis restaurant is a true European at heart. The owners, Fio and Lisa Antognini, are Swiss. In the European tradition of a family restaurant, Fio is in the kitchen leading his staff and creating superior meals, while Lisa runs the dining room, managing service that is balanced perfectly on the fine line between formal and friendly.

The prices at Fio's put it in the rank of the most expensive in town, above $40 a head before wine. A six-course, fixed-price dinner is $53.75, a five-course meal is five dollars less. The pale pink room is clearly designed to be romantic and glamorous, albeit not intimidating. This is a restaurant where a large table of people celebrating a birthday can become decorously rowdy without feeling as though the staff or their fellow diners disapprove.

Fio manages to serve several masters at once, and never misses a moment. There is always a vegetarian dish available in all courses. There's a steak for the gimme-my-meat crowd, and there's always a low-fat meal, with calories and fat grams—and percentages of fat in the dish—printed on the menu. And there are seconds.

Yes. Like at Mom's house. Seconds on anything you order. The portions are moderate-sized, eminently sensible in this society. But if you just have to have a little more of the veal medallions and their succulent, earthy wild mushroom sauce, you may not even have to ask. They'll bring it.

So what should you eat? The menu changes every month or so, slightly, but many dishes are permanent residents. Chilled mussels in a Dijon sauce, sharp and succulent; carpaccio of smoked salmon and horseradish cream; bay scallops and crawfish tails in a sauce of vodka, dill and lemon that is a showstopper. The sauce would be heaven on cold fish, or asparagus, or a bale of scrap paper. Coconut shrimp fritters were a real fritter, more shrimp than coconut and full of flavor. Veal brains lolled seductively in a dark, rich reduction of veal stock

And there are no restrictions on Fio's menu. Mix a low-fat dish with one from the fixed-price meal and one from the a la carte list. It doesn't make the kitchen pause for a moment, nor does it draw quizzical glances from the waiter. The diner is in charge here—and anything goes.

A fascinating low-fat entree is scallops of venison, grilled with a pineapple-mango salsa and gingered broccoli. The venison was as tender as venison gets, and the salsa generous enough to cover the fact that this is a very lean meat. The broccoli had a taste of pineapple, too, and ginger, plus some pepper heat in both items that kept the mouth busy. Those veal medallions we spoke of are consistently outstanding, fork-tender and absolutely magic. Normally thought of as a delicate meat, this was as hearty as an osso bucco but still not heavy. The vegetable, a lump the size of a tennis ball, was a melange of potatoes, broccoli, beans and cauliflower, with a steamed carrot draped limply on top, like one of Salvador Dali's watches.

Grilled tenderloin, succulent roast lobster, striped bass or wild mushroom ravioli may be other menu highlights. Salads, in the European style, follow the main course, with wonderful things like warm crispy potatoes and endive in a creamy garlic dressing (178 calories and two grams of fat!), or assorted beans and tomato, rather than The Same Old Green Stuff. They act almost as a digestif.

If it were not for the strength of the rest of the menu, this would be known as a dessert house. Fio, in the fine tradition of Switzerland, loves desserts and has a deft hand. The signature dessert is an individual souffle. The Grand Marnier and Swiss chocolate ones are omnipresent, lofty and wobbling as they fly to tables, causing heads to swivel as they pass. They come with a creme anglaise sauce poured in the middle. If you haven't had a souffle, or if you haven't had one lately, someone in the party ought to order one, no onerous task. Special souffles include such things as mocha, a delicious chocolate-coffee blend, walnut and others. Fio makes his own ice cream, too, rich vanilla and chocolate, and fruit flavors like raspberry and apricot. How to choose? Don't bother; you get a small scoop of each. On the low-fat side, an apricot mousse, tart and tender and surrounded by a delicious blueberry sauce. A white chocolate-caramel-toffee torte was short of flavor, but maybe that was in contrast to the other desserts.

Every square millimeter of the coffee pot must be scoured by Swiss elves at night. This is outstanding restaurant coffee, not wildly strong but displaying pure coffee flavor, and none of this milk-in-the-creamer business, either. Have a cookie and sigh contentedly.

The wine list is long and as elegant as the restaurant, and on the expensive side. Good wines by the glass are available, as are lots of fancy martinis, but we won't count them against Fio or Lisa. This is an elegant restaurant in every sense of the word, and for some St. Louis diners, the best news of the year was the fact that the planned sale had fallen through, and the Antogninis were in full charge again.

Fitz's

Root Beer/Brewpub Food

6605 Delmar Boulevard, University City
726-9555
Lunch and Dinner, every day
Credit cards: All major
Wheelchair access: Good

We like to think we're sophisticated, even jaded or curmudgeonly on our better days. But some things are irresistible to anyone, even people like us. We're not sure what was more fun at Fitz's—the food, the lurching bottling line, or the faces of the kids aged three to past sixty-five watching the process.

Sure, it's a great building—an old bank (Joe's bank, when he first moved to St. Louis)—that had a brief turn as a Chinese restaurant. It subsequently made a swell marriage with the original Fitz's, a Clayton Road hamburger stand with good burgers and a special sauce. Now the interior is a warm yellow with trompe l'oeil peeling plaster and Italian-industrial lighting, and there's an upstairs balcony with a bar and dart boards and pool tables.

With a menu that concentrates mostly on burgers (nine kinds) and designer pizza (seven kinds), one might expect ho-hum plates. But there are lots of other sandwich choices, some blue plate specials, and desserts that lean heavily on the bottling line. And the food is interesting and tasty. The same menu runs from lunch through dinner, by the way. Appetizer, main course and dessert will run in the neighborhood of $15, and servings are extremely generous.

When a menu says fish and chips, the restaurant has an obligation not to toss out the sort of frozen, bread-crumbed rectangle found in a grocer's freezer case. Further, it has an obligation to supply malt vinegar the same way it does ketchup with burgers and fries. The good British chippie places deliver fillets, not slabs, of fresh, white, flaky fish in a light, crisp and very tasty batter. Fitz's gives exactly that, fish that won't be taken for chicken breast, an excellent batter, well-drained with some fries that have been crisped up with the powder they use nowadays (but which improves boring frozen potatoes), a nice coleslaw, and the offer of malt vinegar. A rousing chorus of "Rule, Britannia!"

This is surely the only place in St. Louis—it might be the only one in the country—that has both outstanding fish and chips and outstanding barbecue. Carolina-style pork, pulled into shreds, is basted with a vinegar-based sauce. The sandwich, jammed with tender meat, comes with a cup of sauce on the side. The sauce is tasty not fiery, despite flecks of floating cracked red pepper. We spiked it up with a little of the Mexican hot sauce on the table, but it was fine solo, too. A side of onion rings probably were not made from scratch, but they were well-seasoned and well-fried without the doughiness that can plague rings.

They do have regular beer here, of course, but the house product and its siblings, including—shades of the Nehi era—grape and orange, are more politically correct. The diet root beer, by the way, is pretty good, a rare compliment from the junior partner who usually is thumbs-down on any artificially-sweetened product.

Dessert is various ice cream floats, plus apple pie and bread pudding. In the interests of seeing how a taste from small-town Missouri in the '50s held up, we tried a chocolate ice cream (from Quezel, St. Louis' best) root beer float. Not quite the same as a chocolate root beer from Green's Drug Store, but amusing. Bread pudding was moist and rich, with a caramel sauce and a lot of nutmeg. Served warm, it was on the verge of sinful, which is where all great desserts live.

The glassed-in bottling line at the back of the dining room gives a full view of the bottlers, who seem to enjoy their jobs and the audience. Someone often comes out to explain what he's doing, and to patiently answer questions from mesmerized kids and grown men poking each other and saying, "Look! Watch him shake up that bottle of root beer!" The shaker, who has put a pressure gauge on top of a fresh bottle, puts on a particularly ebullient and Marcel Marceau-like show. Who needs Las Vegas?

Flaco's Tacos

Fast Food Mexican and Fish, Too

3852 Lindell Boulevard
534-8226
Sixth and Pine Streets
231-8226
2024 McKelvey Road, Maryland Heights
469-2151
Lunch and Dinner every day on Lindell and McKelvey; Lunch only on Sixth Street
Cash only
Wheelchair access: Satisfactory

When Dean Flacco pumped his savings into a former Toddle House on Lindell Boulevard, in the shadow of St. Louis University, and started cooking and selling fish tacos, the first thought among many wiseacres was that he was a few years too late to take advantage of the fish-on-Friday connection.

The wiseacres forgot that there were six other days to the week.

Today, there are three Flaco's Tacos shops around town, and fish tacos are the prime seller. The Flaco's style is for good quality fish, fried fresh and topped with shredded cabbage and tomatillo sauce. On the side is a full set of hot sauces to add, ranging from maiden-aunt mild to wicked witch-wow!

Refried beans are good, and the taco itself has satisfactory flavor. Quesadillas display a couple of cheeses, and are quite chewy. Mexican chicken soup works well, and a banana burrito makes a superior dessert. Lines move rather quickly, and where fish once was described as brain food, it now passes as health food. At Flaco's Tacos, where lunch is only a couple of dollars, it's also fast food and good food.

Frank Papa's Ristorante
Italian Cuisine

2241 South Brentwood Boulevard, Brentwood
961-3344
Lunch Monday-Friday, Dinner Monday-Saturday
Credit cards: All major
Wheelchair access: Difficult

Frank Papa's is unassuming from the outside, a storefront in a suburb. There's no sign at all that some of the finest Italian food in town comes out of the kitchen. Not that this little restaurant isn't popular—just try eating here on a weekend night—but they don't blow their own horn a great deal.

Frank and Diana Papa let their food and service do the talking, and a smart idea it is. In a dining room that reminds us of one or two we've visited in the Italian Alps, Diana Papa runs a tight but very affable ship. This is a white tablecloth restaurant whose patrons are clearly having a good time, especially at dinner. A tab might run $30 to $35 a head.

The don't-miss appetizer here is a flash-fried escarole, the leaves shatteringly crisp and flavorful, sprinkled with Parmesan cheese that doesn't come out of a shaker-top can. This one-ups the deep-fried spinach seen around town, with a more flavorful green. We're also infatuated with the mussels diavolo, Prince Edward Island mussels, fat and tasty, in a chunky tomato sauce pungent with garlic, the mussel juices and a spike of crushed red pepper, which is what makes it "the devil's." Eaters would be foolish to ignore the waiter's advice to mop up the sauce with bread; it's heartbreakingly good. The menu offers both bruschetta (with tomato) and crostini (with goat cheese and spinach), too.

Soup of the day varies by whim and market basket. We've had things like a cold tomato soup drizzled with pesto. For almost any soup, succumb to the suggestion to drizzle it with a little olive oil, a traditional garnish for Italian soups and one that increases their appeal, already high, one more notch.

The house salad is dressed with a balsamic vinaigrette. Aside from the very St. Louis touch of provel cheese, it's classic with good greens lightly dressed, a serious olive, the whole adding up to a successful execution.

Pasta here is wonderful. A simple dish like linguini with escarole, real Italian soul food, comes with the pungent smell of garlic and the full, rounded taste of good olive oil bouncing off the slightly bitter greens. The pappardelle con porcini makes you think of a roaring hearth and the hearty foods of late autumn as the mushrooms and white wine cuddle the wide noodles, still nicely al dente, in a warm, elegant coat. Ziti alla carbonara is heartier than most carbonaras we've found, the sauteed pancetta carrying the sauce along with secondary notes of that good

Parmesan cheese. The amount of sauce is just right, too, with never a puddle in the bottom of the bowl.

The protein-based entrees are good, too. Vitello alla Diana features thin slices of very tender veal with brown mushrooms, a little tomato, shredded fresh basil and a classic brown sauce. The dish came with crispy roasted potatoes seasoned with a little black pepper and oregano, fluffy inside and steaming hot. For lovers of the meat-and-cheese school of St. Louis dining, there's a strip steak topped with Gorgonzola, and several chicken preparations in that style, but most of the entrees, a generous number of which are fish, are cheese-free, like the chicken with a brandy, Dijon and green peppercorn sauce.

Desserts can be yummy here, with a good version of tiramisu and a charming cassata cake, with a nice balance of filling to cake. We're going to try their chocolate ravioli next.

A fine wine list coves both Italian and non-Italian offerings, and includes some offerings from obscure producers that are unsung stars.

But then, that fits right in at Frank Papa's.

Frazer's Traveling Brown Bag
American Eclectic/New Orleans Overtones

1811 Pestalozzi Street
773-8646
Dinner Monday-Saturday
Cash only
Wheelchair access: Passable

He isn't there yet, but he's on his way. And one of these days Frazer Cameron may soon be the best-known denizen of Pestalozzi Street. People asking directions will receive replies like: "You want to get to Anheuser-Busch? Easy, it's right across the highway from Frazer's."

Frazer's Traveling Brown Bag, small and crowded, loose and relaxed, with the look and feel of San Francisco's North Beach in the '60s, blew into St. Louis in the early '90s almost unnoticed, a situation that didn't last long. Many West Countians realized for the first time that their beer came from somewhere besides the supermarket, and a long lunch at Frazer's became one of the city's favorite activities. Shrieks and moans met the news that he had stopped serving lunch, but it wasn't all bad. The long-awaited expansion meant more seats, and the restaurant is a little less funky and considerably less crowded. The singular style persists.

Frazer cooks the way he speaks—slowly and with considerable thought. He comes from the New Orleans tradition, and he can get the spices from his kitchen to swing in the sort of ensemble performance that even the St. Louis Symphony would envy.

A dish coming out of Frazer's kitchen is full, beautifully colored, ruggedly handsome to look at (no frou-frou here), and with hearty flavors that often show that odd combinations work very well. A salad of endive, poached pear, Gorgonzola cheese and walnuts, dressed with a balsamic vinaigrette, was deliriously good, and even the odd-seeming garnish of strawberries was spectacular. Is it us, or do the berries and endive really work well together?

Cioppino, the Italian version of bouillabaisse, comes in an immense serving with lots of fish and shellfish and a generous amount of garlic bread. It's deeply fishy without being salty, and all the various ingredients were cooked to perfection. Crab cakes are wonderfully crabby, even though they're not entirely of lump crabmeat, and they're spiced with just the right amount of cayenne pepper. Chicken Vesuvio, requested without the melted cheese, was sauced with roasted tomatoes and piled with eggplant, mushrooms and sweet red peppers. Very tasty, not spicy-hot. Garlic pasta came alongside, but we subbed some mashed potatoes, reeking merrily of roast garlic and laden with black pepper and a choice of excellent beef or chicken gravy. And even if it isn't lunchtime, the sandwiches are still fine, with both the roast chicken ($5.25) and pork loin ($8.75) in splendid shape.

The drink list is as esoteric as anything else at Frazer's. Excellent Jamaican ginger beer and Miami-made pineapple soda are Joe's favorites, both showing a little extra pop through the carbonation. No colas, but almost everything else is on hand, with good beers, including some from the across-the-street neighbor, and a solid, well-priced selection of wines by the glass. The bottle list is small, but well-chosen and at reasonable prices.

Frazer does a sublime key lime pie. But if the bread pudding with chocolate is unavailable, don't blame us. We're glad bread pudding has come back to St. Louis, and this is among the best in town. Too many are dry, but at Frazer's, chunks of dark and white chocolate (more dark, fortunately) stud a moist square of pudding, and a clear whiskey sauce rests between the pudding and a little whipped cream. They warm it, so the chocolate is melting. You will be, too.

Vince Bommarito did one afternoon. Well, he didn't quite melt, but he and Joe met for lunch there one day. When Joe arrived, Vince was crawling around the floor of the bar area, examining the undersides of stools.

"These were my barstools," he said happily. "Look." He pointed to the head of a screw. "I put that screw in, about ten years ago."

Yes, they had been Vince's, when Tony's Restaurant was on North Broadway. When Bommarito moved to his current location, he sold much of his equipment and furniture, and along the way, Frazer bought it. Vince didn't say so, but it was obvious in his tone, as he enjoyed his lunch, that he thought Frazer must be a smart man to buy such good furniture—even used— for his restaurant. Smart man. Good restaurateur. Good cook. Frazer had another fan.

Gianfabio's
Italian Cuisine
Hilltop Village Center
Olive Boulevard just north of Highway 40 and Clarkson Road, Chesterfield
532-6686
Lunch and Dinner, Monday-Saturday
Credit cards: All major
Wheelchair access: Satisfactory

This West County restaurant could qualify for a dual-personality diagnosis. The south side of Gianfabio's is a casual area subtitled Il Forno Cafe, a family-oriented place where you can watch the giant pizza oven work its way on dough and sauce and toppings. The other side, where we ate, is fairly formal, with black-tie waiters, white tablecloths and the requisite paintings.

The menu, similar to many of the Hill restaurants and their spiritual descendants, meat-with-cheese-on-it and various pastas, distinguishes itself with a couple of small vegetarian pizzas hidden among the appetizers; a classic Margherita ($8.50) of basil, tomato and mozzarella with the pleasant addition of roasted garlic; and a delicious Mediterranean ($9.50) with real mozzarella, nicely stringy, and in generous quantity nestled around roasted eggplant, good black olives, marinated artichoke hearts and mushrooms. The slight bitterness from the olives and artichoke hearts made it distinctive, and the crust was great, thin and crisp on the bottom, nicely chewy at the edges.

One of the listed soups is pasta con fagioli ($3.50). For the generation of Americans who heard comedians refer to "pastafazool"—this is it, pasta with beans, traditionally a thick, tasty soup drizzled with olive oil, peasant food at its best. Ann first tasted it in Mantua and fell head over heels. But there was none this night. After the pizza, the waiter came to say that it wasn't available after all. Maybe a little tortellini in broth, or maybe some—clam chowder? In an Italian restaurant? Actually, it's not the first time it's been the evening's offering. Who knows why? Why not zuppa vongole con panna?

A mixed seafood risotto was quite good. On the plus side, it was a generous amount and with a variety of seafood, not overcooked, just nicely tender. The broth used was essence-of-the-sea, quite fine, and the seasoning was charming, a little red pepper causing a brief flare in the mouth. Alas, the rice was overcooked, making it lose many points on texture. But it was definitely not rice with sauce, which happens too often.

Veal piccata ($16.50), with lemon, white wine and capers, was three generous slices, more thickly cut than is traditional. But they were so tender you could hear the violins. The sauce was a little too bitter (usually caused by introducing the white pith while grating the lemon peel), which is off-putting. Properly cooked broccoli (a little al dente), a little zucchini, a little carrot, and a few potatoes that seemed lost ringed the plate.

This is one of the few places in town that serves zuppa inglese, English soup, or trifle. But here, they do it as a mounded cake, layers of sponge cake and custard and jam and a little booze, covered with a piped meringue that's been browned. Absolutely charming. We'd eat it again. The dessert tray was heavy on chocolate, led by a house-made cake with two layers of truffle filling and three of dark moist chocolate. Occasional (one and a half) dark cherries lurked inside, but be warned: some still have seeds. A dark chocolate frosting of ganache finished it off, and it was excellent chocolate. Two for two on the desserts.

This is a restaurant that sins by not giving prices with the specials. The wine list is adequate but not exciting.

Gian-Peppe's
Italian Cuisine
2126 Marconi Avenue
772-3303
Lunch Tuesday-Friday, Dinner Tuesday-Saturday
Credit cards: All major
Wheelchair access: Difficult

When one considers the number of restaurants on the Hill, we hope Gian-Peppe's doesn't get lost in the crowd. They've been chugging along for close to twenty years, putting out food of the highest quality that's just one short step beyond home cooking —and we mean that as a major compliment.

The waiters are in black tie, and the room is fairly formal, but it's not a stuffy place. Robert Morley, the late British actor and noted trencherman (remember Who Is Killing the Great Chefs of Europe?), said, "No man can be lonely while he's eating spaghetti." A plate of pasta here and you'll be a friend of the house.

The soup is homemade by Peppe Profeta's mother, who does a great deal of the kitchen work. We've had first-rate chicken soup here, and the veal meatball soup is another winner. Calamari can be fried or sauteed with a little tomato sauce, slightly sweetened with a little use of basil. The calamari stays tender, and it becomes almost sweet, too. Gamberi al ferri, shrimp under the fire, is lightly breaded first, and sprinkled with a little olive oil before it's run under the broiler. Why does it taste so good? The response to the question, delivered with a very Italian shrug, is "Who knows!" A little lemon and its essence-of-the-sea flavor spreads all over the plate, and through the mouth, too.

The house salad is fresh and crisp, with supporting roles for mozzarella, artichoke hearts and julienne of hearts of palm. It's lightly dressed, too. First courses begin at $5.75 (the salad), and go up to $10.50 (shrimp).

Pasta can be a first course as well as an entree, of course, and after a substantial opener, one of the lighter pastas works well. Rigatoni with maritriciana sauce is one example, the sauce sparked nicely by a judicious use of red pepper, and another is spaghetti with fresh tomato sauce.

Peppe's pasta of choice for carbonara—"My favorite," he crows. "I've been making it since I was a little kid."—is a bucatini, a slightly stouter spaghetti that is the best example of al dente in a long pasta we've seen in a long time. The sauce itself is dense and rich, not so cheesy that you can't taste anything else, and supported, but not overwhelmed, by a very mild ham. Interestingly, Peppe puts a little mint into his pesto sauce; a fine idea.

Risotto is not so creamy as we might like, but it's fairly firm and the taste of seafood is strong and rich.

Peppe's considers itself a veal house, with the scallopini with mushrooms and Fontana cheese being its biggest seller, but we're fond of the version with lemon, essentially a piccata, with tender veal in a sharp, savory sauce. Listen carefully to the fish specials. The kitchen handles them well, particularly a red snapper that's grilled in much the same fashion as the shrimp. The slight charring of the crumbs sets off the flavor of the fish, asking for nothing more than a judicious squeeze of lemon and perhaps a glass of cold pinot grigio. Pasta runs $14.50 to $20.50 for entrees; other main courses begin at $18.50 for one of several chicken dishes like cacciatore or Parmigiana, and top out at $27.50 for a stuffed filet mignon or $60 for a Chateaubriand for two. Peppe's is an expensive place to dine; figure on over $35 for appetizer, entree and dessert.

Speaking of dessert, if there's room, the standards are available, including a tartufo, pistachio ice cream in a hard chocolate shell, an Italian Eskimo Pie for adults. Often, there's flan, a house specialty, which tends to be a little overcooked but with good flavor in a nutmeggy caramel sauce.

The wine list is solid. Peppe is interested in Italian wines, and there are some fine ones, but they seem on the high side. The list can use some medium-priced wines from Peppe's native Italy; there are many of them available.

This is a popular lunch place, too, with many of the same dishes available. The lunch crowd must leave the way we do—always feeling very well-fed.

Gino's
Italian Cuisine

4502 Hampton Avenue
351-4187
Lunch Tuesday-Friday, Dinner Tuesday-Sunday
Credit cards: AE, MC, V
Wheelchair access: Satisfactory

Give the customers what they want. In St. Louis, they seem to want immense portions, and that's what they get at Gino's, where huge platters roll out of the kitchen and into a dining room that avoids the Italian Restaurant School of Painting. Bright posters and pictures of pizzas dot the walls; a decor that's worked well for over a decade. Owner-chef Giovanni (Gino) Vitale has risen from being a renter of one small space to being the owner of the entire building.

There's a solid appetizer list, and roasted peppers topped with discs of mozzarella cheese and a drizzle of olive oil, simple and tasty, are a strong beginning. The smooth softness of the cheese balances the sweet complexity of the roasted peppers, a dish that's not only honest and elegant, but also authentically Italian. Another first course, large enough for a main course, is seafood salad. Squid is poached just to the point of tenderness, and is bolstered by a few clams and mussels in their shells and a couple of shrimp, all bathed in a lemon and olive oil dressing, with some julienne carrots and celery added. The dressing ends up under the lettuce leaves that form a base, and it's good enough to be scooped up with bread.

Speaking of bread, the warm, crusty slices had arrived earlier with a dish of olive oil, fresh basil and finely-minced garlic, and the waiter had encouraged us to mix it with the Parmesan on the table. It's rare for us to complain about the amount of garlic, but there was an awful lot of it, to the point of its being hot and raw, causing it to run over everything else until it was tamed with the cheese.

The salad served with entrees is mostly iceberg lettuce, made so long beforehand that it was beginning to show signs of wear and weariness. A wedge of tomato was atop the lettuce, along with some onion that seemed to have been marinated first (or perhaps it just picked up some of the dressing during the wait). The dressing was a simple oil and vinegar that was delicious. It would have been more appealing had it not followed the aforementioned tradition of immense portions.

Although there's a full list of meat and fish dishes, most people seem to go for the pastas. Among the twenty-one on Gino's menu are eleven that are listed as vegetarian; most eliminate cheese, as well as meat and fish. We sampled the spaghetti Tarantina, a delightful, old-fashioned, round, tasty spaghetti noodle cooked deliciously al dente, served with the spicy, chunky, basil-laden tomato sauce that Gino terms "marinara," and fat, juicy, excellent mussels.

The same red sauce, solo, sat atop some fettuccine, a side dish with the evening special of trout. Neatly boned, split and broiled, it had almonds and a lemon garlic butter on it. The trout, very thin, had been overcooked. The lemon garlic butter was low on lemon and, once again, very high on the garlic, making it too intense for the delicate fish. The fat, which looked as though it were part butter and part olive oil, covered most of the bottom of the dish.

The pastas, which include cavatelli, penne and ziti, among others, have the standard toppings, and Gino's offers four different risottos, including one with the marinara sauce, lentils and broccoli, and another with a list of garden vegetables that includes arugula, escarole and saffron. Pasta dishes average about $11; other entrees, with a median price of $14 or so. The appetizers are those seen in most upper-level Italian restaurants in the area, and that's not a disparaging remark. Vitale sticks with basic Italian entree combinations, and his kitchen skills give the dishes their individuality. The same holds true for other chefs in his class.

The wine list is of moderate price, but there are no real bargains and few great wines. Service is good, but it became rather annoying as the meal went along. The waiter practically hovered over the table, asking if we were finished with a dish or wanted it wrapped the moment we stopped chewing. Other diners seemed able to eat in peace, but we felt like the waiter was trying to earn a merit badge in a "Shadowing the Subject" course in the Sam Spade School of Becoming a Detective. We also think that linen napkins demand real tablecloths, and not a piece of glass that causes condensation to turn into unabsorbed puddles and water glasses to slide of their own accord.

The dessert selection, like the entrees, is a compendium of the best of Italian St. Louis, except for Italian-made sorbets packed into real fruit, then frozen together. They began arriving from Milan early in 1998, and are available in several places; the dessert fruit includes pineapple (our favorite), peach, tangerine and lemon. The sorbet is smooth and fruity, and the bits of fruit left in the shell add a hint of flavor—and an aura—that is delicious. Tiramisu, made with real lady fingers, had a light, pleasant flavor and a texture that was slightly heavy.

Real Italians often end a meal with fruit, and Giovanni Vitale seems to be saying, "Try it my way!"

Giovanni's
Italian Cuisine with a Swagger
5201 Shaw Avenue
772-5958
Dinner Monday-Saturday
Credit cards: All major
Wheelchair Access: Impossible

Dealing with Giovanni Gabriele is far more difficult than dealing with the restaurant that bears his name. Most of the time, it is one of the bright lights of the Hill, but it often is glaringly in your face as Gabriele himself gets in the way of the fine dinners his kitchen can provide. There is no question but that the man can cook, and can supervise a superior kitchen.

But he can be a pain in the neck. He has an ego to match his talent (like many of his counterparts on the Hill), but he whines and complains and has apparently memorized every word Joe has ever written about his restaurant. He knows the dates of each review, and he also knows the dates of reviews of other Hill restaurants (just for the sake of comparison). Joe isn't complaining that writing about restaurants is tough, but the job—like any job—should be fun, and it's no fun dining at Giovanni's under the constant and penetrating gaze of the boss.

The staff hovers, and it pushes, and it's sycophantic, and when Joe enters, the waiters apparently break into severe cases of what every comedian knows as "flop sweat." They start off by addressing Ann as "young lady," and then proceed to shoot themselves in the other foot. Our waiter, strongly and repeatedly, suggests linguine with seafood, although we ask for pasta with a black sauce made from cuttlefish ink. To the table comes the seafood sauce. We taste it, explain the problem to the waiter. His response is to semi-apologize and tell us how angry Giovanni will be. Then he disappears.

In truth, the meal is very good. The seafood sauce is full of delicious treats, and the pasta is perfectly al dente. Mushroom sauce is wonderful atop a broad, delicate pappardelle pasta. Osso bucco is superb, though the risotto that comes with it is merely rice and not a true risotto. Scallops are overdone and too dry. Desserts are exciting. Giovanni has the classics, and does them in classic style. Mascarpone torte is rich and tasty. Tiramisu is light as angel's breath and richer than Bill Gates.

The word gets around, of course, and Giovanni will not let anyone rest until we agree to return for fettuccine with squid ink. It is quite good, but the sauce lacks the feeling of the sea that a great seafood sauce should bring. Very good, but no cigar. Stuffed eggplant is wondrous. The eggplant's inside is removed, chopped, sauteed in a little olive oil with basil, pepper, tomatoes, onions and some angolotti pasta, then replaced in the skin and baked. Simple and super-delicious. The same holds true for some swordfish, grilled, served in a sauce with roasted vegetables, including some flash-fried zucchini that marked the first time Joe has ever termed the vegetable "delicious." The kitchen does these things regularly at Giovanni's.

The meal ends on a diva's clear, high note with a grappa granita. A few raisins are thrown in for emphasis and it's wonderful; sweet but not cloying with a slight punch from the booze, light in the mouth and quite endearing.

There are many who think Giovanni's ranks with the best restaurants in the Midwest, maybe in the United States. The wine list is deep and filled with delightful flavors to match anything he creates, and we've experienced great meals here for many years. We've also experienced Giovanni for many years.

Giuseppe's
Basic St. Louis-Italian Cuisine
4141 South Grand Boulevard
832-3779
Lunch Tuesday-Friday, Dinner Tuesday-Sunday
Credit cards: All major
Wheelchair access: Passable

Once upon a time, back in the mid-1950s, Franklin Avenue was the main street of the northern edge of downtown St. Louis. It was a bustling main street, with streetcars and traffic, and it buzzed with urban life. People lived along Franklin Avenue, and they loved there, ate there, worked there, shopped there, died there. After Dr. Martin Luther King Jr. was assassinated, the Power Structure of St. Louis re-named Franklin Avenue in his honor. Then they did to the street what they were afraid to do when both the man and the street were alive: They killed it.

In place of shops and houses, pulsing with life, they built little office boxes, made of ticky-tacky, and sealed them off from the world and filled them with people who lived in the suburbs. The boxes cut through Franklin Avenue, and Dr. Martin Luther King Jr. Drive was chopped into fragments. No one used Dr. King's name in downtown St. Louis; he wasn't remembered anymore. A street called Cole took its place as an urban artery. Even the *Post-Dispatch*, once a bastion of liberalism, stopped using 1133 Franklin Avenue as its address and turned the corner to use 900 North Twelfth Street, later Tucker Boulevard.

A major highlight of Franklin Avenue was Rose's Restaurant, where many of downtown's movers and shakers ate and drank and talked and dreamed. All for naught, it now seems. Rose's kept some tradition alive in the face of "urban renewal" and "master plans." It moved to the heart of south St. Louis, the corner of Grand Boulevard and Meramec Avenue, where it became Giuseppe's. More important, it satisfied several more generations of St. Louisans as another of those exquisitely traditional restaurants where things seem to have remained unchanged for decades. We like it a lot, for the memories it conjures up and for the food it serves.

On Saturday nights, the joint jumps, at least as much as an essentially genteel place can jump. The crowd is quiet and a little older, with many couples having dinner together to catch up on news and gossip. White tablecloths gleam; smiling, competent waitresses speed hither and yon.

Appetizers are few and familiar, like crisp, hot garlic bread and, of course, the ubiquitous toasted ravioli. Calamari is crisp and drained to be greaseless, and is a popular dish. Sauteed peppers are probably green bell peppers, but they're well-seasoned and have picked up the flavor of the olive oil that cooks them. Smaller appetizers, at $6, will satisfy one or two, a few dollars more bring enough for the table to share. The house salad, despite an extra hint of sweetness in the dressing, retains its charm, and the addition of fresh salami and good cheese is welcome.

There must be something about kids and meatballs. Maybe it's the visual effect of a food that looks like a toy. Maybe it's just the name. Sophisticated adults, of course, would never order such a dish—unless they thought no other adult was watching—because the lure of old-fashioned spaghetti and meatballs is strong, and Giuseppe's basic red sauce, with a generous addition of basil, is outstanding.

Chicken liver lovers, a hardy breed, flock here, happy to hear the news over what must be an underground network. Livers are pan-fried, tender and moist inside, and though the livers-and-spaghetti isn't often on the menu, it seems to always be in the kitchen, ready to go. Joe is weak for chicken livers and finds it difficult to restrain himself, though occasionally a length of Italian sausage will lure him away. Chicken cacciatore can be half a boneless, skinless breast, or half an entire chicken in a dish filled with onions and pepper, saucy and succulent. Pastas average about $12, other entrees come near to $20. There's a modest wine list, limited but inexpensive, but there's usually a decent Chianti available.

This is not much of a dessert house. Cannoli is slightly soggy; cheesecake and ice cream are dependable, so finish your pasta and, as Mom used to say, it'll be a fair day tomorrow.

Great Chef Garden
Chinese

17 National Way Center (Manchester Boulevard and Woods Mill Road), Manchester
394-8008
Lunch and Dinner, every day
Credit cards: All major
Wheelchair access: Difficult (steps at door)

Many of us remember egg drop soup, chop suey, egg foo yung and fried rice as a series of wildly experimental choices at the old Orient Restaurant, in the shadows of Famous-Barr downtown. We're also the group that felt we deserved excessive praise when we sampled the Szechuan wares at Yen Ching, or ate clams with black bean sauce from Chef Tom Hsu's kitchen.

Well, it's time for another great leap forward.

Onward to Manchester, to the Great Chef Garden, where the weekend dinner buffet has the widest selection we've ever seen in St. Louis. It's a setup that matches many we've seen in San Francisco and Vancouver, both of which qualify as North American dim sum heaven.

Traditional dim sum fans will moan (and we moan, too) that the buffet system is all wrong, that dim sum should be served from a cart, as it is at the China Royal on North Lindbergh Boulevard, or at the one thousand-seat (no kidding) dim sum halls in Vancouver, London or Hong Kong, to name a few. Joe asked about it at the Great Chef and was told that the carts made things too crowded, and that Americans preferred to see their choices with labels on them, avoiding the necessity for asking questions and possibly running into a language barrier.

Joe still prefers the carts, where smaller quantities of food ensure that it is fresher and hotter than from a steam table. Besides, language barriers can be a plus. He's tasted many a dish and gone back for seconds not knowing its name, but knowing that a pretty cart driver smilingly—if unintelligibly—recommended it, and that he liked eating it. Earlier knowledge may have dissuaded him before the first effort.

The dinner buffet at the Great Chef Garden is staggering in size and display, and the owners have taken an interesting, all-inclusive approach. They are appealing to the St. Louis Chinese food fan with many of the items, and reaching toward a predominantly Asian audience with many others. On the night we visited, there were more than one hundred diners, with Asians holding about a 60-40 majority. Dinner was $11, including beverage, a serious bargain.

The buffet table is a large square, with one side partially open so that one can eat from either inside or outside three sides of the box (a trendy advertising term, we're told, though we don't know what it means). One side features soups (at least four kinds), and appetizers like egg rolls and dumplings; a second side is for dishes like beef and broccoli, steamed mussels, fried rice and green beans that will appeal to conservative diners. The third side is farther out—kim chee (hot and spicy Korean pickled cabbage, the ultimate sauerkraut), two kinds of pigs' feet, jellyfish, marinated beef tendon, and a dozen or so other dishes not often found on St. Louisans' short lists.

The Great Chef Garden offers the opportunity to wander around, to look at the many dishes. Dishes change as empty platters are removed and replaced by full ones, and sometimes the contents change, too. On a few circuits, we also saw, in no particular order, noodles with sesame sauce, green beans, five or six different dumplings, several baked whole fish, chicken wings, bean curd, roast beef, roast duck, crab legs, several kinds of shrimp, chicken salad with wide rice noodles, excellent sauteed mushrooms, shrimp salad with fruit, green pepper stuffed with shrimp, meatballs and several dozen other things. For an adventurous diner, it's truly mind-boggling.

Condiments, cookies and pastries, fresh and canned fruit and other desserts, including a delicious, cooling cantaloupe soup with tapioca, are on tables beyond the big hollow square.

There are several foraging styles. We saw a pair at one table start by making three or four trips to the buffet, returning each time with two plates filled with food. When the table was full, they sat down and went to work. We were different, making more visits, each time filling one plate with a variety of food.

We enjoyed dinner, relishing a number of different experiences. High spots were the cantaloupe soup, chicken salad, mushrooms, shrimp, dumplings and fresh fruit. Less exciting were roast chicken, sushi-style rice rolls, roast pork and egg rolls.

The regular menu is not particularly imaginative, with selections identical to those in restaurants all over town. In cases like this, the chef makes the difference, but the staying power of Asian chefs is like that of professional athletes. We've also thought there was just one print shop, and one menu, for all Chinese restaurants in St. Louis, with only the names changed to protect the guilty.

We enjoyed Great Chef Garden. There's a lot to watch in terms of both food and people, the buffet dinner is inexpensive and much of the food was excellent. That which isn't can be written off to experience.

Harry's Restaurant & Bar
Modern American Cuisine
2144 Market Street
421-6969
15415 Clayton Road, Ballwin
256-0221
Lunch Monday-Friday, Dinner every day; Brunch on Sunday at Clayton Road
Credit cards: All major
Wheelchair access: Passable

After opening in a blaze of glory as the first new and elegant downtown restaurant in many years, Harry's immediately became known as a watering hole (or more accurately, a feeding trough) for the sort of people who populate newspaper columns, as well as for hordes of well-dressed young urban professionals after work or in the hours surrounding downtown sports events. The terrace overlooking the Arch rocked with music and conversation; inside, the sound levels were almost as high.

Now, more than five years after its phoenix-like rise from the shell of a radiator repair shop, the kitchen still is going strong. So, it seems, are the crowds, although the dress seems a little more casual, and Harry Belli is serving a glorious brunch at Harry's West (just beyond the intersection of Clayton and Kehrs Mill Roads, shortly before the dragons' heads rear up over the end of the earth).

The menus are similar at both, well-rounded though not immense. The wine list is large, always an encouraging sign, made more encouraging by the wide selection of wines by the glass, all with impressive labels and most at moderate prices. Menus, like those at most restaurants that mean to be taken seriously, change with the seasons. A cold-weather dish of polenta was wonderful, fried and topped with a duck ragout that sang of the mushrooms that had been cooked with the rich meat. The flavor was deep and satisfying; this dish would reach greatness with a little more emphasis in the seasoning.

Shrimp salad is a full plate of mixed greens and a generous handful of noticeably tasty shrimp. The greens wear a judicious amount of dressing that presents the mouth with, successively, sweet, toasted sesame and hot tastes. Despite our general disdain for sweet dressings, this was sensational, especially when one of the shrimp was added to a forkful of the greens. Most dishes stop surprising the mouth after a number of bites. Every bite of this, right down to the end, gave a little extra touch of surprise and pleasure. Other first courses could be oyster fritters, lobster macaroni and cheese, or ahi tuna. Crab cakes have too much filling, not enough lump meat.

Liver and onions is often a sleeper. Restaurateurs say they're surprised at how well it moves. People either love it or hate it; we fall in the former camp. Harry's is tender veal liver, quickly sauteed, smothered in slightly browned onions and mounded over Yukon gold potatoes, roasted with garlic and then mashed with it. The mix was excellent, and special kudos go to potatoes that not only pick up all the other flavors, but also taste good on their own. There are a lot of garlic mashers out there these days; too many taste of garlic but not potato. Good steaks and smoked things, several fish selections and a lot of imagination on these plates, with dinner in the $35 range.

An in-house, brioche-pecan bread pudding with vanilla ice cream is a winner, and ice cream, not normally a topping for bread pudding, worked satisfactorily here. The brioche's buttery richness showed off the pecans, which had kept their crispness, not an easy thing to do in a bath of custard. However, this would be a great place for a whiskey sauce, since bourbon and pecans are such a natural pair. Good coffee, too.

Service keeps up with things smoothly, and manages to be very easygoing with parties who aren't in a hurry, surprising and laudable in a restaurant paced like this.

Brunch is available only at Harry's West, and we think it's one of the best in town. For one thing, it seems to concentrate more on breakfast-type foods, an emphasis we like. While there's a cold salad table, nearly all of the main course line is breakfast entrees. Ham and bacon, sausage gravy and tiny drop biscuits, eggs scrambled or Benedict and blintzes—real breakfast food. Biscuits and gravy is apparently exotica in this neighborhood. A gentleman of perhaps nine was pondering the line. Was that stuff oatmeal? No, Ann explained, it was gravy with sausage in it. "Weird," was the verdict, and he went on to content himself with some of the very spicy pepperoni in chunks on the cheese-and-sausage platter. The Benedicts aren't overcooked, the blintzes are tender and good, French toast is made from cinnamon swirl bread, and the potatoes—oh, the potatoes! New potatoes, cut in quarters, are roasted to crisp them nicely, and onions are added at some point in the process, to produce what's technically an oven-fried potato, we guess, but, wow! are they good.

There's an omelet station with a gifted egg flipper who also carves up beef as needed. Nearby is a platter of fruit. The variety isn't huge, but the flavor is consistently excellent, with pineapple in a class with what we had in Hawaii. On the salad table is a Caesar with lots of anchovy in the dressing, poached plain and peppered salmon, small, sweet shrimp in the shell that aren't overcooked, and a bland pasta salad. The mixed green salad is from a mesclun mix, and the sausage and cheese platter also features a wonderfully pungent Italian salami. We suspect it's from Volpi.

Desserts vary depending on the hour, but could be small creme brulees, tiny scoops of blueberry bread pudding, fingers of incredibly moist carrot cake or tiny versions of the chocolate upside-down cupcake that several bakeries in town make, except this one is more moist.

The coffee is good, too, and so is the small army of servers who keeps the tables clean. Most incredible of all is that it's less than $12, but please, please give us something besides the bare tabletop to put our silverware on.

Harvest
Modern American Cuisine
1059 South Big Bend Boulevard, Richmond Heights
645-3522
Dinner Tuesday-Sunday
Credit cards: All major
Wheelchair access: Satisfactory

Happily raucous and as fashionable as a morning in Milan, Harvest continues to be hotter than most recent rock groups, with a string of hits that goes back to its 1996 opening. Fashionable does not always mean good food, whether in St. Louis or anyplace else, but in the case of Harvest, both the trendy and the un-hip are extremely well-fed, at a cost of about $35 a head before drinks, tax and tip.

Located in the old Cyrano's, Harvest still gets people wandering in after movies in search of a Cleopatra sundae. The lost ones must feel like Alice falling down the rabbit hole when they walk into a room with California decor and a noise level to match a gold strike.

The menu changes several times a year, and the inevitable specials, well-conceived and often written like Shakespearean sonnets, make for some agonizing decisions. It's difficult to think while hunger pangs are racking the soul.

Appetizers probably are the hardest choices. Roasted mussels arrive in a fajita pan, simply and sizzlingly done with just a little lemon and garlic adding flavor to their own juices. Chicken liver pate rang with earthy, unctuous herbs and garlic. Fritto misto, almost an Italian version of Japanese tempura, adds a few French-fried vegetables to a seafood medley in an airy, well-seasoned batter. And there are the onion rings. Oh, are there ever the onion rings! Shatteringly crisp, desperately hot, the buttermilk batter on them is excellent. Lying on the plate next to the immense mound of rings is a dip of blue cheese with the nip of cayenne pepper, a combination that should become an instant classic.

Main courses jam the plate. Each has at least one vegetable side, but we're not talking succotash here. We're not even—thank heaven!—talking the ubiquitous "seasonal vegetable medley" that surrounds every other St. Louis entree with the same vegetables that are ripe year-round. A roasted organic chicken breast sits on a casserole of potatoes, oyster mushrooms and French green beans with a pinot noir reduction. Sliced New York strip steak stretches out luxuriously on garlic mashed potatoes with sauteed spinach, a grilled red onion and cabernet sauce. Pasta? Fettuccine wears scallops, portobello mushrooms, asparagus and a sherry mushroom sauce.

One of the best dishes we sampled was a whole-roasted black bass sitting on a bed of fat Israeli couscous mixed with sauteed bok choy and chanterelle mushrooms. The fish is perfectly cooked, flaking with a nudge of the fork, still very moist, and extremely easy to bone. The couscous is complex, slightly chewy and teaming perfectly with the bass notes of the mushrooms and the tenor of the bok choy. It was quite fine.

Duck breast, always one of Joe's favorites, was well-nigh perfect. It was served on the rare side, in a Marsala wine reduction that added a hint of sweetness from grapes, rather than the usual cherries. It accompanied a cassoulet of beans, tangy sausage and caramelized onion, and the blend of flavors made the whole far more than the sum of its parts.

Dessert presents another set of agonizing choices. The bread pudding seems to be a constant, and it's special, but when there's room, we go ranging off into the cakes and fruit crisps. Good combinations and excellent pastry crusts are common, and the ice creams are deliciously rich.

The wine list is impressive but generally on the high side. California and imported wines, often from small vineyards and wineries, come in a wide variety of styles, aimed at every taste. The by-the-glass selection is admirable, offering the diner a chance to experiment with wines and grapes he or she doesn't know. It's a grand opportunity to broaden one's wine knowledge. Service is zippy and reasonably attentive, and the Harvest experience continues to be a bountiful one.

Hot Locust Cantina
Modern American with a Bang

2005 Locust Street
231-3666
Lunch and Dinner, Monday-Saturday
Credit cards: AE, MC, V
Wheelchair access: Passable

In India, we understand, people believe that eating new things increases mental capacity. It makes sense. Just like hearing new music or seeing new visual art, it expands the horizons of the imagination. And yet, there are some people who might avoid the Hot Locust Cantina because they take its first name as a dire warning.

A great deal of the food cooked at this spot, which sits on the edge of a reviving downtown, does include some sort of the Americas' gift to gastronomy—the chile pepper—and many dishes pay homage to south-of-the-border traditions. However, not much on the menu is actually fiery, and often the heat is the soft warmth in the mouth that tingles briefly and disappears, leaving only a Cheshire cat kind of smile. It's an interesting way to realize what the peppers can do, and a visit here will help expand tolerance for spicy food. Small doses get those endorphins stirring, and the pleasant, very natural buzz is one reason people have come to enjoy spicy food. Good bargain for maybe $20 a person, but don't tell John Ashcroft about endorphins. He'll try to ban them.

This is a brick-walled joint with an immense chalkboard menu on one side. Fortunately, the staff has mastered it and can explain it to those sitting nearby, avoiding the uninsured cost of a neck brace the next day. There's also a regular menu, as detailed as its hanging counterpart.

The brick walls also mean this place is loud with the sound of happy conversation. At night there's often a band, but that area is well soundproofed.

Much of the staff is twenty-somethings with bobby-pinned hair and fashionably ugly shoes. Despite their garb, these folks are professionals; they hustle, and they know their stuff. They also don't hesitate to give opinions about what's good and what's better.

The soup list alone is enough to cause a major attack of indecision—vegetarian blue corn posole, green chicken noodle soup with penne, chili from scratch, seafood stew. Too much to choose from. And then there are three kinds of chicken wings, and good guacamole, too.

Shrimp blackened with Indian spices, if not actually from a tandoori oven, teamed with grilled green onions, a raita-style yogurt sauce with mint and a grilled ring of pineapple, a delightful combination. The shrimp was properly cooked, although a little salty. A chalkboard special burrito appetizer turned out to be a huge, thin, almost fragile flour tortilla bearing chorizo sausage, a little shrimp and some cheese, with a salsa made of tomatillos (those little things that look like green tomatoes). The tomatillos have an almost lemony taste, adding to the sensation that the salsa was much like a chopped salad. Sweet potato fries are addictive, with a tropical ketchup that is sweet at first bite, hot at second.

Lamb chops were delivered in a different version than was offered on the menu. Instead of the two loin chops with a jalapeno lime marmalade and minted apple couscous, the chops, cooked to the correct degree of rareness, came with a sauce sparingly spooned across them. It resembled the bright green topping on real, cheese-free oysters Rockefeller. No spinach in this—it was sharp and full of mint and lemon with the chile finishing third. The bouncy counterpoint to the meat was fascinating and perfect. The couscous was unspiced but carried red and green peppers, carrots, two kinds of squash and half an onion.

Ropa Vieja (old clothes) is an old Cuban dish, described on the menu as Ric Orlando's recipe. Stand up and take a bow, Ric. This is beef brisket the way a Cuban-Jewish mother could only hope to carry off. Big chunks of beef, fork tender, cooked in a sauce with tomatoes, wine, olives and capers, mouth-filling in its flavor, slightly to moderately hot, and exceptionally good. The side dishes were white rice and black beans, the latter tender without mushiness but with a slight sweetness that finished with a little warmth; red cabbage whose slight caramelizing gave the impression it had been fried like onions (and a touch, just a touch, of heat, very, very far back). The house mashed sweet potatoes show lots of citrus flavor, and though they are not sweet, they remind a diner that they could be if they wanted to. Outstanding.

There are vegetarian dishes like blue corn nachos, an eggplant and goat cheese melt, burritos and a new approach to catfish, baked in a creole sauce. Sensitive palates might avoid chicken wings with habanero sauce, but seared tuna with soba noodles or a pan-grilled porterhouse steak will be mild. Most display a blend of flavors with a peak here and there. This kitchen knows how to find flavors in some dishes and create them in others, a pair of superb attributes.

Dessert is a cheesecake with Mexican chocolate (that probably means with cinnamon) and a little ancho chile laced across the top. They were out of it, and we went for the house-made pecan pie. It suffered from having been refrigerated, making the pecans soggy. But the filling itself was remarkable, with a little orange and tequila giving the faint taste of candied fruit, sometimes almost unnoticeable and other times right there and easy to identify.

The wine list is brief; this is a margarita and beer house.

House of India
Indian Cuisine
8501 Delmar Boulevard, University City
567-6850
Lunch and Dinner, every day
Credit cards: All major
Wheelchair access: Passable

An adventurous diner may start to worry when walking into House of India. Do the taupe-colored walls mean prettied-up, toned-down Indian cuisine? Does the scalloped awning dilute the subcontinental experience?

Not to worry. There's not a trace of creeping panculturalism in the food. The papadum, a crisp cross between a cracker and a chip, is the spiciest we've tasted in St. Louis. A green sauce, full of cilantro, and a red sweet-hot sauce, arrive with them, a promise of what's to come. Samosas (turnovers) and pakoras (fritters) are the most common appetizers, and the soups are tantalizing, especially the dal, or lentil. Onion ring eaters should leap upon the bhajia, onion rings dipped into a seasoned batter of chickpea flour and deep-fried. The batter is dense but tender, the bhajia well-drained. The dish is common in English takeaway (carry-out) places where they are pronounced "onion bajees." We've also liked the chane-ki-chat, or chilled chickpeas, diced potatoes, cucumbers and onions in a minty yogurt sauce.

Bread is also something to pay attention to. There are several stuffed breads, which are tasty, but they always seem more like an appetizer. We like the paratha, flakily-layered unleavened bread, served hot and glistening with butter, and the roti, which is very much like a whole-wheat tortilla, rolled out and cooked on a grill. Especially with a kebab of some sort, bread is a good idea.

Biryani is the classical celebration dish. House of India's lamb version (one of five variations) had basmati rice with a tomato sauce and lots of meaty chunks of lean lamb. It's not spicy-hot, for the more conservative of palate, but it doesn't need to be. The rice mixture included almonds and peanuts, as much for texture as taste, and the occasional raisin for a little burst of sweet in the midst of the savory rice.

The tandoori is good here, but instead of the usual seekh kebab or chicken tandoori, we tried a ginger chicken kebab. Chunks of skinless boneless white meat were tangy with their yogurt and herb marinade, very tender and nicely moist. They come on a fajita-type pan, sizzling with sliced onions and green peppers, and are very nice plain or rolled up in a little bread with some raita and/or chutney as seasoning.

About those two items: Raita comes as a side with the biryani, or otherwise must be ordered separately. This version is heavily cumin-laden and rather salty compared to some. It cuts the heat in dishes that are too spicy, and adds another note of flavor. The mango chutney tastes like it's made in-house, a lovely peach-pink, zingy but not killer-hot. It, too, is an extra item, but definitely worth trying.

The Eggplant King ordered baingan bhartha, a tandoori-cooked eggplant smashed and seasoned and mixed with tomatoes and peas. It's very creamy, full of ginger and coriander and onions. House of India's vegetarian menu is particularly deep, with a baker's dozen of entrees and several appetizers.

The wine list is limited, and lacks the sweet, fruity German-style whites that work so well with curry, so we went for Kingfisher, an Indian beer. Dessert was a mango lassi, the yogurt-and-mango drink similar to a non-sweet milkshake, and some kheer, creamy rice pudding, dotted with almonds, coconut and ground pistachios.

Our standard indicator (appetizer, main course, dessert) shows a $16 tab. Extra bread and condiments could raise it another $5. They're worth it.

Hunan & Peking Garden
Northern Chinese Cuisine
1264 Old Orchard Center, Manchester
227-6445
Lunch and Dinner, every day
Credit Cards: All major
Wheelchair access: Satisfactory

On Fridays, Joe's grandfather would sit in the living room window of his apartment, three flights up in a four-story Brooklyn walkup, read his Hebrew newspaper, and wait for his children and grandchildren to arrive for dinner. Joe's family would walk on the Eastern Parkway sidewalk, and when he looked up, Grandpa would be waving. In far west St. Louis County, Mr. Lin sits in the window of the Hunan & Peking Garden Restaurant, reads his Chinese newspaper, and waits for the customers to arrive for dinner. There's little resemblance between them, but a thought of connection looms upon entering the restaurant, all decked out in red plush and red lanterns.

The Hunan & Peking is high on our list of Chinese restaurants, especially when we're in the mood for fried oysters, an uncommonly fine appetizer here. Cooked in a light batter (almost in the tempura style but not quite), they're large, juicy and absolutely delicious, perhaps the best in the area. They are large enough to be comfortably cut in half, and, knowing oyster prices, $5 for four giants is not out of line.

Fried oysters, however, are only the beginning. The wide-ranging menu is like many in the area, but the Frank Lin family excels with its dedication to detail and the careful use of spicing. Like many other Asian menus, the Hunan & Peking notes that it will adjust the spicing to taste, but unlike many of its counterparts, the waiters and the kitchen staff here pay attention when the diner speaks.

Therefore, asking for medium heat brings dishes that emphasize flavor, not just spice. Shanghai-style ribs, with a superior taste from ginger and garlic, are delicious, as are green jade scallops, with snow peas, green peppers and water chestnuts. Besides the oysters, superior appetizers include all soups; our favorites are the classic hot and sour, tangy and tingly to the tongue, and chicken and black mushrooms, which includes lychee fruits and dates for different tastes and textures that bring something different to the palate.

The black bean sauce displays hints of garlic along with the warm, dark beans, and it's perfect over clams or squid. Twice-cooked pork, beef with orange flavor and squid with five spices are other favorites, and there's a special nod to the Hunan & Peking's duck dishes. Asians do special things with duck, our favorite fowl, which benefits in dishes like crisp smoked duck, steamed duck with sour plums, and Hunan roast duck.

Asian cooking is wondrous, but we don't think Americans are experimental—or maybe courageous—enough to take full advantage of the variety of marinades and rubs before cooking and the many techniques used during it. Chat with the server, or else just try a new and/or unfamiliar dish and see what happens. At best, it might derail an entire train of thought. At worst, it's a minor expense because an entire dinner at Hunan & Peking rarely costs more than $15 a person.

India Palace

Indian Cuisine

4534 N. Lindbergh Blvd. (11th floor Howard Johnson Motor Lodge), Bridgeton
731-3333
Lunch and Dinner, daily
Credit cards: All major
Wheelchair access: Satisfactory

The trick to eating at India Palace is in finding it. Located atop a building that includes a motel, a bank and offices, it overlooks the airport at the northeast corner of Lindbergh and I-70. Moreover, coming from the south, a driver must drive by it and make right turns, followed by a left, to loop back to the building—and then figure out which door to enter. (It's the door nearest the inner corner of the building.)

From the elevator, the decor resembles the late Trader Vic's, with plants and bamboo everywhere. There's even a wicker outrigger canoe suspended from the ceiling. And there are lots of windows. The view is better at night, when the lights outside don't reveal suburban sprawl and the Boeing plant.

The clientele, however, often includes a sizeable percentage from the Indian subcontinent, to judge from the conversation overheard, leaving a Westerner with the understandable urge to gesture toward a nearby table and say, "I'll have what they're having."

The diner who followed this urge would probably eat well. We didn't encounter a single miss on the menu. On arrival, a plate appears with a couple of papadums, crispy wafers of lentil flour, and two sauces, one sweet-sour tamarind, and another green spicy one with lots of cilantro. Gently shatter the papadums into chunks, then dip them while you read the menu.

Vegetable samosas were packets—knishes or dumplings or ravioli, if you will—of potatoes and peas, happily spiced, folded into a jacket of dough and deep-fried. They weren't greasy, but they certainly were dense, which is the nature of samosas. Pakoras, on the other hand, were lighter; a sort of tempura with a chickpea batter that's used on vegetable slices.

Indian breads are a significant part of the meal. We like nan, which is a little like pita, and roti, which is tortilla-like, as well as paratha. We also tried the onion-stuffed nan recommended by our waiter.

Soup is often an unsung pleasure at an Indian restaurant. A maitre d', who looked as if he'd sampled well, suggested the chicken soup as we debated it against the tomato. It deserved the recommendation, arriving as a small serving, but tasty and warming, with bits of tandoori chicken in it.

That tandoori, by the way, refers to the oven where the food is—for lack of another word—barbecued. It gets very hot, and in skillful hands, produces succulent meat and fish, an excellent introduction to Indian food for the inexperienced eater. The tandoori here is as good as any we've had in St. Louis. The chicken and fish were juicy and utterly tender. They were out of lamb, and substituted the seekh kebab, a minced lamb that's sausage-shaped. It's spicier than the other, but imaginatively so.

A rogan josh lamb was tasty, and spicy-hot at just the level ordered, the rice was the rich-smelling basmati, and a vegetable dish of eggplant and potatoes was milder, bringing an almost sweet taste in contrast to the spice. The menu also lists several goat dishes, a superior animal for the tandoori.

The raita, a yogurt dish with cumin and a few small vegetables, was particularly thick and rich—one is tempted to eat it like soup—and it's another good dish for beginners. Mango chutney was smooth and a little fiery, with an almost buttery note to it. There's an extra charge for both these items.

There's a wine list, and it has some gewurtztraminer on it, although not by the glass. Frankly, though, we'd just as soon order cold Indian beers and let them cool the heat.

Indian desserts are always interesting. Sometimes we order a mango lassi, the yogurt semi-milkshake that is officially a beverage, but which is so good, you can drink two before the food comes. Be careful, though, it can fill you up. But the favorite is rasmalai, cheese patties that come soaked in a milk sauce, thickened and rather sweet with ground pistachios in it. Strange, but curiously pleasant.

Figure about $20 per person before you start dabbling in the breads and the side condiments.

India's Rasoi
Indian Cuisine
7923 Forsyth Boulevard, Clayton
727-1414
1101 E. Broadway, Columbia, Mo.
(573) 817-2009
Lunch and Dinner, every day
Credit cards: All major
Wheelchair access: Satisfactory

When Rasoi moved from its cubbyhole in west St. Louis County to smack dab in the middle of Clayton, across the street from the County Courthouse, there were a few doubters who gloated at a few stumbles. But the Indian restaurant seems to have regained its glow, and its claim to the rank of being the best of its style in the area.

First courses at Rasoi are bicultural, not just the samosas, which are like stuffed turnovers, and pakoras, which involve items battered in chickpea flour and deep-fried, and not unlike tempura in Rasoi's version. There often is a salad topped with tandoori chicken and tandoori chicken wings—Bombayed, instead of Buffaloed, is the operative word. In addition, it's a good idea to try some of the stuffed breads like naan and paratha, loaded with meat, vegetables or cheese. Dahiwada, steamed lentil patties, are served cold with a yogurt sauce much like raita, and are curiously satisfying for all their wet-bread texture.

Soups are enticing, too. Dal is lighter than what one pictures as a lentil soup, with a gentle slow glow in the mouth. Mulligatawny, with chicken and vegetables, is deeper, darker and seemingly more complex. The lemon that comes alongside adds a great deal in flavors both on the surface and extremely deep.

Tandoori, with meat rubbed with mild spices and roasted in a clay oven to help bring out the orange color, is superb. Hot and juicy, it's something to endear even the timid eater. Lamb curry, in a tomato sauce with tender, lean chunks of meat, was a delight in every respect. A Balti shrimp and crab korma didn't seem to have the almonds and raisins that the menu spoke of, but it was nicely spiced and the seafood cooked just long enough, lots of flavor and not tough. Rasoi also is a fine spot for vegetarians, with eleven meatless entrees. Roasted eggplant with tomatoes and onions is delicious, and chickpeas, cooked with herbs and spices, reach new heights of flavor.

Garlic naan was not shockingly garlicky; roti is reminiscent of pita but thinner and more crisp. Raita and papadums cost extra here, by the way, but the papadum order is two large ones and comes with tamarind and mint sauces. Masala chai, tea enriched with herbs, comes with hot milk already in it—very British—and is fragrant and warming.

Dessert involves kulfi, various Indian ice creams; kheer, rice pudding flavored with saffron; gulab jamun, which an Indian once described as doughnuts in syrup and came close, but not enough for a cigar; and ras malai, cheese patties in a sweet milk sauce. These are addictive, though they don't seem like cheese. The wet-bread texture, which bothers some diners, can be very cooling, and the sauce and spicing are fascinating.

Wine by the glass includes a Kendall-Jackson Johannsberg Riesling, a good match. There's beer, of course, which is also good. Service is sharper and more brisk, but Indian's Rasoi is still one-forking it, which it should not. With linen tablecloths, and dinners close to $20 a person, replacing a fork soiled in the first course would seem to be a reasonable courtesy.

J.P. Field's and John P. Field's

American Food

34 South Old Orchard Avenue, Webster Groves
962-3445
26 North Central Avenue, Clayton
862-1886
Lunch and Dinner, Monday-Saturday
Credit cards: All major
Wheelchair access: Passable

John P. Field's in Clayton wasted no time in becoming a regular lunch and watering hole for businesspeople. Its clubby atmosphere fit right in with the law offices and corporate boardrooms in the neighborhood. When change was decided upon, in came Michael Holmes, one of St. Louis' best-known and well-traveled chefs. Soon thereafter, or perhaps simultaneously, a second location was needed, and a Webster Groves' site was chosen.

Starting with a building that had housed a record store for many years, the Fields' group put in a bar, a fireplace and a kitchen, their trademark wooden Venetian blinds and green walls, and gave Holmes a new fiefdom. He and his right-hand guy, Brian Fuchs, are adjusting the menu to reflect the different crowd in quiet Webster Groves.

Originally, for example, they figured the evening crowd in what the Rep's David Frank called "the quiet little village of Webster Groves," wouldn't be interested in burgers and wings—but sure enough, they're back. Pre-theater dinners are large, and the restaurant serves food until 11:30 on Friday and Saturday nights. Dinner prices will be about $20 per person, higher for steaks.

First courses are in the $7 range, and there's a wide selection, including fish and chips, a shrimp salad, a Cajun shrimp dish, potato skins and a cheese plate. One of the soups is a wild mushroom bisque, creamy and carrying the standard mushroom tastes, and topped with a slice of Gruyere toast.

All entrees, except sandwiches and dinner-size salads, come with either a soup or salad, which makes the prices, from $10.95 for a vegetarian stir-fry to $24.95 for a 12-ounce sirloin strip, quite reasonable. The house salad is a good mixture of greens with a little tomato. The dressings are a creamy basil, the basil being grown on the restaurant grounds in warm weather, and a tomato vinaigrette. We chose the vinaigrette, which was quite thick, and slightly sweet. The salad was only lightly dressed, a quality we admire. Basil isn't the only crop that Holmes is doing on the grounds. There are banana peppers growing, and some cilantro, too. Frazer Cameron of Frazer's, and Steve Komorek of Trattoria Marcella also are growing herbs and things at home; Holmes is the first countian to join in. We look for State Fair entries next summer.

A salmon of the day was crusted with pecans and grilled. The coating (or maybe the farm-pond where it grew up) seemed to tame the fish's natural flavor, making the overall effect rather bland. It came, however, with a sweet potato casserole that was dynamite, chunks of fresh sweet potato cooked with sliced tart apple and tiny currants, almost a sweet potato-apple crisp. The portobello steak is one of the big mushrooms caps marinated in oil and vinegar and a lot of dandy things, baked and then finished on the grill. It was superb, moist and meaty and full of wonderful, wonderful flavors. Holmes says he occasionally offers it as a lunch sandwich special. Can you imagine it with a slice of ripe, juicy tomato? At night it comes with potato (mashers are pungent with the scent of roasted garlic), sweet onions, and a little Gorgonzola cheese. Quite splendid, indeed.

Holmes et al are tinkering with sticky toffee pudding, working on getting it just right, or as good as the one at the Tap Room. The current one is extremely moist, too wet if it were a cake, but fine for a pudding whose first name is sticky, and which shows a silky texture. We'd move the nice warm sauce away from butterscotch and toward caramel or toffee, though. The cream, though, is definitely not the stuff from a pressurized nozzle, but droops down the sides in an elegant swoon.

About ten wines by the glass head a solid wine list, and servers give the price with each special, which deserves a big hurrah. We're told that there's already a pool on just how long the peripatetic Holmes will last.

Jack Carl's Two Cents Plain
Kosher-style Delicatessen
1114 Olive Street
436-1070
Breakfast and Lunch, Monday-Friday
Cash only
Wheelchair access: Passable

Spending time close to a bar or a delicatessen meat-slicer turns a person into a psychiatrist, a lawyer, a minister and a fount of knowledge on everything from pasta to pastrami. Jack Carl stands behind his downtown delicatessen counter and, all in the interest of helping his customers, litigates cases, criticizes restaurants and theater and movies, counsels both parents and children, and collects photographs for his wall.

Among them is an autographed photo of a striptease queen named Jada, the headliner at Jack Ruby's club in Dallas when John F. Kennedy was assassinated. Coincidentally, she was the headliner at the old Grand Theatre in Louis six months later when Ruby was convicted of the murder of Lee Harvey Oswald, and she presented the photo to Carl at his Two Cents Plain in Gaslight Square.

Carl has been slicing meat and giving advice for about a half-century. His father had Carl's Delicatessen on Delmar Boulevard in the University City Loop (where Jay Brandt now is located) when Joe first arrived in St. Louis. Jack subsequently moved to Gaslight Square (and lived just down the hall from Joe in Laclede Park), then to Clayton, before settling in downtown.

Since Woody Allen introduced mayonnaise to Jewish delicatessens, and Meg Ryan made them sexy in When Harry Met Sally, the place of the deli in American life has changed a lot. Being kosher is no longer as important as it once was to owners and customers, and Carl offers a wide variety of sandwiches to suit almost any taste. Smoked meats like pastrami and corned beef are excellent, and so is the selection of German, Jewish and Italian salamis. Many people think (and we're often among them) that kosher bologna and hot dogs, being all beef, have extra flavor. There are many salads, and lox and bagels make for an elegant breakfast. Coffee, soda and beer, and a chance to get into some serious—or not so serious—dialogue with Jack. Eating here is only part of the fun.

Joe and Charlie's
Bar Food—and More

8040 Clayton Road, Richmond Heights
721-9597
Bar food for Lunch and Dinner, every day
Credit cards: All major
Wheelchair access: Satisfactory

Charlie Becker and Joe Scopolite had a Gaslight Square saloon in the mid-1950s, just as the Square was first achieving national prominence. They did well, but they showed Branch Rickey wisdom when they were among the first to leave the neighborhood. (Rickey's maxim, in trading players, was to trade a player a year too early rather than a year too late.) They moved to Brentwood Boulevard and re-established the business, drawing young urban professionals before people started designing acronyms.

Lawyers and various executives flocked to the Brentwood location, and on St. Patrick's Day, the boulevard was closed by a sea of humanity, mostly wearing green.

The partnership dissolved, as partnerships are wont to do, and Becker used creosote when he painted the Clayton Road interior, leaving a penetrating aroma for several years.

Anyway, in a closet-sized kitchen, a series of fry cooks have created outstanding sandwiches—at first just cold ones—with liverwurst on rye and a slice of onion being a personal favorite. When a grill was added, so were superb Reuben sandwiches. Chili is excellent, and the sandwiches all up and down the menu are winners.

John D. McGurk's
Irish Pub, American Food

1200 Russell Boulevard
776-8309
Lunch and Dinner, every day
Credit cards: All major
Wheelchair access: Difficult

If we needed a place to hole up on a rainy afternoon, McGurk's would be the answer. It's a big joint, with several rooms, walls of brick and dark wood and pictures of Irish musicians and athletes practically covering them. A quiet place at that time of day, but like a proper pub, it becomes various degrees of rowdy at night. McGurk's has hosted more than one wake, too. Not that it's gloomy—not at all. Because of the way it's divided, it can be cozy and surprisingly private.

Another much-admired attribute is that it seems to serve happily as the classroom for Pub 101 for any number of properly respectful children. Not long ago, a young fellow wearing a Cardinals cap sat at the bar eating lunch with his dad. Their quiet discussion was occasionally interrupted when Da chatted with the publican. The boy contented himself with ESPN reruns of Mark McGwire home runs.

While the traditional American pub food is available here, with hamburgers and chicken wings heading the list, things go much further and much better. For instance, McGurk's has the only vegetarian toasted ravioli we've seen, spinach and artichoke, with a spicy honey dipping sauce. Of course, the old-fashioned kind also is available. But why not the crab cakes or smoked salmon pate or soup? Potato soup is thick and creamy, the occasional cube of carrot thrown in for eye appeal, but the taste is unsullied beyond potato, onion and milk. More potatoes, boiled new ones, team up with thick slices of two kinds of sausage and a few onions, alongside some coarse-ground mustard. A potentially glorious dish undone by overcooking the sausage. There's also help for salad eaters; first courses range from $2.50 to $8.95.

Beyond the burgers, a hungry lad runs into Irish stew, corned beef hash and chicken sausage farfalle. Club sandwiches work with pan-roasted salmon or smoked turkey. The pork loin sandwich has smoked cheddar and onions stewed to sweetness in Guinness stout adorning it. The sourdough baguette it rests on is far, far too fat, and the easiest way to manage (unless you are a veteran of several potato famines) is to remove the top layer of bread and eat it open-faced, like a gigantic Danish smorrebrod. Roast pork, seasoned with maple syrup and spices, is sliced thinly and snuggles happily with its mates, a good gathering of flavors. Many draft beers, too.

Corned-beef hash consists of hash-brown potatoes, chunks of beef, onion and the occasional hit of spicy pepper, all cooked together long enough for the ever-friendly potato to pick up the juices of the meat and onion, erasing all memory of canned hash and its itty-bitty dice. Irish chips accompany sandwiches. These are crispy rather than chewy, russet-brown and not so large a portion that one is driven to eat them despite waistline conscience. Lunch specialties are $4.95 to $9.95; at night, a few entrees in the $15 range replace a few sandwiches.

Bread pudding and Bailey's cheesecake work well for dessert.

Whatever you do, don't mention the potato blight.

John Mineo's
Italian Cuisine
13490 Clayton Road, Town & Country
434-5244
Lunch Tuesday-Friday, Dinner Monday-Saturday
Credit cards: All major
Wheelchair access: Satisfactory

John Mineo's seems on a definite upswing. Another of the Hill-away-from-the-Hill restaurants, it has begun to sparkle like its chandeliers again. Where once was dignity to the point of stodginess, service now is wreathed in smiles. Not to the point of casualness—this is still a black tie and white tablecloth restaurant—but still a marked and welcome change.

The food, too, has perked up. While there are certainly a lot of the old standbys—cannelloni and shrimp cocktail, veal Marsala and penne al salmone—diners can now find new sauces, new versions of old sauces, and a wider range of variety meats and seafood.

An order of mussels Provenzale brought a dozen or so large ones in a chunky tomato sauce, which at first brought to mind the oregano seasoning for a steak pizzaiola, but then grew in the mouth to finish more like an arrabiata, pungent with red pepper and with hints of sherry. The hearty mussel flavor can stand up to a big taste like this, and it's a good match.

Fettuccine verdi alla pirata involved green fettuccine surrounded by mussels and fat shrimp. The sauce was the unlikely combination of curry and cheese, much like a highly aromatic Alfredo. The combination worked, bringing a new perspective on what a judicious use of curry can do. The mussels took to it like they'd been doing so for generations. The shrimp were having a bad night, unfortunately, without much flavor of their own, but the entire dish was extremely satisfying, even to the junior partner who normally views guest appearances by curry powder with a dubious eye.

Baby squid in a spicy tomato sauce appear as calamari alla Luciana, and at the suggestion of John Mineo Jr., we had it over pasta, an al dente linguini that picked up and carried the sauce very well. This also was a spicy red sauce, but in an entirely different style than the one with the mussels—less tomato sweetness, more basil and some chopped green olives. The calamari was cooked just to tenderness, keeping it full of that briny, fresh-from-the-ocean flavor. Eminently satisfactory.

Desserts come in from outside—there's no crime in that now that St. Louis has several first-rate suppliers—except for the Brown Squirrel, an ice cream drink with creme de cacao and amaretto. Every so often, something like this is a fine finish to a good meal, and this hit the spot.

The wine list is both long and strong, with many excellent bottles at the top end of the price spectrum. First-rate Italians lead the way.

Why all this change? We're not sure. Sometimes restaurants, like people, just go through cycles. Young John is running the kitchen, and he reports that some of the clientele have more adventurous tastes. As a result, he now offers dishes like risotto al Nero, squid risotto flavored with squid ink, when the ingredients are available. While heavy on seafood and shellfish, the menu also offers liver Veneziana and tenderloin topped with eggplant. This is clearly becoming a restaurant for serious eaters, but not necessarily stuffy ones.

Joseph's Italian Cafe

Contemporary Italian

107 North Sixth Street
421-6366
451 South Kirkwood Road, Kirkwood
909-0455
Lunch Monday-Friday, Dinner Monday-Saturday
Credit cards: All major
Wheelchair access: Satisfactory (Kirkwood); Difficult (Sixth Street)

Ernie Trova began as a window-dresser at Famous-Barr, and went on to great fame as an artist. He also is a considerable gourmet.

Joseph Consolo Jr., also is a window-dresser, at Famous-Barr and the other stores of the May Company. A few years ago, he decorated a restaurant, designing everything from the menu to the chairs and tables, using stainless steel photographers' tripods for the legs of the latter. His son, Joseph Consolo III, operated it, and it has been enough of a success that the family opened a suburban branch with similar decor and menu.

Joseph's is a gorgeous restaurant. Steel and black go very well together, and both restaurants have a high-tech, sleek look that feels hip and modern. The Kirkwood site also has a jazz room and a cigar bar next door, equally sleek and elegant to eye and ear.

And the food is very good, too, though a notch behind the top-drawer establishments of our city. Dinner will be upwards of $30 in Kirkwood, a little less downtown.

Joseph's downtown is a favorite lunch spot, with sandwiches, pizzas and pastas that are imaginatively designed and properly executed. Fresh ingredients are featured, and the spicing is just right. The Caesar salad works with the fresh, crisp romaine, and the romano cheese shavings help the overall flavor.

The pizzas, with artichoke hearts, or with a four-cheese combination, or with sausage and roasted red peppers, are splendid; and strombolis, meals in themselves, are a meat-eater's dream. All have mozzarella cheese, which combines with spinach, pepperoni or sausage and pepperoni.

For dinner, the Kirkwood spot serves crab cakes or a steamed mussels-clams combination, marinated shrimp, bruschetta and an eggplant canneloni, rolled around ricotta cheese into a superior combination of flavors. Shrimp-and-artichoke salad was a good idea, but watery shrimp hurt the final effect.

Among entrees, grouper served atop apple mashed potatoes was an exciting dish, with the apple's tartness helping the potatoes. The grouper itself was wonderful, its delicate flavor coming forth in all its richness. Penne pasta with an Alfredo sauce was good, arriving with sun-dried tomatoes, fresh basil and pine nuts, but it lacked the snap to turn it into a great dish. Still, it provided memories. When Joe was a small boy, he and his father often would sit on the front stoop of their Brooklyn home and listen to the baseball games being broadcast by Red Barber. They lived close enough to Ebbets Field to hear the roar of the crowd when the Dodgers did something good, and as they sat, they munched on pine nuts, also known as pinon nuts or, to people who lived in Brooklyn, as Indian nuts.

Dessert includes Italian-American standards like creme brulee, tiramisu and apple crisp; the tiramisu fell far short of excellence. If it had tasted as good as Joseph's looks, it would have been a winner, and not in a photo finish.

Kemoll's

Italian Cuisine

#1 Metropolitan Square (Broadway between Olive and Pine)
421-0555
Dinner every day
Credit cards: All major
Wheelchair access: Comfortable

If restaurants are judged by the way they set their prices, and it's a large weight on our scales, Kemoll's has set itself a good-sized task. Another venerable, traditional St. Louis-Italian restaurant, it holds memories from its beginnings in the 1920s and its location in north St. Louis near the late Sportsman's Park. Still family-owned, it always has been a standard-setter for St. Louis diners, and when it moved downtown about a decade ago, an era ended. In today's terms, however, with dinner about $35 per person and non-pasta entrees in the mid-$20 range, it no longer is the value or the dining experience it once was.

Tucked in a ground-floor corner of a newish office tower, the restaurant has a very European feeling. To get there, however, means traversing miles of rose-colored marble across a lobby whose paintings honor the working man while the building itself pays tribute to capitalism. Kemoll's, with a long hall and doors and alcoves opening onto it, is reminiscent of some places in Northern Italy. The main dining room is warm and friendly without being imposing, its terra-cotta-colored walls dotted with plants, mirrors and sconces. Customers are exuberant rather than restrained. The staff is surprisingly young and female for a traditional establishment.

This is big food, old-fashioned in the size of its servings. Everyone walks out carrying doggie bags. First courses are marked by the fritto misto, to serve either two or four. An old Kemoll specialty, it's different from the usual mixed seafood fry. This is all vegetables, almost an Italian tempura. Pieces of eggplant, green pepper, zucchini and mushroom are dipped in a light batter and flash-fried. They arrive hot and greaseless, nestled in a white linen napkin around a bowl of horseradish-mayonnaise sauce. The batter is basically neutral, providing a gentle crunch around the vegetables, inoffensive but not exciting, and setting the tone for the entire meal.

Things perk up with the main courses. A mixed grill of lamb, beefsteak and an Italian sausage from Volpi's came with a particularly remarkable currant-mustard sauce. It's their usual accompaniment to grilled lamb, closer to the English Cumberland sauce than anything in the old Roman Empire, and it's outstanding. The meats, tasty and grilled as requested, were the high spot of the evening. A veal piccata was three slices of tender veal, not thin enough to be perfect. The sauce was classic, with lemon and capers in ideal proportions. Side dishes were farfalle with a vigorous marinara sauce or an oil and garlic sauce that had been served too generously; sauce pooled in the plate.

We sampled cannoli with a sticky filling, tasting faintly of orange and showing pistachio nuts, and a tartufo, the chocolate-covered ice cream ball. This was chocolate ice cream molded around a maraschino cherry. The size of a baseball, it had been cut into segments, a smart way to serve it. The chocolate coating, which traditionally hardens like the cover on an ice cream bar, was quite thin. Unexciting but easy to eat. Coffee was very strong and European roast, with specialty dessert coffees available. The wine list is long and well-selected, with some excellent values, and it is balanced by some good by-the-glass offerings.

Service was attentive and not overly formal, but Kemoll's downtown proves that in some respects, the good old days really were better.

Key West Cafe
Sunburned Cuisine

St. Louis Union Station, 1820 Market Street
241-2566
Lunch and Dinner, daily
Credit cards: All major
Wheelchair access: Comfortable

We're great fans of Metrolink. Rapid transit is just plain good sense, and people in cities that have it will tell anyone that proximity to a stop is an asset to real estate values. Another good reason for us is that it's the easiest way to get to the Key West Cafe.

Union Station seems to be on another upswing. One of its stalwarts is the Key West, which offers good food and a kitchen wisely open until 2 a.m. Tom Burnham has been running saloons in St. Louis, and dreaming about Key West, for many years, so the bar side is not just for appearance. But he s serious about food, too, putting out dishes that no one else in St. Louis has. The mix of good food and eclectic menu tends to attract the sort of diners who eat late, like actors and athletes, who come with anecdotes attached. (Such as the time when Cathy Rigby, in town for *Peter Pan*, was thrown around the table by a bunch of stagehands.)

Key West also boasts what may be the only photo in existence of Henry Aaron, Roger Maris and Dan Dierdorf—plus, of course, Burnham—taken by Mike Shannon. It's hard to find, though, because so many things hang on the wall.

But it's food that we want to talk about. Yes, there are chicken wings and hamburgers here. But try the unusual stuff, like conch chowder, pronounced "conk." The ground mollusk goes into homemade vegetable soup with extra potatoes and spices, producing a slow warmth that grows on you. There's a fresh oyster chowder and turtle soup, too.

They smoke their own fish here, and the smoked fish salad is wonderful. The fish of the day—maybe blue marlin, maybe red mullet—is cut into chunks and piled over shredded iceberg lettuce, and iceberg is just what's needed to provide a contrasting crunch. It's then dressed with a mustard sauce, and topped with—our only quibble—tasteless, black sliced California olives. But it's still delicious, just the thing for a day when St. Louis feels like Key West in terms of heat and humidity.

Lots of fresh fish hang out here—grouper, mahi mahi and red snapper—and cultures are combined in fajitas made with grouper. Conch fritters, either a first course or an entree, are a superb entry in the deep-fried dough category of food. These are good-sized chunks of sweet conch in a batter made heady with pepper and pimentos. Not fiery hot, but flavorful and slightly chewy, they intrigue and then addict.

One of the great sandwiches of St. Louis is Key West's version of the Cuban sandwich, a sort of sub. But this one features mortadella, ham, roast pork and salami, along with just a little cheese and some tomato. The length of French bread is then press-grilled until the bread flattens a little, the inside is warm, the cheese softens and things get nice and crispy. It's a winner, in any state. We salute the Cuban.

Barbara Burnham makes the pie—Key Lime, of course—and it is served in generous pieces with weak whipped cream. If it isn't a work day, we advise cold beer or one of those joyously goofy tropical drinks. Two ingredients make a cocktail, three make a goofy tropical drink. Under $20 a head, unless you spend several hours here eating and philosophizing over what Harry Truman would have thought of Key West today, and what Jimmy Buffet would have thought of Harry Truman.

King and I Restaurant
Thai Cuisine
3157 South Grand Boulevard
771-1777
Lunch and Dinner, Tuesday-Sunday
Credit cards: All major
Wheelchair access: Passable

Unlike the woman who drove W.C. Fields to drink, the pal who introduced Ann to Thai food has been thanked. Several times, in fact, because he bears the same responsibility for Indian food, a double blessing on his head. It took a long time to get used to the taste of cilantro, one of those pungent things that don't come easily for some of us. Cilantro is a trademark of Thai food, just like lemon grass, that wonderful-smelling stuff that scented long-past childhoods in its guise of citronella.

But would-be bold eaters, take heart. It can be done. Large numbers of St. Louisans have learned to eat Thai food at the King and I, from the days when it was a small storefront on South Grand through its move up the street into a big double storefront, with far more elegant surroundings. Still, this is a sweaters-and-backpack sort of place, not so much youth-oriented as it is casual and welcoming, though a "No Tank Tops," sign went up last summer.

Prices for first courses average about $3, entrees run $7-$10, but even though they're tasty, we don't do a lot of serious business with first courses here. The Bangkok wings are stuffed with meat, shrimp, and thin noodles, and come with spicy sweet and sour sauce. The fish cakes are deep-fried rather like meatballs, and are tangy but not killer hot on their own. Papaya salad, a favorite in the homeland, is made with green papaya, peanuts and tomato, and can be cranked to severe heat if desired. It's strikingly good.

Some of the entrees, though, turn out to be salad-like, or just a soup. The spicy soup tom yum, and another, tom kha, made with coconut, are available as appetizers or as main courses. We like both of them a lot, but have a soft spot for the tom yum because it's available with mussels. Yum seafood is like a ceviche, cold seafood in a zingy sauce of lime juice and chili with onions and cilantro. It's available as a mixture (including those so-called crab sticks, which have absolutely no relation to a crab) or as just shrimp or squid, which are particularly good because their solidity stands up to the softening qualities of lime juice. The result produces a splendid feel in the mouth.

The curries, unlike those from India, seem quite liquid, with flavorful coconut milk carrying the ingredients. We haven't found any we don't like, but the masman curry and the green curry with shrimp are particularly good. Lots of rice is at hand to help carry the lovely juice. Servings are generous, and the staff is observant about instructions as to how spicy-hot a dish should be made.

Noodles are as ubiquitous here as in the rest of Asia. Pad Thai, the basic dish that almost everyone starts with at Thai restaurants, is excellent at the King and I. It involves rice noodles topped with small strips of pork, shrimp, a little tofu, bits of scrambled egg and green onion in a mild, slightly sweet sauce. Nearby, or piled on top, is a small hill of fresh, cool, crunchy bean sprouts. In addition, a mound of crushed peanuts and a lemon quarter are on hand, along with perhaps a half-teaspoonful of chili powder. The bean sprouts go on top, with peanuts a level higher, and lemon is squeezed over the entire thing. Chili powder is at your discretion. It's a wonderful contrast of textures (crunchy, chewy, smooth), of temperatures (cool, warm) and of flavors (sweet, salty, sour). It's heaven.

We were in Thailand two years ago, and were surprised to find the food so similar to what we'd been eating at the King and I. If it's Americanized, it doesn't seem to be very much. The one thing from Thailand we'd like to have at the King and I is the bridal-white, silky-smooth coconut ice cream, maybe with a little un-Thai chocolate sauce on top.

King Louie's
Beyond Bar Food
3800 Chouteau Avenue
865-3662
Lunch and Dinner, Monday-Saturday
Credit cards: All major
Wheelchair access: Satisfactory

While Matt McGuire was a student at the Art Institute of Chicago, one of his many part-time jobs was as a bicycle messenger in the Loop. A great leap of faith is necessary here—but Joe believes that (1) Chicago may be the best American casual restaurant/bar town in the country these days, and (2) King Louie's has the most Chicago feel he's seen in any St. Louis restaurant besides Trattoria Marcella. Make the leap of faith, please, and don't ask him to explain, though it has something to do with a relaxed attitude, lots of bare walls (be they wood or brick), and an aura of enjoyment that bounces from owners to cooks to bartenders to customers and back again.

Light wood and a large patio are positive aspects. So are the newspapers, arranged on old-fashioned wooden racks, which make us think of the sort of dignified clubs that would blackball us immediately.

King Louie's sits on the site of the old Billie Goat Hill, at the corner where the elephants turn to lead the circus parade down the hill and onto the train. If this were another time, King Louie's would be the quintessential newspaperman's hangout. There are not nearly enough drinking newspapermen to support such a place these days, but it is good that some of them have drinking friends, and some come in to eat and assuage their guilt. Louie's is rather clean to be that type of hangout, but then again, it's also rather new. Give the customers a chance.

King Louie's has lots of microbrewery beer taps, and a couple to handle both apple and pear cider on draught, plus a superior selection of Irish whiskey, fine California wines and a menu that takes bar food in new directions.

Trying to mix the dual, and conflicting, roles of artist and publican is not easy, but so far, McGuire is making it work. To replace newspapermen, he has reached out to lawyers and advertising executives and medical students on what are sometimes described as "liver rounds." He lives in the city, which helps, and he obviously thinks about the road he is following. As a result, King Louie's is one of the few saloons with a vegetarian entree, and with salads that are more than just some torn-up lettuce. The grilled vegetable sandwich involves a portobello mushroom, tomatoes, onions and eggplant, all grilled and served on a hamburger roll. When all the juices start to mingle, the sandwich becomes sloppy, but the tummy remembers the Sinatra song about the tingles intermingling, and that's what happens.

Hummus is garlicky and smooth, and makes a wonderful addition to a chunk of pita, warm and crisp. Pastrami-style smoked salmon, in thick slices, is a delicate, yet extremely rich and flavorful dish, and chicken wings are rather standard. They're hot, but much hotter would require asbestos linings in the cheeks, and we all know how bad for you asbestos can be. Mussels and crayfish, in a spicy broth with lots of leeks, is superior and probably our favorite appetizer.

Appetizers run $5-$8, for good-sized servings, and King Louie's other prices are $5-$9 for salads, $7-$10 for pastas and pizzas, $5-$7 for sandwiches.

One of three regular soups on the menu (potato-leek and tortilla-corn are the others), the Guinness stew is a beef stew laden with tender, tasty chunks of meat, all wrapped in a soup stock based on Guinness Stout. It's a brilliant soup, especially on a chilly day.

Salads may sound like an oxymoron in a bar owned by a McGuire, but these are special, all in large portions with good amounts of meat, plus vegetables that are man-sized and man-chewy.

Some pizzas and pastas are available, and there's a roasted garlic and shrimp pizza that is exemplary, with the garlic soft and sweet, the shrimp chewy and sweet. All the pizzas are brilliant, and the sandwiches, once we get past the portobello, include the usual, highly satisfactory hamburger. More exciting than the hamburger are the pan-fried Louisiana catfish, the pork loin and the turkey, joined by bacon, smoked gouda cheese and slaw.

All the sandwiches are messy, but that goes with the territory, and the territory is as wide as the entire Northwest, given the style and imagination of the publican, his parents and his pals. In the interest of fairness, let us also point out that Matt McGuire's father is Joe's long-time buddy from the *Post-Dispatch*—a duo who understands a newspaperman's bar better than anybody.

Kirk's American Bistro & Bar
New American Food
512 N. Euclid Avenue
361-1456
Lunch Monday-Friday, Dinner Monday-Saturday
Credit cards: All major
Wheelchair access: Satisfactory

The new popularity of martinis has come a long way from the days when the classic of gin and vermouth turned one into a clear-eyed seeker of wisdom and truth. At most bars and restaurants, even hoping-to-be-hip places like Kirk's, they are just another fad, often without either of the prime ingredients, and experienced St. Louisans know that River City is where fads come to die. So even if they still are around, it is best to ignore the lengthy list of too-cute martinis, and head for the sophisticated-looking dining room. After all, not many restaurants in St. Louis serve fried chicken and martinis, though the bird is a Tuesday-only special.

Despite the rather sophisticated interior, Kirk's displays plastic tablecloths, which do not belong in a place where entrees are $17 to $25—and 8:30 p.m., even on a quiet night, is too early to send a busboy out to clean the tables with a spray bottle.

A portobello mushroom grilled in a Marsala sauce topped the appetizer list. The mushroom was delicious, rich and charcoal-ey and tender, but the sauce was not as sweet as many local Marsala sauces. Another appetizer was one of the night's pasta specials, available as a first course or as an entree. This was a lobster ravioli in a lemon cream sauce, rich and comforting. The sauce was fine, smooth and slightly tart, and the pasta was tasty, if a little doughy.

A Caesar salad drew a divided response. One of us thought it was underdressed; the other, who believes that salads, like women, can almost never be underdressed, faulted it for the romaine lettuce, which not only was cut instead of torn, but also was cut into too-large pieces that needed recutting. But the Parmesan was shredded generously, the croutons fresh and not from a package. We agreed it could have had more anchovy, and that the dressing itself was tasty.

Tuna, crusted in black pepper and seasoned with sesame oil, came beautifully cooked and very peppery. Catfish, another special, was described as grilled with a lemon tequila sauce, but showed little evidence of a sauce. The fish itself was just not quite … catfishy enough, as though part of the flavor had gone elsewhere. Side dishes were rice—white for catfish, brown for the tuna—and the ubiquitous zucchini stir-fry, here made less tedious by the addition of some grilled red pepper and a handful of mushrooms.

Service, however, was the big sticking point. An order for pork chops produced the gasp of, "Oh, gosh, I forgot to tell you those aren't available, and neither is the pork loin." "How about the flank steak?" "Flank steak? That's not on the menu." But it was. "We meant to take it off."

At least he was pleasant and apologetic.

Nevertheless, bread didn't arrive until the salad, well after the appetizers had left. However, the warm rolls exemplified ordinary, and really were not worth the wait. Dessert wasn't suggested, and wasn't ordered, either. The check arrived unrequested at about 8:30; too early, even on a Monday, to be scooting people out.

The wine list showed about a dozen by the glass, and overall, there were many good, representative, tasty, medium-priced California wines.

Even ignoring dessert, dinner was just under $25 a head.

Kreis' Restaurant

Traditional American Steak and Trimmings

535 South Lindbergh Boulevard, Frontenac
993-0735
Dinner every day
Credit cards: All major
Wheelchair access: Passable

A friend recalls coming to Kreis' as a grade-schooler and very quietly ordering a steak he thought his father would veto because it cost $3.95. (Dad, by the way, played along with the game every time.) That was about 1958. Our guess is the menu hasn't changed much since then.

No more frog legs, Joe sadly points out, but neither zucchini nor thirteen seafood entrees were around in 1958. But for every "lite raspberry vinegarette," there's still a Mayfair and a Thousand-Island dressing. Dover sole and veal Oscar populate the menu, but the main thing here is meat, and while lamb, pork, veal, and chicken are plentiful, roasted or broiled beef remains king, in quantities and varieties to gladden even the heartiest meat-and-potatoes person.

For whatever reason, prime rib is out of favor, which is good for people who go to sports banquets (though Joe thinks people who go to sports banquets deserve whatever they get). But it's bad for those who really like the flavor of the cut, one which Kreis' serves in basic, classic, beautiful style. The smaller of the two available cuts is about 18 ounces, at least an inch-and-a-half-thick, and as big as one of Mark McGwire's hands. The larger size would need McGwire to carry it. Delivered as pink as ordered, it was remarkably tender and full of flavor, the way a prime rib was designed to be, with a sharp horseradish sauce alongside. A filet mignon gives the same sort of satisfaction, and is equally tender, but the flavor is slightly different and, perhaps, slightly less. Lamb chops are rubbed with oregano and probably a little garlic, and arrived nicely seasoned, properly cooked and very good.

The menu also has several German dishes, and a traditional schnitzel a la Holstein was a pleasant change. There were three boneless cutlets of veal, larger than a scallopine and fork tender, quite flavorful and, most important, not overcooked. They had been lightly breaded and topped with the requisite fried egg and an anchovy fillet. Breaded veal cutlets have overtones of chicken fried steak, but these were much tastier, and the smooth egg and salty little fish added a lovely contrast. When German dishes are prepared properly, we wonder why there aren't more German restaurants in town. When they're prepared poorly, we know.

With all this meat, it seems that a salad—just something light—would be the only logical first course. Unfortunately, we are troubled with the slow seepage of resolutions, and we were faced with a bowl of clam chowder. This is presumably New England style, because it was creamy, although tan rather than white. It carries a smokiness, so there's probably some bacon, and we found a few bits of tomato, as well. It was hot enough, with a generous amount of clams, and was not loaded with vegetables used to stretch it.

Fried eggplant, a longtime favorite of Joe's, comes as long, fat wedges, lightly breaded, but not very flavorful, and available with a choice of several sauces. A tomato sauce was sweet and rich, with more flavor than vegetable. And speaking of tomatoes, they and some fresh onion turned out to be a solid bet. A simple vinegar and oil topping did the trick, though a couple of anchovies would have been an improvement.

Side dishes are potatoes or rice. Double-baked potatoes, whipped and returned to a half-shell, seemed pretty flat. The German fries are essentially fried potatoes, sliced and fried with a generous amount of onion, almost good enough to eat for breakfast. The potato pancakes were crisp, but not cooked to death, and came with some pink applesauce, another homey touch.

It's a stretch to think about dessert after such immense pieces of protein, but we did check the apple strudel. Not cloyingly sweet, but lacking strong apple flavor, any crispness of crust succumbed to a blanket of what seemed to be a simple vanilla sauce. Next time we'll investigate the three-layer fudge cake.

The wine list is adequate, and prices seem reasonable. Appetizer, entree and dessert at Kreis', to be saved for a special occasion or when hunger is strong, is about $30 per person, with the exceptions of the 20-ounce filet mignon ($30.95), the two-pound New York strip ($34), and the extra large cut of prime rib ($38). Kreis' may be the area's ultimate beef house, and if not, it's certainly among 'em.

Lemmons Restaurant
Basic American Fare
5800 Gravois
352-2626
Lunch Tuesday-Friday and Sunday, Dinner Tuesday-Sunday
Credit cards: MC, V
Wheelchair access: Difficult

With a name like this, how could we not visit? We point out that the spelling is different, and that there is absolutely no relation between a former owner (for whom the place was named) and the co-author of this book. Nevertheless, with a reputation for lemon pie, it seemed foolish to ignore a south side tradition.

This is a classic of its type—with wood paneling, a corps of waitresses roving the two dining rooms with pitchers of iced tea, and patrons whose parents ate there in the years right after World War II. Not that this place is just for seniors; a young engaged couple was sharing spaghetti and meatballs, and a family with three kids filled a big back table. It's nostalgia on the hoof, and the menu reflects it.

We passed the soup of the day in favor of pan-fried chicken livers, which were among the best we've found, lightly floured and tossed in the pan, cooked just long enough to remove the pink but leave them tender and us smiling. A small order, maybe six full-sized livers, came with an unneccessary bowl of gravy. A good red sauce with a little pop might have been an interesting change from the gravy.

The dinner comes with salad and vegetable, and the salad, a combination salad, was right out of 1950s Missouri—a little shredded carrot and a radish slice or two mixed in with diced iceberg lettuce. The dressings include blue cheese and Thousand Island, dense and poured with a heavy hand. In this place, somehow, it seems right and proper.

Half a fried chicken came as four pieces lightly battered and fried, still tender and moist, and an absolutely glorious golden color. We also had jack salmon, another St. Louis tradition, which is really skinned whiting, served with tail intact. It's a tasty fish, easy to bone and handle with a knife and fork. The breading was a dense cornmeal, quite proper, albeit a little tough, and the fish was a tad overcooked. None of these fried things—livers, chicken or fish—seemed to have been seasoned much. Part of this may be the contemporary aversion to dietary sodium; part may be the old-time south St. Louis aversion to spicy food. But salt and pepper were quite helpful.

Side dishes are secondary at best. An old-fashioned place like this should peel and mash its own potatoes instead of using instant ones. And the gravy bore a taste that was reminiscent of bouillon cubes. The pasta was cavatelli that hadn't been drained well, and the sauce featured very mild tomatoes.

Dessert? A piece of the lemon pie had meringue up to there, a filling that was lemon-ier than had seemed at first bite, and a crust that was extremely flaky. The peach cobbler, also made in-house and served warm, was full of nutmeg. The crust was on the soggy side, but that's part of the fun of cobbler.

Serious nostalgia for about $14 a person. Serious dinner with better potatoes.

Llywelyn's Pub
Bar Food
4747 McPherson Avenue
361-3003
Lunch and Dinner, every day
Credit cards: All major
Wheelchair access: Satisfactory

Information operators hate this restaurant and bar. Directory assistance operators hate it, too. Few can pronounce it, even fewer can spell it. First-time customers have been known to use the phone, tell friends to meet them at "Lou and Ellen's," and then ask when the Country and Western music would begin.

In the days before the most recent coat of polish was applied to the Central West End, this spot on McPherson Avenue was known as the Castlewood Lounge, providing 10 a.m. eye-openers for a rather specialized clientele. After Herb and Adalaide Balaban bought it, it was nicknamed Camp Castlewood. Then Jack Brangle and Jon Dressel bought it in the 1970s, and named it Llywelyn's. (Dressel is of Welsh descent; Brangle is about as Welsh as Herb Balaban.) When Brangle and Dressel split, Dressel moved around the corner to open Dressel's (where he remains to this day), and Brangle kept the name Llywelyn's.

Brangle's entrepreneurial skills and the artistic and culinary talents of his wife, Patricia, lifted Llywelyn's to some high points, but they then let it suffer through a major period of benign neglect before they sold it in the winter of 1997-98. Brangle was a Hollywood casting office idea of a barman—a man who could mix a drink and tell a story at the same time. He did both well, provided the former was simple and the latter complex.

He liked to tell of the wintry morning he was on hand, saving a few customers' lives, when a derelict entered and took a seat at the end of the bar. Jack went over and heard the expected sob story about hunger and cold and joblessness and the hopes for something to eat. Jack nodded, prepared to donate, and headed for the other end. Jack filled a bowl with chili and started back, stopping (he swears) for not more than a minute to speak to a new arrival or two. When he looked up, the derelict was gone. Vanished. Split. Jack returned to the derelict's end, and, sure enough, no derelict. He looked over the bar, a feat his six feet, six inches permitted. No derelict on the floor. He turned to a customer, and the customer said, "I thought it was kind of weird. There you were dishing the chili, and he looked at his watch, and he mumbled, 'If this is the kind of service I'm going to have to put up with, it just isn't worth it.' And he walked out."

The new Llywelyn's has been scrubbed and painted. The big booths of the back room are gone, adding light and space, and the banquette row in the front room also is gone, with some high tables in place. Some of the food is excellent, but strangely, some notes we made when he stopped in a month or so after it opened were still valid six months later. Minor problems, but irritating and guaranteed to take the edge off the experience. Burgers were excellent, fat and flavorful, but they could have been charred a little more. The buns, however, were cold, the fried onions were chilly and the chips were cool, all situations that should not exist.

Joe remembers the first time he had written about Llywelyn's, sometime in 1976. Chilly hamburger buns, a fact that was in his *Post-Dispatch* column. Brangle and Joe were longtime friends, and Joe ate there regularly, but cold buns are cold buns. A few weeks later, he stopped in for lunch, sat down across from the bar and quickly ducked, because bartender-cook Mark Offner was firing frozen buns at him.

However, the bun around the hamburger was warm, and buns remained warm as long as Brangle owned the bar.

The new menu has many of its predecessor's prime dishes—like the Welsh potato chips ($1.75 and $2.50), which began here and may have become the most copied dish in town; the rarebit ($4.25) and the ploughman's lunch ($6.95); along with the London broil, either plain ($8.50) or topped with rarebit sauce, making it a Welsh broil ($8.95). Newcomers include roast lamb ($8.95), grilled Irish salmon ($11.50), a Welsh onion and potato pie and a Celtic steak and vegetable pie (each $8.25; citizenship courtesy of the menu-writer).

Fish and chips are first-rate, the fish benefiting from a light, tasty batter but slightly overcooked. There's also a potential language problem. English chips are our French fries, and the English ask for crisps when they want our chips. Other appetizers are superior: Partan Bree, a Scottish soup with crabmeat, was rich with tarragon and very creamy; and a Fenian stew, with lamb and vegetables, was delicious. Welsh beef soup also is hearty and filled with meat, and the white bean-and-chicken chili is spicy and a pleasant change from tomato-based chilis.

The only disappointment was in the summer pudding, and although the dish is tasty, it's short of English splendor. More disappointing, while the menu says it's served with clotted cream, we got a cheap imitation of whipped cream, squirted from a can. Even real whipped cream is a long way from clotted cream. Llywelyn's menu runs from lunch through dinner, and the red-and-green dragon remains a beacon.

Lombardo's
Italian and American Cuisine

10488 Natural Bridge Road, Edmundson
429-5151
Lunch Monday-Friday, Dinner Monday-Saturday
Credit cards: All major
Wheelchair access: Satisfactory

The last place in town—any town—we'd look for comfort food is around the airport. But we found it at Lombardo's, which offers a nice view of Metrolink and some impressive soundproofing. Lombardo's started serving traditional Italian food in 1934 at Jennings Station Road and Goodfellow Boulevard in north St. Louis, and not much has changed since its move four years ago to the Drury Inn south of I-70. Tabs vary widely, but it might be about $25 a person.

It's a family business. The sons have the Lombardo's Trattoria downtown at the Drury Inn, with higher prices and a more upscale menu, but there's nearly always someone from the family here to greet you and, if necessary, bus tables.

Appetizers cover a spectrum from calzone and oysters Rockefeller to turtle soup. We knocked back some clams and mussels, a special appetizer, cooked in a tomato sauce punched up with a little red pepper. The fresh and tender shellfish rested in a sauce that was slightly too salty. Still, it rested nicely on the old-fashioned Italian bread that we used to sop up the last drops.

Generous chunks of meat marked the ham and bean soup; no Tuscan zuppa fagiole but good old-fashioned American style, simple and full of the flavor of the ham. The salad situation got a little sticky. We'd asked if the house vinegar-and-oil had sugar in it, explaining that we didn't care for that. The server said she wasn't sure, but she thought maybe it did. Fine, we said, and chose the blue cheese dressing instead. The salad arrived with tidy chunks of fresh iceberg lettuce, a bit of tomato—and shredded cheese peeking out at us from under the generous serving of blue cheese dressing. Cheese on cheese? Oh, well, we said, and took a bite. The blue cheese dressing? It was sweet, an absolute first for both of us.

This is the sort of place that offers liver and onions and pork chops on the meat side of the menu, keeping company with the beef. Sauteed mushrooms, crunchy green pepper and onions ringed the pepper steak, a carefully cooked piece of good beef, just rare enough, and lolling in a nice bordelaise sauce. On the pasta side, there's not a smidgen of goat cheese or baby vegetables. The closest you can get is bowties with broccoli and ricotta. An old-fashioned fettuccine Alfredo arrived with the noodles cooked al dente, and the cheesy sauce provided a socially acceptable way to eat macaroni and cheese and not relinquish one's credentials as a grownup. It was extremely satisfying, and a huge serving.

Stuffed, we skipped dessert, mostly the traditional Italian restaurant items like cheesecake.

LoRusso's Cucina
Italian Cuisine
3122 Watson Road
647-6222
Lunch Tuesday-Friday, Dinner Tuesday-Saturday
Credit cards: All major
Wheelchair access: Comfortable

LoRusso's is another of the Italian restaurants not far from the Hill, which began in a storefront slightly larger than a walk-in closet and has prospered, growing in floor space and menu since its inception. Unlike many of the others, Rich LoRusso is American-born, so is most familiar with the interpretation of Italian food with American ingredients; for him, a significant difference. On his menu, he tries very hard to get the spirit of authenticity, not just what he thinks Americans will eat, and he mostly succeeds. Sure, there's toasted ravioli and spiedini and a filet mudega, which sell quite well. But there's sauteed escarole with linguini, too, and imported anchovies and even prosecco, the light sparkling wine you seldom find in St. Louis.

We're not sure quite how long it takes a place to become an institution, but we think LoRusso's may have reached that status during its twelve years of existence. There are longtime employees and longtime customers. At the next table, we heard a man with a strong Canadian accent say, "I come here every year when I come to visit my daughter." And like any good institution, LoRusso's participates in the community. Sales from the escarole, for example, benefit the St. Louis Food Bank.

It's a comfortable, slightly dark dining room; toward the back, there's a view of the cooking line as the steam flies up and the cooks fly around. The art on the walls is—pleasantly so—mostly Italian food posters and a little Italian porcelain.

Now about those anchovies. We like anchovies. We like fish that tastes like fish, and that defines anchovies. Milder fish, especially those from fresh water, are nice, but we bliss out on mackerel and bluefish, the delicious oily fish from Atlantic waters that you rarely see here. Anchovies are as much a staple in our house as a chunk of fresh real Parmesan cheese and coffee beans and dark chocolate. So when we saw them on the menu (listed under appetizers as alici), we asked LoRusso about them. "They're marinated and packed in glass," he said. "I had them in Rome and I love them," he added. So, it turns out, do we.

They arrive, five boned anchovies, startlingly pale, laid out in a star on a plate. Take one and place it on the bread from the bread basket and eat it like an open-faced sandwich. Rich and tangy, the only thing we could faintly compare them to is a fine grade of marinated herring. The bread, by the way, is particularly good here, compared to many of its peers. But why do all St. Louis Italian restaurants insist that their bread wear sesame seeds? It's not a universal practice in Italy. This bread is chewier than most, nearly a sourdough, but sure enough, wearing sesame seeds.

The dinner salad is fairly ordinary lettuce but of good quality, simply dressed in vinegar and oil. A little red onion and slivers of roasted pepper crown it, and there is the omnipresent cheese. But the balance of cheese with greens and dressing is superior, the best example of this St. Louis salad we've found. The tomato and rice soup was more of a vegetable and rice, full of the taste of the aromatic onion, celery and carrot, but nothing wildly exciting.

A slice of wahoo was broiled and put on some ratatouille, and topped with a cup of broiled asiago cheese. Yes, broiled until crisp, and shaped into a cup. Inside was a handful of julienned carrots and onions that had been run through a light batter, almost tempura-style, and quickly fried. Showy, and quite tasty, although the fish was overcooked. Still, the ratatouille was extremely good, full of the flavors of the sun with tomato and garlic and onion and eggplant.

Risotto is the subject of much discussion in Italian cooking. Just how al dente should the rice be? How wet should it be? Stiff or soupy? LoRusso falls into the wet side of the category, and far from the al dente school. But a duck risotto with mushrooms, garnished with carrots and broccoli and some fresh tomato, was incredibly satisfying, with a rich broth thickened by the rice and sparked by more garlic than traditional, but feeling right at home with the duck. Too soft, perhaps, but it was one of the best risottos we've had.

Several innovative vegetarian pastas and a risotto here, and most of the standard beef and veal dishes, plus a wine list that has some unexpected offerings, all at prices that can often be called modest, and at most, moderate. Expect to have a tab that comes to $20 to $25 a person.

Dessert features cheesecake and cannoli, a couple of chocolate items, and the Milanese fruit-and-sorbet (more accurately sorbet-in-fruit) desserts that are new in town—and so good. Delicious sorbet is stuffed in a real fruit, and all frozen together. Every flavor of this specialty (lemon, tangerine, pineapple, coconut and peach) we've had is shockingly good, and the peach at LoRusso's captured the elusive taste of the fresh fruit to perfection. In terms of "waste not, want not," just let the scooped-out peach holding the sorbet thaw a while (or maybe a kind waitress will pop it in the microwave a few seconds). It's a nice bit to nibble on while lingering over dinner—a very Italian habit. Cannoli was fresh, but the pastry was hard and the filling the grainy sort that reminds you of cake frosting. Lots of pistachios and chocolate chips, though. A Bellini, the Venetian cocktail made of pureed peaches and prosecco, might be a better idea.

Lou Boccardi's
Pizza and More
5424 Magnolia Avenue
647-1151
Lunch Tuesday-Saturday, Dinner Tuesday-Sunday
Credit cards: MC, V
Wheelchair access: Difficult

One of the quietest of the Hill restaurants, Lou Boccardi's is unselfconsciously nostalgic. The decor is so earnest and sincere that it would be embarrassing to even suggest that it's kitsch. The menu, too, is a throwback to a time when the customer pretty much knew what was going to be offered in an Italian restaurant. It would have been thrilling to eaters in the early '60s with offerings like fried artichokes, linguini with clam sauce and veal francese. In the '90s, figure $15 for a meal unless it involves veal or a steak, then go to $20, and enjoy.

We succumbed to toasted ravioli here. We like it meaty, a little chewy and non-greasy, and that's just how it came. The red sauce really wasn't necessary. The house salad is a little tired, with shreds of provel cheese. The creamy Italian dressing was pretty good, but the house dressing is heavy on the celery with some anchovies. We overheard the waitress describe the latter to a group of conventioneers, saying, "People either love it or hate it. I'll bring it on the side. (They loved it.) The eternal tomatoes and onions wear wine vinegar and olive oil with a pinch of sugar and a mouth-nudge of black pepper, with white chopped onion sprinkled across the top. This is the first time we've ever seen the dish with cheese on it.

Time was when this was where you came for pizza; the other things, as we recall, were nothing more than a polite gesture. The pizza still charms, a hand-stretched rectangle of a crust that is about as thick as a really expensive wedding invitation, but considerably more tender. The tomato sauce is simple, the cheese is provel, provoking mutters from the East Coast purist who disdains such heresy, and the other toppings are spaced judiciously, rather than piled, on. The result is pizza so light that it can be knocked back as quickly as an iced tea in August, and the taste evokes a St. Louis that existed before there were pizza chains.

Pasta here is pretty standard. They've gotten as far as cavatelli with broccoli or cauliflower, but mostly it's the basics—spaghetti, ravioli, lasagna, rigatoni. This is where visitors can try wedding-reception mostaccioli, by the way. A little fish, chicken cacciatore, a half-dozen veal dishes—like we said before, classic.

Lots of eggplant flavor characterized the rigatoni with eggplant and mushrooms. The basic red sauce of the house is not so great on its own, and calls for salt or the shakers of cracked red pepper or cheese. Meatballs are extremely good, beefy without much filler and also without the heaviness that an all-meat product can give. Pasta, both the rigatoni and some spaghetti under the meatballs, was al dente, a condition that didn't exist in most St. Louis restaurants in the '60s and '70s. Progress is good.

A tartufo of chocolate and pistachio ice creams, coated in a thin layer of bittersweet chocolate, had been allowed to soften enough that it was easy to eat and didn't scoot around on the plate.

"All Food Cooked To Order" says the menu, and the pace can be as slow as in the Old Country. Service, in our experience, has been unflappable but often stretched thin. Still, it's a fun place to go when you're in the mood for a leisurely meal with a lot of time to reminisce.

Lynch Street Bistro
Modern American Cuisine
1031 Lynch Street
772-5777
Lunch and Dinner, Monday-Saturday
Credit cards: All major
Wheelchair access: Satisfactory (enter in rear)

On the night we visited the Lynch Street Bistro, it was the calm after the storm. A round of severe wind and hail had passed outside, and much of the loud, flamboyant aura that once characterized the restaurant's inside was no longer there. When it first opened, with Michael Holmes at the stove, Lynch Street shook the neighborhood with its crowds and the volume of business, and the sound level in its rooms—stark as Milan—wasn't far behind on the Richter scale.

Today, or rather on that night, it seemed almost grown-up, quieter and without any sense of turmoil. Whether the calm comes from the arrival of newer restaurants, or just a few months of maturity, is difficult to figure, but the dining room's stark beauty stands out better in the midst of calm.

Located across the street from Anheuser-Busch, the Bistro gets a good lunch crowd from the brewery offices, especially now that Frazer's is no longer is open for lunch. Both the prices, about $30 per person for dinner, and the atmosphere, are more rarified here. Suits, three of which occupied a table across the dining room, are probably more comfortable here than in a storefront that serves pineapple soda.

A very good, if somewhat pricey, wine list is on the back of the menu. Requests for wine by the glass bring a verbal recitation that probably varies from day to day. Service is, as it always has been, casual but effective. The menu, with many promises of good things, aims somewhat toward the spicy, with things like Thai-fried shrimp and several dishes with major Cajun and Southwest influences. Bread was a welcome surprise, arriving as a medium-sized loaf of herbed white not long out of the oven, served with a mixture of asiago cheese and herbed olive oil. The oil kept the herbs at a nice balance, and the mixture was one of the best of its type.

Four shrimp came in the appetizer, in a tasty tempura batter and very shrimpy (some would say heavy on iodine). However, it's a strong taste we like, and the wild rice stir fry that came alongside was sparkling with flavor. It was, we were warned, pretty hot, and though it fit that description, we found it excellent. The "paint" on the plate was what they called "rooster sauce," the chili garlic sauce found on almost every table in Southeast Asia. For those accustomed to hot food, the intensity was quite tolerable. The seasoning seemed to be missing something, a layer of flavor that wasn't there. It was good, but at Lynch Street prices, it should be better. Barbecued duck pizza was on a supermarket-style crust, slightly sweet, nothing remarkable, though the duck had a good flavor.

A list of entrees showcases things like duck breast with dried cherry and port sauce, lobster and portobello risotto, and beef tenderloin. The roast chicken breast arrived as two boneless skinless breasts, with the first joint of the wings attached and grilled quickly enough to retain some flavor. The sauce, roasted shallots and mushrooms, didn't contribute much. Chili potatoes au gratin were splendid, showing a series of interesting tastes, cheesy and interesting and non-cliched. Vegetables on the side were juliennes of orange and green with some rather bland asparagus. A Cajun grill showed another lightly-seasoned, boneless, skinless chicken breast, a couple of shrimp and some andouille sausage, tasty but a little dry. The meat was arranged over a Cajun cream sauce—thick and tasting of bottled seasoning—around some unsauced linguini.

Desserts included a chocolate cake that didn't have a deep chocolate flavor but offered lots of whipped cream instead; a chocolate pecan pie that was full of good, crisp pecans and a delicious crust; some of the fine sorbets from Quezel; and a creme brulee that put everything else served before in the shade. Rich and eggy, and carefully browned to give that faint, fabulous, never-forgotten taste of toasted marshmallows at a campout. It was a clear winner. The Lynch Street Grill, however, remains slightly fuzzy, with hopes raised by moments of delight, then subdued by dishes that don't work as they should.

Mai Lee Restaurant
Vietnamese Cuisine
8440 Delmar Boulevard, University City
993-3754
Lunch and Dinner, Tuesday-Sunday
Credit cards: All major
Wheelchair access: Satisfactory

Walking into Mai Lee just makes a customer grin, even before dining. Whoever heard of a cozy Asian restaurant? Mai Lee is, and that's in addition to being the area's first successful Vietnamese restaurant, now more than a decade old. The wallpaper is a stylized crewel flower pattern, happy pictures adorn the walls and, best of all, embroidered tablecloths drape every table. The cloths, white with red accents, say "Mai Lee" right in the middle, a step not even Tony's has taken. Messy eaters like us don't have to worry, however, because glass tops cover them, not a good solution. In addition to big front windows, there is a large amount of interior light, making the interior somewhere between airy-looking and bright enough to perform surgery.

The crowds of mostly young people, both Asian and Western, probably don't worry much about the tablecloths or the lighting. They're too busy chowing down on sizzling-hot platters of food. There's a Chinese section to the menu, but the most interesting food comes from the Vietnamese selections. It's good for the budget, too, with soups and rice dishes coming in under $5, and Vietnamese main courses averaging about $8.

There is some Asian overlap. In the appetizers, the first listing is kim chi, the spicy fermented cabbage that began in Korea and seems to have spread throughout the continent. There also are sesame noodles, Mai Lee's version of the Szechuan-style Chinese restaurant standard. The noodles are fat round babes, their slight irregularities lending an air of home-made-ness to them. The sauce is very thin, puddling on the platter, but it's flavorful, and not over spicy.

Five different condiments share space on the table—traditional fish sauce, without fish but tangy and salty; red chile sauce that can fly and burn; a thick brown sauce that is soy-based, but spicier; standard soy; and the thin sweet and sour sauce that is often used with appetizer rolls. Ours had shredded pork and vegetables, along with a little crunchy rice, a not unusual ingredient here, and several different textures including those from fresh cilantro leaves and stems. Both appetizers were cold, the noodles in particular suited to a warm evening. Vietnamese food in general seems better in such weather than other south Asian cuisines like Thai and Indian. Perhaps it's the delicate flavors and heavy use of fresh, uncooked vegetables.

There certainly seemed to be some Thai influence in tom xao lan, described as "shrimp fried in coconut milk, lemon grass, and curry sauce." The shrimp were sauteed, not deep-fried, and came with onion, both green and white, wood ear mushrooms and glass noodles (the tiny clear ones) under a garnish of chopped peanuts. Curry was yellow and hot (we asked for medium hot) but far from mouth-burning, and singing a clear song of the lemon grass. The noodles had soaked up a great deal of the seasoning, making them almost as tasty as the sweet and extremely tasty shrimp.

A vegetarian dish, dau hu xao xa ot, explained as "golden tofu stir-fried in hot chili, garlic, lemon grass," came out shining. The tofu, or bean curd, absolutely deserved the word silky. The exterior was chewy from the cooking, the interior as fragile and smooth as a perfectly cooked custard. It seemed even less peppery than the curry, although it was marked as being hot and spicy, and wore a rather elusive sweetness whose source was hard to pinpoint. The Man Who Mutters About Broccoli even managed a few flowerets. The serving seemed particularly generous, too.

There are lots of pork, beef and chicken dishes here, like stir-fried ribs, clay pot beef and smoked chicken salad, more traditionally Vietnamese, as well as a large selection of noodle dishes and twenty-three different soups.

Vietnamese coffee comes in what we suspect is the traditional way. Two glasses, one full of ice cubes and bearing an iced tea spoon, the other with an inch or two of sweetened condensed milk in the bottom and a small drip container of coffee perched on the top, arrive at the table. The coffee drips into the milk. When it's done, the container goes onto an accompanying saucer. The milk and coffee are stirred together to make a liquid that s the color of milk chocolate. Ice cubes are then added, and the whole thing is sipped. It's the ultimate iced coffee—very strong, very sweet, very creamy, meant to be sipped slowly, and evoking memories of shady terraces and tropical heat.

Malmaison
Near-classic French

St. Albans Road (off Hwy. T from Missouri 100), St. Albans
458-0131
Dinner Wednesday-Sunday
Credit cards: AE, MC, V
Wheelchair access: Satisfactory

These days it seems to be a big deal to come up with an original way to propose marriage. We propose an old-fashioned proposal. It's not hard to imagine taking one's nicely dressed beloved on a short drive in the country, stopping at a beautiful restaurant, having a romantic dinner by the fireplace and declaring great intentions.

However, a word of caution: It's best to conduct such business after dinner. The food at Malmaison is too good to be swept away, even in thoughts of white orchids and string quartets.

This is the real thing, an authentic French auberge, except in a switch of the traditional roles (Vive la libération!), Papa, the suave Gilbert Andujar, works the front of the house while Maman, Mme. Simone, and son Norbert, take care of the kitchen. (Mme. Simone also is the green thumb responsible for the flower-bedecked grounds surrounding the lovely restaurant.)

There are two dining rooms; one cozy with a low ceiling and a glass wall overlooking the terrace, the other with log and half-timbered walls that are two stories tall. With fireplaces in both, the smaller room has the aroma of wood fires, as if someone has lived here for generations. The menu is not long, but there is always a generous number of off-the-menu specials. The wine list is considerably longer, expensive and of superior quality, including the French Bandol rose from Domaine Tempier imported by the savvy Kermit Lynch, a top-flight importer.

Not surprisingly, there are pates as appetizers, one of goose liver and another of wild game, served with Cumberland sauce, a traditional English accompaniment to game and other red meats. It's made from red currants, punched up with a little orange to make a fine sweet-sharp contrast to the richer meats. We chose the goose liver, which came topped with capers, lots of black peppercorns and a clear, dense aspic full of flavor. No one would think about capers with Cumberland (and this is about as close to modern fusion cuisine as this kitchen gets) but it worked well, the pate smooth and rich and unctuous on the tongue.

There's always onion soup around, and one or two others. Someone in the kitchen here has been seriously schooled in Creole cooking, and a gumbo born in the richness of a good roux and full of seafood and smokiness was a glorious treat. Interestingly, unlike any gumbo we've eaten before, it carried all that without the heaviness traditionally associated with the dish. A fine first course—kept light, we suspect, for just that purpose, and succeeding perfectly.

The house salad dressings are a raspberry vinaigrette, or a creamy one. Mixed greens—the French were the originators of mesclun, the now-fashionable combination of unusual lettuces—were drizzled with a little of the dressing and sprinkled with some toasted chopped walnuts, a nice touch. It was, by the way, one of the rare times a St. Louis restaurant has offered a choice of salad before entree, in the overwhelmingly popular California style, or afterward, the way it still is done in Europe.

This is a game house, appropriately enough, although the specials often emphasize fish, and the written menu has classics like filet mignon with a bearnaise and a soubise, or onion, sauce. One of the evening's specials was partridge, which came boned except for the drumsticks. About the size of a Cornish hen but more flavorful, the meat was light in color and delicate and very tender in texture. It was stuffed with a mixture of aromatic vegetables, herbs and some pear. We can only hope they mean to keep the partridge and pear available through the Christmas holidays. The stuffing was quite fine, and a good match for the meat, which had no gaminess at all. It came with a little of that fat, pearly Israeli couscous that is growing in popularity.

Duck with apricot sauce, from the regular menu, arrived with skin almost as crisp as a deep-fried pork rind in spots, always a ducky virtue. This was not your pink-rare bird, but the old-fashioned sort, cooked all the way through but not greasy. The sauce was appropriately rich, but not sweet and gooey so that it provided a delightful contrast to the duck.

Rice was alongside, but the star of the accompaniments was a portion of asparagus with hollandaise. While the asparagus were good, the hollandaise was spectacular. It was light but not runny, and particularly lemony. In addition, it carried a slight—a very slight—pop, achieved by a little white or cayenne pepper. The overall style of sauce again carried us back to New Orleans, where hollandaise has more spice and lemon than in the Mother Country.

Dessert was a fine chocolate mousse, dark chocolate rather than milk, fluffy but still fairly firm, and rich on the tongue. Creme brulee sported a few excellent berries and a generous amount of strawberry puree and creme anglaise for mixing and matching. The custard itself was rich with egg, and there was a fine ratio of custard to crust, although the latter could have been a little browner.

Malmaison was the name given by Napoleon Bonaparte's first wife, Josephine, to her country home. It's in an elegant location in the St. Louis suburbs, about forty-five minutes from Clayton. And since elegance is expensive, so is dinner at Malmaison. Figure on $35 for an appetizer, dinner and dessert, more if the wine list seduces or if Champagne is necessary to accompany the ring.

The Mansion at LakePointe
Modern American Cuisine

1680 Mansion Way (I-64 east, exit at Illinois 158, go north toward O Fallon.
Turn left at the first traffic light. Turn right, 1/2 mile, onto Lake Pointe Centre Drive,
and right again onto Mansion Way), O Fallon, Ill.
(618) 628-0800.
Lunch and Dinner, every day; Brunch on Sunday
Credit cards: All major
Wheelchair access: Difficult

Fine dining in semi-rural O Fallon, Ill.? Twenty-five dollar entrees in a pre-Civil War house? If a restaurant really does set its own standards by the way it sets its prices, can The Mansion at LakePointe carry it off?

This elegant, obviously much-loved, old farm house (with a contemporary addition that includes a fireplace), is run by Michael and Ellen Miller, former owners of the Stockpot in Belleville. The Millers try hard, and much of their ambitious menu (which is as different as the restaurant itself) succeeds, but it falls short in some areas. In addition, where there are service problems, the facile excuse is that it's difficult to find experienced, black-tie waiters this far from a city. With prices close to $30 a person here, this excuse is unacceptable.

Appetizers are available only in sizes for two or more, and run into double-digit prices. Entrees, whose price includes a salad and side dish, are heavy on beef, but all are beyond just meat and potatoes. Everything, we were told, is made in-house.

Gravlax, or cured salmon, is different in flavor from smoked salmon and is served as an appetizer. Garnished with a seafood sausage, said the menu. It arrived with four large slices of gravlax, homemade melba toast, and four slices of sausage on what tasted like crispy-fried onions. The sausage had ice crystals inside. Was it, perhaps, supposed to be hot? No, cold, but not that cold. The waiter apologized, and whisked the plates away. After a wait, replacements. These, he promised, were fresh. But they were still cold inside, and had the watery consistency of something thawed too fast. The gravlax was good salmon, sliced thickly, but it wasn't the image of the vigorously seasoned fish that comes to mind at the word. There were surges of black pepper and dill, but nothing more, leaving the high-quality salmon not properly cured, or cured long enough.

The appetizer the Millers call their signature is a triangle of mushroom strudel, stuffed with portobello and shiitake mushrooms with Swiss cheese. The pastry was crisp and full of flavor, although a tad too greasy.

One salad involves pears, walnuts and Gorgonzola with a balsamic vinaigrette. At a time of year when pears were at their peak, and fresh pears honey-sweet, these were poached and diced. The cheese was used sparingly. The vinaigrette was slightly sweet. It could have been excellent with fresh pears and no added sweetness. The house salad had the same vinaigrette, and was basically greens, tomato and a little onion. A Caesar is available, too.

A Thai duck breast arrived over a sweet potato galette with a "straw" of vegetables. The breast came rare, in a reasonably tasty glaze. The galette was two sweet potato patties. The "straw" turned out to be a julienne of mixed vegetables stir-fried and arranged over what seemed to be sun-dried tomato halves, rather on the chewy side. A filet of beef, split and stuffed with crawfish tails, had its bearnaise on the side, which we prefer. The meat itself was tender and tasty, good beef. The bearnaise had some cayenne to match the New Orleans aura of much of the menu, but it was faintly bitter and lacked the unctuousness of serious egg-based sauces, which give you the feeling of eating butter with your spoon. "Smashed" potatoes were successful indeed, steaming hot and full of real potato flavor.

Dessert and coffee proved to be the most consistent course of the meal. Coffee is advertised as freshly ground and it tasted it. The Earl Grey chocolate cake—yes, like the tea—lives up to the name. Oil of bergamot is what makes Earl Grey tea distinctive. It's hard to tell if the cake had bergamot or just the tea in it, but it was wonderful, very different, very moist. A singular dessert.

The wine list fails to list all vintages, a major annoyance, and the by-the-glass selections are few. The beer selection was quite good.

Service is always a hard call when eating at an upscale restaurant in a non-urban area. Servers with little experience have been innocent of both meaning and pronunciation of foreign words. And many local people are not much taken with detached, uninvolved service, no matter how cool and professional it would seem in the city. The service at The Mansion was attentive, interested, full of details on the food. The table was crumbed— twice—water glasses were kept full, management kept an eye on things. What more is needed?

And by the way, there's a swan in the lake.

Market in the Loop
This, That and Everything Else—Fast

6655 Delmar Boulevard, University City
Lunch and Dinner, Monday-Saturday, St. Louis Bread Co. open Sunday, too
Mama's Coal Pot (Barbecue), 727-8034
Racanelli's (Pizza, Calzone, Stromboli), 727-7227
Sombrero Taqueria (Mexican), 721-6474
St. Louis Bread Co. (Sandwiches), 721-8007
Wong's Wok (Chinese), 726-0976
Credit cards: All major at Bread Co., others cash only
Wheelchair access: Satisfactory

The Market in the Loop is one of the great meadows in the St. Louis area. After all, isn't a meadow—even a concrete one—a place to graze, to relax and to enjoy life? The University City market is, in some respects, a memorial to the late Harry Wald, and it offers much more than the average food court.

First, there are no franchises or national chains, with the exception of St. Louis Bread Co. The others, whether selling eat-in or carry-out meals or the raw materials to make them, are all small operations, mostly with real dedication to what they sell. Second, they're a chance to sample well-cooked ethnic food at good prices. Third, the customers and the passers-by at the market provide some of the finest people-watching anywhere. Every imaginable group, in every imaginable T-shirt, will wander by to eat or shop, or to do both.

We're there often to eat and shop (especially at the wonderful Bob's Seafood), or to visit stores in the area, and we admire Jeff Wald's work with the market. Of course, Joe remembers Harry, Jeff's dad and a local entertainment entrepreneur who ran the Grand Theatre, on Market Street, for many years. It was the city's primary burlesque house, a proud downtown monument to beauty and the art of the ecdysiast, until it was torn down to make room for Busch Stadium, making St. Louis the first American city to choose night baseball over sex.

MAMA'S COAL POT: The sign reminds us to order our smoked ducks and turkeys early, but Ann orders rib tips on the spot. For folks in need of a barbecue fix, Mama's is a hot spot. The tomato-based sauce covers smoky tips that have a higher-than-average ratio of meat to gristle, bone and fat. Potato salad tends to be the sweet style, and there's the requisite two slices of white bread. Sweet potato pie shows good crust and subtle spicing. And there's a sink near the inside tables for after-meal cleanup, which makes things darn near perfect. Hot links are hot, pork steaks sing. Under $7.

RACANELLI'S: New York-style pizza, rolled at the edges and thin in the middle, and fat, cheese-filled calzone are winners here. Pizza, in 14-, 16, and 18-inch sizes, climbing up from $8.50, is nicely cheesed, and there are a dozen available toppings, including anchovies, a personal favorite. Calzone is a fat turnover of bread dough stuffed with cheeses and pizza toppings, and is extremely filling. Mozzarella, Parmesan, ricotta and Romano cheeses start the calzone, a full meal for $4, and a stromboli, for another buck, is a winner with peppers and onions. Lots of cracked red pepper and cheese to add at the diner's whim, and always some badinage from the guys behind the counter. A splendid deal.

SOMBRERO TAQUERIA: Tacos here definitely aren't fast finger food. They're open-faced knife-and-fork soft tacos piled with chunks of meat or fish, beans, tomato and lettuce, with a good salsa alongside ($1.75-$2.75). The spicy guacamole succeeds despite its frigid temperature. Chicken burritos, in large flour tortillas, are less successful, with lots of rice, but horchata, a traditional Mexican milk drink with rice and cinnamon ($1.25), is uncommon and yummy. Chicken or steak fajitas are $5.25, the burritos are $2.75-$5.25, and if the Mexican market doesn't work, they can go back to felafel and hummus, which they also make well and used to sell, in the same location, before fashions changed.

ST. LOUIS BREAD CO. is dear to the heart of many St. Louisans. They do a particularly good, if quite messy, tuna salad sandwich, along with their other cold sandwiches. Good combinations, and the seven-grain bread offers lots of flavor to help the meat or cheese. For mass-produced breads, theirs are pretty good, with Ann admitting a distinct affection for the pumpkin muffins. Soups, too, and a generally good lunch for about $5.

WONG'S WOK: The best bargain in the market is the Friday-Saturday spicy beef noodle bowl at Wong's Wok, where less than $5 brings a huge bowl of spicy beef noodle soup, stuffed with tangy beef and thick, soft noodles. Like a lot of beef at Chinese and other Third World restaurants, Wong's Wok is variable, with too much gristle and fat sometimes interfering. But the noodles and the soup are delightfully spiced. Plenty of the usual items, from fried rice to kung pao shrimp, and many chop sueys and chow meins, also under $5.

None of these places has great food, but they're inexpensive and generally tasty. And afterward, if the spirit to duplicate at home strikes, well, Bob's has all the necessary seafood and there are two produce markets just outside to fill the market basket with good things.

Mike Shannon's Steaks and Seafood

Steak House

100 North Seventh Street
421-1540
Lunch, Dinner and Supper, every day
Credit cards: All major
Wheelchair access: Satisfactory

Mike Shannon's looks right and feels right. This is a steak house in the style of the great New York dining palaces like Gallagher's, The Palm, Smith & Wollensky. Dark wood paneling, dark green paint and big leather chairs to match, lots of pictures on the walls—déjà vu all over again, as Yogi Berra reportedly said.

As all of St. Louis knows, Shannon's, owned by the former St. Louis Cardinal player and longtime colorful color man for the team's broadcasts, is where the sports crowd hangs out. The restaurant (located in the shadow of Busch Stadium) began as a Pasta House operation, with Shannon as the front man, but Shannon and his partner, Tony Marino, purchased it a few years ago. Shannon hosts a post-home game radio show from here, interviewing various sports figures and swapping yarns, and the place does a good supper business at that time. A lighter menu is offered after 10 p.m., although we can't imagine them refusing to cook a steak at any hour, especially if an athlete is ordering.

Interestingly, with all this and the concomitant piles of sports memorabilia, the restaurant doesn't reek of testosterone. On a quiet evening, it can be relaxed and quite civilized. Shannon is pictured with dozens of interesting people, and the souvenirs and decorations are worth a careful look.

We saw some foreign tourists on our last visit. On reflection, we could have told them that this is real American food. Chicken noodle soup to escargot and mussels to steak, the menu is full of classics most Americans would recognize. However, the immense individual Yorkshire pudding with the prime rib left several young people visibly puzzled. It's not cheap. Everything is a la carte, and our usual measure of three courses would average above $35 without a vegetable. A big Idaho baker is $4.50, and French fries, at $3.95, cost as much as wild rice.

Maryland crab cakes were a slow start, and would have been booed in Baltimore, where not only are crab cakes and crabmeat practically a religion, but also the one area where the late, lamented St. Louis Browns got a good deal in their move. Pink inside, crisp outside, the cakes had a fair degree of crabbiness but not a sign of lump crabmeat. They were nothing more than adequate, until we tasted the relish that came alongside—an excellent, sweet-tangy dish with corn, fat, marinated raisins, and what we think were tomatoes. (Imagine how we must have looked in the dimly lit dining room, picking up a small piece, examining it closely, tasting it.) If they were tomatoes, like the raisins, they were imbued with the dressing, and it was a very successful match.

One of our favorite ways to serve tomatoes is as bruschetta, slabs of bread toasted and piled with fresh tomatoes chopped and dressed with olive oil, garlic and basil. Shannon's rendition comes in a soup plate, a pile of the tomato surrounded by long slabs of crunchy bread. While the tomato itself wasn't gorgeously red, piling it on the bread and dribbling some juice over it made for a tasty, first-rate combination, an example of the whole being more than just the components. It was a solid hit.

Spinach salad is traditionally sweet or savory with bacon, egg and mushroom. Here, someone wisely chose the savory route. Glossy dark leaves hid slices of mushroom, bacon and several chunks of roasted red pepper. Hard-boiled egg halves sat on each side. The salad was dressed with a judicious hand, but the dressing was so full of bacon flavor you could taste (but not feel) it in the eggs, and the result was satisfying.

Once upon a time in St. Louis, frog legs were fairly common. No more, and now that they are folk heroes for Budweiser, the delicate meat will suffer the same fate as venison, where many complain about "eating Bambi." Their loss. Frog legs, small and tender, are dusted lightly with Italian bread crumbs and quickly run under a broiler. They are delicious and need nothing more than a squeeze of lemon. The senior partner was thrilled. A 16-ounce strip was perfectly cooked, although just a little tough. The baked potato has a tender skin, but was flaky and flavorful. The menu offers "Irish potatoes," a Southernism to differentiate them from sweets; the result is new potatoes, quartered and buttered and parslied.

Desserts are done in-house, ringing some significant and imaginative notes on great American dessert themes. Upside-down apple pie comes a la mode, the chocolate cake wears caramel and pecans for a turtle title, and there's a nice simple rum cake. A blueberry lemon pie had a graham cracker crust, a layer of berry puree and some wonderful lemon mousse. European-style strawberry shortcake had two thin circles of sponge cake with berries in a honey sauce. It was handsome, but the strawberry sauce had been thickened and didn't soak into the cake, leaving us with the naturally slightly chewy nature of sponge cake. With just a little adjustment, this could come in a winner.

The wine list is remarkably good and not overpriced. A pinot noir from Oregon's Elk Cove Winery gave a great bounce to the bruschetta, an odd combination that really swung. So does Shannon's, more in the front porch than the Carnaby Street manner, and in a very nice way.

Molina's Wishing Well
Modern American Cuisine
12949 Olive Boulevard
205-2299
Dinner Monday-Saturday
Credit cards: All major
Wheelchair access: Satisfactory

It isn't easy being green, as we all learned from Kermit. It's no easier being in the restaurant business for nearly three-quarters of a century. The Molina family restaurant, now a multi-generational business, began as the Hollywood on North Grand Boulevard, in the area near Olive Street that was the center of the motion picture business. Before it reached West County, however, it stopped near old Busch Stadium on Dodier Street, then reached new heights as the Wishing Well on Brown Road, where it served glorious catfish and prime rib before it succumbed to fire.

Now, reaching toward Chesterfield, Steve Molina has made the family name prominent once again. He has left the catfish and prime rib behind; the menu, describing what they serve today as "seasonal continental cuisine," is really so mixed that it exemplifies what Americans eat today.

If the first courses range from turtle soup to crab cakes, that's American. If there's lots of pasta, a couple of steaks, grilled tuna and French-fried lobster tail, that's American, too. It's what we eat today; a variety of foods the majority of which wouldn't have been seen on a St. Louis menu forty years ago. Flash-fried spinach is now seen around town more and more. In Molina's rendition, he first lines the dish with a balsamic vinegar reduction because dribbling it on top will reduce the exquisite crispness of the vegetable. Some shavings of pecorino cheese are a sharp final touch. The dish is a dandy.

Another very American ingredient we don't see often enough is Maytag Blue cheese. Made in Iowa (your washer dollars at work), it's delicious, and just as good with a dessert wine. The mixed salad is a wide variety of greens, fresh and properly handled, available with a balsamic vinaigrette or the Maytag Blue dressing. It satisfies on many counts, starting with the fact that it is tossed in the kitchen with just enough dressing to coat the leaves of lettuce.

The entree list involves a familiar group of steaks and chops, both veal and lamb, along with fresh fish dishes, pasta and risotto.

A filet mignon, unusually flavorful for that rather quiet cut, was stuffed with crabmeat and served with a really good bordelaise sauce and a delicious three-onion sauce, a nice balance of flavors. The double-thick pork chop held cornbread, very spicy andouille sausage and tart apples, blending to yield a big-taste result. The pork chop came a little rare even for us, but the tarragon mustard sauce, which would seem too light given the ingredients of the stuffing, worked very well. Altogether a dish for a pig to be proud of. Potato pancakes were crisp outside, very dense inside, and the other vegetable dishes included ratatouille and sweet-and-sour red cabbage.

The wine list has about a dozen wines of reasonable quality by the glass. Among desserts, the bread pudding souffle seemed to be of a whole-grain bread, rather dense and seemingly unsouffled at all, a square with raisins and nuts and a bourbon caramel sauce dizzyingly striped on the plate. But the winner was a tarte tatin, an upside-down apple tart that becomes almost ethereal when properly done. Molina's was near-perfect, with more of those tart apples and a thin, crispy crust, slightly warm. Did we hear Paris outside the door?

Service is very attentive; the crowd is mostly in casual dress. Three courses should run about $25 a person.

Morton's of Chicago
Steakhouse
7822 Bonhomme Avenue, Clayton
725-4008
Dinner every night
Credit cards: All major
Wheelchair access: Passable

The sound of Morton's is different than it once was. In the early years in St. Louis, the bass and tenor pitch of men pretending to play, but usually working, was the backup for a seemingly endless loop of Frank Sinatra music. The voices were low in volume as well as pitch, because this was, to be sure, A Serious Steakhouse. There were women there, of course, but mostly in power suits, holding their own against the men during those dour years when cigars and senses of humor were out of fashion.

Close to the end of the second millennium, the pitch and the volume are higher than they once were, and the atmosphere definitely more relaxed. We noticed men in shirtsleeves, families with well-behaved children, a couple of tables of women, and, a little before 9 p.m., a group of three was seated wearing shorts and T-shirts that weren't tucked in. The times are a-changing, yes, they are.

It's still one of the stiffest tariffs in town. The cheapest piece of red meat is a tenderloin brochette for $19.95. The lobsters run three to four pounds at market price, which will be upward of $18 a pound. Everything except the bread and butter is a la carte. Clearly, this is a place that's ready to be judged with an extremely skeptical eye.

All but two of the appetizers are seafood, and they're about $10. Bean soup is $5.25, sauteed mushrooms $7.95. Oysters were cockenoes, opened but not loosened from the shell, and served with a chunky, rather sweet cocktail sauce. They came in one of those pressed fake wood salad bowls, resting on ice, and hadn't been there long because they were at room temperature, something of concern when you're dealing with raw shellfish. They were nothing special in terms of flavor, either. On the other hand, the crab cocktail was, as promised, honest lump crab, served on a huge leaf of romaine with a little mayonnaise flavored with mustard and a half lemon. The lemon did far more for the delicate meat than the mayo, and it was a fine, light, beginning.

Salads are all $5.50; a Caesar, sliced tomato with onion or blue cheese, spinach with a sweet and sour dressing, or a Morton's salad. The latter is romaine and iceberg, dressed with blue cheese, chopped boiled egg, and an anchovy, which is optional. The salad is dressed in the kitchen, and the egg and anchovy placed atop it. The lettuce was fresh and cold, but some pieces were six inches long, leaving the customer only an immense steak knife to cut it. The same knife must be used to slice and butter the eight-inch loaves of onion bread that are brought to each table, making diners look like Fred Flintstone. The salad dressing itself was quite sharp and tasty, but portioned with the too-generous hand that often marks steak house servings.

The tenderloin brochette comes on white rice, surrounded by what's described as a diablo sauce. Traditionally, that means mustard, but this adobe-colored sauce was considerably more than that, with considerable snap, but not enough to get in the way of the other complex flavors. It reminded Joe of Hack Ulrich's special steak sauce at the old Tenderloin Room, and made him hope it would be revived at the Chase-Park Plaza. The meat was ordered rare, and came out closer to medium, but it was tender and considerably tastier than one might expect for the least expensive cut in a very expensive restaurant.

A porterhouse was not giant-sized, perhaps 18 ounces, but the larger side was as succulent as the smaller one. That's unusual in a porterhouse, and worthy of special note. The meat juices that surrounded it and its solitary sprig of watercress showed a faint taste of spicing like a seasoned salt, but it was so subtle that all it did when matched with the meat was to accentuate the innate steak taste. Someday, though, someone will imitate the French and use those good juices to dress a small salad after the main course, a platonic combination.

Desserts are the standard fruit, ice cream and cheesecake, a creme caramel, the individual hot chocolate cakes that have melting chocolate inside, and souffles for two. These are small enough that someone who had eaten lightly could kill a whole one. We wouldn't blame them. They're idyllic, fluffy and perfectly done to give a little taste of something fun and un-filling at the end of a heavy meal. A classic Grand Marnier souffle was accentuated only with a little grated orange rind and served with what looks like dense, chunky whipped cream, but is actually a sabayon sauce, with the Marsala so faint it's difficult to identify, and not a great deal of sugar. Nicely done, and a cheer to the souffle cooks.

Service is attentive and fast-moving. The wine list is deep and priced in accordance with the rest of the meal. Dinner at Morton's is not inexpensive, but it is very good.

Nachomama's
Mexican Cuisine in a Hurry
9643 Manchester Road, Rock Hill
961-9110
Lunch and Dinner, Monday-Saturday
Cash only
Wheelchair access: Satisfactory

We admit to being suckers for a good pun. Nachomama's, however, is one of our favorite lunch stops for far more than the name. The food is cooked to order, they have those wonderfully silly fruit sodas that go so well with tropical food, and you can make your own tacos al carbon with their fajita platters and the three varieties of salsa, including a fine pico de gallo, or raw salsa, which are offered on a help-yourself basis.

In addition, they roast chicken over a wood fire, and there's nothing better than some of that chicken with the pico de gallo wrapped up in a fresh tortilla, finger food Ann considers worth licking to the last drop.

Nachomama's is located in an old fast-food joint with a drive-up window, and its decor is a long way from the burger wars. Beer signs, old soda coolers, galvanized tin signs and a variety of roadside art give it the bright colors of a fiesta. From mechanics to soccer moms, everybody chows down on things like their enchiladas, excellent corn tortillas wrapped around a hearty rich filling. Joe's favorite is the chicken, sweet and tender, cut into strips of just the right size. Some of the hotter salsas work well with it, and you can put whatever salsa is left over onto the refried beans (which are good, but need some spicing).

Stuff yourself silly for less than $10.

Neruda

Modern American Cuisine

1 Club Center, Highway 157, Edwardsville, Ill.
(618) 659-9866
Lunch and Dinner, Monday-Saturday
Credit cards: All major
Wheelchair access: Satisfactory

Pablo Neruda was a Chilean poet and politician, exiled for his views, and later, the hero's hero in the book and movie, *The Postman*. Not exactly a food-related sort of image, admittedly, but he had a St. Louis connection with Antonio Skarmata, the Washington University visiting professor who wrote the novel.

Sean Gallagher named the restaurant for his favorite poet just because he wanted to. It's not Chilean, nor even South American. Influence on the menu items clearly comes from Asia and the American southwest. The setting is glamorous, contemporary and crisp without being chilly. Dinner runs about $25 per person before wine or drinks.

First courses include things like a grilled portobello mushroom with Gorgonzola and Marsala sauce, and a seared carpaccio of beef. A smoked-chicken pot sticker minus the dumpling skin reminded us more of a crab cake. The sauce of shiitake mushrooms and tomato was delicious, and the combination a solid hit. Rangoons are stuffed with salmon instead of crab or its imitators, and arrive with absolutely delicious sides of sweet-hot vinaigrette and wasabi sour cream.

The house salad comes with first-rate greens, red onions, artichoke hearts and shavings of good Parmesan cheese. The piquant vinaigrette dressing arrives with a light hand, and the result is eminently satisfactory.

Dinner ranges from the safe—like pan-fried catfish that rises to the setting with black bean salsa and polenta fries—to the considerably more exotic, red curry-glazed salmon with sweet-potato "hay" on top.

What was described as an hibachi steak turned out to be a strip, with Asian seasonings of soy sauce and garlic, a fine piece of meat. The mashed potatoes were real, made of Yukon gold potatoes, though cool to the taste. Some green beans were near-perfect, well-seasoned and slightly firm to the bite. A rainbow trout bulged with a generous serving of seafood stuffing, the main bone removed and the seasoning slightly spicy with cumin and garlic.

Desserts run the same spectrum. An apple pie exhibited a fine, fine crust that even survived the refrigerator, proving that it belonged in such a hip setting. On the other hand, a fallen chocolate cake had a layer of hazelnut filling and ganache on the top, but it was dry and not enough to raise the pulse rate.

Very good service, too, matching the level of the menu and decor, and the wine list is extensive enough and well-selected to go with the seasoning in the food. The poet, the author, and the filmmaker all would be happy.

Nobu's Japanese Restaurant

Sushi and other Japanese Cuisine

8643 Olive Boulevard, University City
997-2303
Lunch Monday, Tuesday, Thursday, Friday; Dinner Thursday-Tuesday
Credit cards: AE, MC, V
Wheelchair access: Difficult

When someone says "Japanese cuisine," the usual response is, "Sushi, tempura and noodles."

True as far as it goes, but not nearly far enough when it comes to a Japanese restaurant like Nobu's, where sushi, noodles and tempura are fresh and delicious, but a simple piece of grilled fish is so good as to leave a simple description such as "delicious" in its dust.

Noboru Kidera began in St. Louis in 1983 as a sushi chef at Tachibana, then moved a few times before settling in at a one-time pancake house in a small shopping center just east of I-170. All the sushi and tempura and noodles are there, and watching Nobu work the sushi bar is like watching a great sleight-of-hand artist deal cards. (Think of Ricky Jay.)

The action is complex, almost choreographed. Observing Nobu slice one of a dozen or so different types of glistening fish into delicate pieces, shape the slightly-vinegared rice into the proper oblong shape, add just a dab of the sharp, green wasabi horseradish, combine rice and fish and place it carefully onto a tray, is part of the tradition. But it doesn't end there. The pieces of sushi—shiny, color-balanced, startlingly beautiful—are composed like a picture on the trays that carry them to the table.

Sushi has as strong a pull on us today as a penny candy display case had when we were children, and the urge for "one of each, please," is as strong as ever. Unfortunately, as lovely and tasty as sushi can be, it also can dent a budget. The selection at Nobu's is large and fresh, and he turns mackerel, tuna, salmon, yellowtail, octopus and many other denizens of the deep into delectable morsels. A highlight is a soft shell crab roll in which that delightful crustacean comes out of the fryer and onto the chopping block, to be rolled up, with rice and vegetables, inside seaweed. Salmon and tuna are immediately identifiable; temperature doesn't affect the flavor. Mackerel is strong and briny, yellowtail soft and mellow.

Joe keeps wondering which is his favorite, but it seems to change from meal to meal, depending on freshness and texture of what's on the table and, of course, the mood of the eater. He's especially fond of the pickled ginger and the green horseradish (the latter in extremely small amounts), and tends to dip the sushi into the soy sauce, even if purists sneer. The only problem is that sushi clicks the bill into the stratosphere a lot faster than penny candy.

Sushi is a lot more common than it used to be, but Noboru seems above all others, and he stands even taller when it comes to fish. Both types of mackerel, Spanish and non-Spanish, were memorable. Spanish was brushed with soy, then grilled quickly, and the thin fish arrived with a wonderful crunchiness around the edges and a rich, slightly oily, fishiness in the center. The other mackerel had been marinated in ginger and saki before broiling. The chunk was thicker, and softer inside, with the same rich flavor. A couple of pieces of an unfamiliar Japanese squash, bright green outside, bright orange inside, were slightly starchy and totally a winner.

Tuna belly was a sybarite's dream, soft and succulent, from the fattest, most tender part of the fish (just as "belly lox," from the center of the smoked salmon, was the most desired to go on a bagel on Sunday morning. Joe remembers, as a small boy, seeing people stand outside the delicatessen, peering through the window and trying to estimate exactly when to enter, depending on the slicer's distance from the center and the number of waiting customers).

Tempura is crisp and dry, and it may be the best way to eat vegetables. A single string bean, or a slice of sweet potato, or certainly a ring of onion, becomes a thing of beauty, which we all know is a joy forever.

Noboru Kidera uses a lot of ginger in his cooking, and it adds a wonderful dimension to meats and vegetables. There are noodles, of course, cold or pan-fried and delicious, and various dishes, either grilled or fried, and accompanied with teriyaki sauce. Rice is a standard side dish, and so are dishes of splendidly crisp and lightly marinated cucumbers. Entrees are under $15, and dinner at Nobu's is almost a bargain at about $22-$35 per person (as long as the sushi dreams don't escalate into sushi nightmares).

Green tea ice cream makes for a pleasant dessert, but if there's fresh pineapple on the menu, leap to it because it's the closest thing to fresh, at-site, Hawaiian pineapple we've ever had.

Norton's Cafe
Cajun-American Casual
808 Geyer Street
436-0828
Lunch and Dinner, daily
Credit cards: MC, V
Wheelchair access: Satisfactory

Another of the saloons in Soulard that has, like Topsy, "just growed," Norton's now sports a charming back patio. The entrance was moved a couple of doors to the west, and leads into it. The action marked "paid" to one of the common problems in Soulard watering holes, blasts of icy air from arrivals and departures on frigid nights. A real fireplace completes the atmosphere.

This isn't a tourist pub, though. There's a generous number of regulars congregating at the bar to give and receive genial abuse. They're fairly well fed, too, from a kitchen that takes food a little more seriously than some of its peers—although the general food quality around Soulard is rising, and Norton's and others should pick up the pace. A dinner should cost around $25.

Norton's usually has at least two soups on the blackboards that serve as menus. A mushroom-celery bisque may have had some ancestry in a can or package, but the end result turned out to be creamy and soothing, fine to the mushroom maniac's mouth and surprisingly good to the celery-reluctant one. It also was hot enough. Chicken cigars turned out to be something of a cross between flautas and tacquitos, crisp rolls, about the diameter of a cigarillo, with a chunky chicken filling and some pop. The un-greasy rolls were served with a cup of salsa and sour cream for dipping. Blackened shrimp, almost fiery enough, is another popular appetizer.

Dinners include a salad, unremarkable except that it came in a bowl large enough for the diner to toss his own, and with dressing on the side. A house vinaigrette is very herbal, tart, and certainly without sugar. Iceberg lettuce, boiled egg quarters and some decent croutons were the primary components.

The main courses are where the New Orleans tendencies of the kitchen take over. Besides the usual contingent of sandwiches—including a good steak sandwich, by the way—there are things like jambalaya, shrimp Creole, red beans and rice, and similar favorites of the Big Easy.

There are also a couple of steaks, plain and poivre, for those who search for simplicity.

Shrimp Creole came on perfectly cooked rice, lots of shrimp but surprisingly few vegetables, in a very smooth, deeply red sauce that had some Cajun spicing but didn't really ignite flame. The shrimp weren't overcooked, and the combination was pleasant for folks who want their Creole uncomplicated. Norton's Cajun spice mixture, sold commercially around town, will help.

A crawfish pot pie arrived looking a little like nachos, crisp brown squares covered with melting cheese, until we found the mudbugs, complete with celery and onions, underneath. The cheese makes no sense, but the pie crust was a rare example of great crust—flaky, fresh—and excellent. The gravy with the crawfish was thick and tasted more of vegetables and crawfish than of added seasoning. On the side was an order of jambalaya, slightly sticky but extremely tasty with tomato and pepper—and a little more pepper—to go with the chunks of chicken breast and sausage.

Move fast on dessert. The peach pie listing was erased right under our noses a couple of minutes before we could get to it. But if the crust was anything like the one on the pot pie, whoever got it was lucky.

O'Connell's Pub
Classic Burgers and Bar Food
4652 Shaw Avenue
773-6600
Lunch and Dinner, every day
Credit cards: MC, V
Wheelchair access: Passable

Jack Parker, as the last to leave, finally turned out the lights in Gaslight Square in 1972. Conventional wisdom stated that the lights would go out in O'Connell's Pub, too, when he moved to Shaw Avenue at Kingshighway. But Parker, never one to pay attention to conventional wisdom, moved the twenty-some blocks to the corner at the edge of the Hill, just west of the Missouri Botanical Garden. He took Nora, Red and Lenard with him. More than twenty-five years later, the score stands at Parker: 1, Conventional Wisdom: 0.

And despite Joe's adding to the conventional wisdom in 1972, O'Connell's remains one of his favorite places for lunch and socializing.

The menu has expanded, and so has the number of beer taps. Parker spends most of his time upstairs, overseeing his antiques business. But Nora, the world's greatest waitress, and Red and Lenard, two of the world's greatest bartenders, are still there, dispensing wit and wisdom, fine drinks and excellent sandwiches.

There are credit cards now, and daily specials and printed menus. The pool table, which came from Gaslight Square, disappeared when Parker discovered he needed more space for tables. But basically, it's the same as ever—Irish poets, playwrights and poseurs on the walls, comfortable chairs, and a tradition of feisty waitresses who once wore T-shirts lettered, "Tip-ping is not a city in China."

When Parker opened in Gaslight Square, in its fading days, he was directly across Boyle Street from the Gaslight Bar, and Joe remembers, one day in the spring of 1964, taking Jada, the headline stripper at the Grand Theatre, into O'Connell's for lunch. What made the day memorable is that a few hours earlier a jury in Dallas convicted Jack Ruby of the murder of Lee Harvey Oswald, and on the weekend of the Kennedy assassination, Jada had been dancing at

Ruby's club. He still owed her money (he treated all his strippers badly) and when she heard the verdict, she let out a howl of triumph. She's gone now, but a photo of her remains on the wall in Jack Carl's Two Cents Plain at 1114 Olive Street. (In those days, Jack was in Gaslight Square, too, and Jada needed a pastrami sandwich after her show.)

O'Connell's hung on in Gaslight Square for almost another decade, but the Shaw Avenue years have been just as triumphant for Parker. He earned his triumph, however, with some of the best bar food in the city, led by a hamburger that Joe claims is the best grilled burger in the nation. A warm bun and a slice of raw onion is all it needs. Ann is a fan of the Thursday special, the roast pork, and when the Italian sausage and green peppers are hot (which they too seldom are), they're outstanding, too. Rib tips, the Saturday special, usually are excellent, and the secret to Parker's barbecue sauce in the early days was the last inch or so of ketchup he collected out of the bottles through the week.

Soup and fries also are strong, the latter arriving thin, crisp and hot, with a minimum of grease, the former almost thick enough for a spoon to stand by itself—unassisted—in the middle of the bowl. Skip the fried mushrooms, battered somewhere else and completely flavorless.

O'Connell's is a wonderful bar for conversation, and the bartenders are worthy conversationalists. The huge round table in the back room was once the Saturday lunch-and-meeting spot for *Post-Dispatch* editorial writers, and the editorials had more punch and more wit in those days. It must have been something in the whiskey, or just in the Irish breeze that still blows through O'Connell's.

Oh, My Darlin' Cafe in Clementine's
Almost Home Cooking

2001 Menard Street
664-7869
Dinner every day; Brunch Saturday and Sunday
Credit cards: All major
Wheelchair access: Impossible

Colossal chicken pot pie behind a bar in Soulard? You bet.

One never knows, do one, as someone must have said. Oh, My Darlin' is a classic Soulard spot in terms of decor, with brick walls, Mardi Gras posters, a mirror or two. But opening the menu, the eater encounters a whole page of daily specials. Monday, for example, involves fried chicken livers, meat loaf, breaded pork chops or chicken fried chicken. This is not a typographical error. Honest.

The rest of the week proceeds in the same vein, although by Friday, the Oh, My Darlin' gussies up for the weekend by adding a prime rib that is served through Sunday, and several seafood specials.

Finding the restaurant is only slightly tricky. One enters through the door to Clementine's, one of Soulard's oldest gay bars. Catty-cornered from the entrance, with a neon sign over its arched doorway, is the cafe itself, considerably quieter than the bar. The cafe seems to draw a mixed crowd.

There are hors d'oeuvres, as the menu calls them, mostly deep-fried things like zucchini sticks and—yes—toasted ravioli. We tried some pot stickers, which were too salty, but with a piquant anise flavor and with a duck sauce that added a little pepper to the usual ingredients. Hors d'oeuvres range from $3.95 to $5.50 for a mixed platter.

Dinners come with soup du jour or a salad. The salad is generous and fresh, with red onion, a little cabbage and carrot, chopped egg and a drift of cheese across the top. The oil and vinegar is sweet, and so is the raspberry vinaigrette, but there's also ranch, poppy seed, and, for fifty cents extra, blue cheese. The Bubbles Salad, by the way, is named for the chef, and has some meat in it as well.

Besides the specials, entrees in the $8.50-$11.50 range include ham steak, shrimp scampi, chicken Parmesan, and a 10-ounce strip steak. We tried the pork chops, which were simply grilled, not too thick—real home cooking. The vegetable of the day was a tomato gratin, a couple of ripe tomato halves briefly broiled with basil and cheese. There are also baked potatoes available, as well as fries, and sour cream carries no surcharge. Chicken pot pie is available Monday through Thursday only. (Thursday, it's joined by its cousin, a steak and mushroom pie.) As large as a three-pound chicken, its arrival will cause the unsuspecting to gasp. The dome of golden brown puff pastry surrounded by outward curving points would resemble a crown if it were only round instead of oval. Inside the dome, it's devilishly hot—the pie is whisked from the oven to the table, still bubbling inside. Spectacles may steam over when the crust is pierced.

How does it taste? Full of large pieces of tender white meat, with a few carrots and fewer peas around more for visual accent than serious vegetable eating. The pale gravy is one step beyond what the mouth expects, a little more chickeny and a little more pepper than one usually finds. It's the kind of chicken pot pie that was made for a snowy winter night, which also qualifies as a sort of pale-colored drama.

Desserts aren't made in-house, not surprising in a kitchen not much larger than the ones that used to be in the Missouri Pacific's dining cars. Still, we had a berry tart—almost more of a torte given the kind of pastry—with good berries, not too sweet, and closer to room temperature than refrigerator temperature, always a pleasant gesture to customers.

No wine list to speak of, but full bar service, and a dart game and pool table in the next room, if you're interested in post-prandial sport.

Brunch begins at 8:30 on Saturdays, 11 on Sundays. The star is the chicken fried chicken, a lightly battered boneless breast that's pan-fried and served with a cream gravy. Seasoned with garlic and maybe a little sage, plus a hint of cayenne pepper, it's sensational, not what you'd expect with eggs over easy. But then again, why not?

Creole omelets are doused in a little too much tomato sauce, seasoned well but not ragingly hot, and the omelet is full of sausage and bacon and vegetables. Eggs Clementine start with homemade biscuits. On top are layered a slice of ripe tomato, grilled ham, poached eggs and then the house hollandaise, which is remarkably lemony. The whole feel here is glorified home cooking, and when an egg yolk broke on its way from the poacher to the plate, no one was upset. Breakfasts begin with a fruit cup, and includes American fries (deep-fried crispy), hash browns (sauteed) or potatoes O'Brien (sauteed with onions and peppers). We vote for the latter. Coffee is really good, too, and they don't serve fake cream, either. The tab for fruit cup, main dish, potatoes and hot bread is $5.75 across the board. Everything is very casual—bring a newspaper.

Old 66 Brewery & Restaurant
Microbrewery Pub Food

9856 Watson Road, Crestwood
965-8866
Lunch and Dinner, every day
Credit cards: All major
Wheelchair access: Satisfactory

Microbreweries may be the best thing that's happened to bar food since the deep fryer. There are exceptions, but most of the micros seem to be run by folks whose interests are more in their mouths than in their pockets. They're proud of their beer, and they want to put out good food to go with it.

When we heard that Mike Wilson, an alum of the kitchens of Tim Mallett (Remy's, Big Sky, Blue Water Grill), was the chef at the Old 66 Brewery and Restaurant, that was sufficient encouragement to investigate lunch. The Old 66, on Watson Road (where it actually was U.S. 66 at one time), has a menu featuring a few pizzas, some plate lunches like meat loaf, chicken pasta, the ubiquitous chicken Caesar, a fish entree, and some sandwiches. We heard diners at a nearby table raving about the flash-fried spinach, and some guys grunting happily into their mashed potatoes with shallot gravy. Two lunch courses here will be under $15.

"Boneless Chicken Wings," says the menu, but they're actually wingless chicken, strips of boneless, skinless breast cooked and tossed with the traditional spicy sauce. Not surprisingly, it's not as succulent as a wing, but it must be lower in fat and the sauce was properly hot. An order is only six small pieces, joined by four dried-out celery cuts and a dish of blue cheese dressing. Not much for $5.25.

Hamburgers, available with cheddar and bacon or barbecue sauce, rode on an onion bun and were good beef, well-cooked to the requested medium rare, but lacking the necessary searing on the edges. Condiments aren't on the table, but are delivered happily. Boneless pork steak sandwiches wear a thick brown sweet-hot sauce, with pieces of onion cooked to brownness, and are thicker than the average pork steak. Leaner would be better, but such is the nature of the cut. Onion rings and fries are both described as beer-battered, but the kitchen was in enough chaos that the rings arrived after the sandwich was finished.

Desserts go beyond the chocolate bread pudding, but we probably won't. This bread pudding swings. Even though an attempt to warm it left it warm at the corners and cold inside, it was still fabulous. This is dark chocolate, crispy on top, sauced with a little creme anglaise and raspberry coulis, but mainly just chocolate, not sweet, very dense, and absolute heaven. The lady who makes the bread pudding bakes other things, including pies, and we look forward to the lemon meringue (Joe's favorite), but only if there's a piece of chocolate bread pudding held in reserve.

Rao Palamand, the brewer and one of the owners (his son, Shashi, and Ron Miller are the others), plans on about a half-dozen beer varieties, depending on the season. There's a good wheat beer for summer, and a passable raspberry ale, though it's no match for the Belgian lambic raspberry. Blond and red ale are satisfactory, and there's an oatmeal stout, too.

And no Route 66 puns, either.

Olympia Kebob House and Taverna
Greek Cuisine
1543 McCausland Avenue
781-1299
16 South Central, Clayton
725-4976
Lunch and Dinner, every day
Credit cards: All major
Wheelchair access: Passable (McCausland); Difficult (South Central)

The world of restaurants and St. Louis Greek immigrants goes back to the beginning of the twentieth century and even before. A couple of kids named Skouras came here, found work in the dining room of the old Jefferson Hotel, then went off to Hollywood and fame and fortune as owners of the nation's largest movie chain. Their spiritual descendants were Steve Johnoff and Steve Boianoff, whose Bismarck Cafe downtown had the state's first liquor license after Prohibition, and was a wonderful restaurant and hangout that not enough people remember.

But these men, and their sons and grandsons, and many other Greek-Americans, emphasized the American half of the title, and their many restaurants were primarily American coffee shops. When Joe arrived, Mestika Jim's was a notable dining spot in the neighborhood that is now Busch Stadium, but it soon closed. Smokey Joe's Grecian Terrace was a standout on Olive Street before and during the glory days of Gaslight Square, but neither lived much after the mid-'60s.

But like the Grecian phoenix, some things arise from ashes, and St. Louis was reintroduced to Greek food in the '60s by the late and much-lamented (at least by us) Grecian Gardens. Located in a pair of half-basements on Euclid Avenue, the Gardens, and Aris Pappademos, the affable waiter, taught many of us about the pleasures of lamb, feta, and even roditis, the Greek rosé wine about which Joe wrote in one of his early *Post-Dispatch* reviews. (It was something to the effect that if you asked the waiter what the vintage was, he would look thoughtful and say, "June was a nice month.") Weekends, the place, especially the bar side, became a big party as a Greek band played and couples on dates mixed with multi-generational Greek families celebrating Uncle Pete's safe return from a visit home to Corfu. The place closed late, alcohol being only peripherally necessary to the good time. It was, in many ways, a "platonic place," if you'll pardon the expression.

But time marches on, and we have fewer white-tablecloth Greek restaurants. The city has never lost its taste for Greek food, however, as shown by the immense holiday weekend festivals bookending summer, and—even more steadfastly—the continued thriving of the Olympia. Gradually, slowly, it has expanded, and added a second location with a smaller menu so that gyro-deprived office workers in Clayton can grab and go, or stay, because there are some tables, too.

The Olympia feels like a neighborhood place. No one dresses up, almost all the diners sound as though they've been here before. The decor is fern bar, with lots of beer signs and a big steam table. There's a back room for overflow dining.

With Greek food, the appetizers are immensely endearing. The eastern Mediterranean tendency to have a lot of nibbles reaches its apogee on Mount Olympus, it seems. Leading the list is babaganous, their spelling of the traditional eggplant dip. The Olympia's version is particularly creamy and tastes of a little tahini. Folks who like salty things will be ecstatic over taramosalata, a pale pink spread made of salmon or pink lumpfish roe—don't say no, just try it—mixed with olive oil and lemon juice. Each comes with warmed pita bread to scoop up the goods.

Saganaki, which is melted kasseri cheese topped with brandy and flamed at the table with an "Opa!" from the server, is lovely and gooey, requiring only a squeeze of lemon to make it perfect. There are also cheese and olive plates, and tiropitas, melt-in-the-mouth triangles of phyllo filled with feta cheese or spinach. Dolmades, or stuffed grape leaves, are lemony and delicious, and the chickpea-and-garlic dip known as hummus, so popular throughout the eastern Mediterranean, is of superior quality.

Greek salad doesn't come up to snuff, alas. It was violently overdressed, tasted as though it had been dressed in advance, and the lettuce was so tired it had already gone to bed.

Lots of vegetarian dishes, including spanokopita, a tasty combination of spinach and feta and phyllo dough, served here as a main course rather than as an appetizer. A vegetarian platter had two slices of fried eggplant, a spinach-rice mixture, and mixed vegetables, with potatoes, onions, carrots, string beans and a few other things, all cooked down to a soft and savory mixture.

Pastitsio, macaroni layered with a white sauce, cheese, ground beef and seasonings like onion and cinnamon, a common ingredient in savory dishes in Greece, was probably a precursor to many of the 1950s casserole. Despite the hint of sweetness the cinnamon gives, it's essentially comfort food, hearty and easy to eat.

Shish kebob comes as lamb, chicken or pork, a full order atop rice, or a smaller one, wrapped in pita and known as souvlaki at festivals, where it is grilled in huge quantities and is mostly pork, a meat that takes this treatment well. Our choice is lamb, more authentic and harder to come by. The server asked if we wanted it medium. No, we said, rare, please. It arrived medium-well, very lightly seasoned with salt, pepper, very little oregano.

Aris taught Ann to pronounce gyro "YEE-ro," flipping the "r" slightly. It's actually a big pressed loaf of various parts of beef and lamb, seasoned and cooked on a rotisserie where it stands vertically. It's a great sandwich piled on warmed pita with tomato and onion and some tzatziki, the yogurt-cucumber sauce. Rolled up, it out-tacos a taco, and was a wrap long before rap music. The Olympia's version is very good, nicely juicy and generous in its use of the meat.

Desserts? Galactoboureko is traditionally a cold-weather dish. If they have any when you're there, get some. It's custard layered between phyllo dough, mildly sweet and very flaky. Baklava, nuts in phyllo, is too sweet for some people, but the version served here is less so, and comes in very generous servings.

If you don't get lost in the appetizers, you can eat well and heartily for $15 to $20 here. Wine? June really was a nice month.

Once Upon a Vine
New American Cuisine
3559 Arsenal Street
776-2828
Lunch and Dinner, Monday-Saturday
Credit cards: All major
Wheelchair access: Good

How nice to have a restaurant that looks out over a landscaped gate to Tower Grove Park. The expansion of Once Upon a Vine has taken it all the way to the corner of Grand Boulevard and the restaurant takes full advantage of the large windows. The interior design is pleasant and soothing, with amusing wine posters and genteel white tablecloths. If there's anywhere on South Grand that gets The Ladies Who Lunch, this must be it.

The name reflects the restaurant's concentration on wine, and about twenty by the glass are usually available. The list changes frequently, so you may miss the Argentinian merlot or the Australian sherry, but the usual California suspects are always hanging around, and some of their neighbors as well.

Appetizers are referred to as "small appetites," which include things like a cheese plate, crab cakes, a hot spinach and artichoke dip, and crostini. The crostini were three large, angular slices of exemplary French bread. Each was toasted and had a different topping. The herbed spinach and ricotta cheese was the most successful, followed by roasted garlic with pancetta bacon, but all three looked like they'd been passed under the broiler just long enough to dry them out, giving them a very unencouraging appearance. Fortunately, they tasted better than they looked.

Sandwiches can wear one of five different kinds of bread. A five-grain worked well with a BLT, which was jam-packed with thick, crisp apple-smoked bacon. The tomatoes were sliced Romas, a good choice during the off-season for tomatoes but a little surprising in July. Still, they were juicy but firm. The only discordant note was the herb mayonnaise, which allowed the rosemary to run roughshod over all the other tastes. (We looked for a good pun about disciplining her, but....) A pasta salad was lackluster, tasting of nothing but a little of the sliver of red pepper that came with the tricolor corkscrews.

Entrees come with soup or your choice of any of the salads on the menu. A spinach salad was dressed in the kitchen—good for them—with a good blue cheese vinaigrette. Matchsticks of red onion might have been expected, but roasted grapes and glazed walnuts were a surprise. Roasting grapes concentrates the sugar and caramelizes the outside a little, browning them. The walnuts had only a paper-thin shell of sugar, so the taste was still basically nutty after a quick sensation of sweet. They got mixed reviews—Ann was surprised to find she liked the sweet additions, Joe nixed them, but both the dressing and spinach were excellent.

Entrees are split between pasta and non-pasta items. We were intrigued by linguini with smoked mussels and the smoked pork chops, but went with a salmon risotto. Seasoned with dill and lots of lemon, it was seemingly unsalted, which made it flat, lemon or not, until salted. The rice was quite long and cooked beyond any hint of al dente. It seemed much more like a fish-and-rice than a real risotto, but the seasoning gave it some charm.

Desserts are mostly from outside the restaurant, and they have taken advantage of excellent purveyors like Quezel ice cream and Hank's cheesecake. But one of Tim Brennan's great cakes from Cravings won out. The chocolate cranberry showed a truly superb butter cream covering layers of dark chocolate cake and cranberry mousse. It was surprising we didn't lick the plate.

A full dinner runs more than $25 before you get to the wine, and attractive as it is, for that price, they still have a ways to go.

O.T. Hodge Chile Parlor

Chili and Friends

1622 South Jefferson Avenue
772-1215
510 Pine Street
421-9060
3523 North Broadway
342-9562
9705 Watson Road, Crestwood
966-5151
Union Station, 1820 Market Street
421-9938
Breakfast and Lunch, Monday-Saturday; Dinner varies by location
Credit cards: Varies by location; some cash only
Wheelchair access: Varies by location

Once upon a time there were establishments known as chile parlors. They were a sort of workingman's joint where a fellow could get a steaming bowl and a big handful of crackers for a nickel, even in the midst of the Depression. That probably was the time when chile (its correct spelling back then) got more like soup and less than a spicy meat-and-beans stew as more and more water was added to keep the proprietor from going broke.

In Ann's childhood, chili was doled out almost every week by the harassed ladies in the cafeteria, and generally held to be a treat by most kids except the picky eater who grew up to co-author this book.

We're going to avoid arguments about things like beans or tomatoes or mushrooms or bell peppers in chili, whether cheese or onions or sour cream belong on top or even nearby, and how the word should be spelled. To us, "chile" is a vegetable and "chili" is a creation like bouilla-baisse.

O.T. Hodge is a relic of chili history, the sort of place that St. Louis rightly enshrines. The chili is well-seasoned, although not blisteringly hot—there's hot sauce on the tables to spike it—and beans are an option. It's thick, too, thick enough to serve as a gravy for things like chili mac.

But the legendary use for it is on the slinger, a dish that has paid college tuition for generations of kids whose surgeon fathers and mothers removed gall bladders. Who knows where the name came from? A slinger is an oval platter that begins with fried potatoes, thinly sliced and with some onions, piled on an egg, either fried or scrambled, and two cheeseburger patties. Then the heap of food is showered with chili and served up with a couple of pieces of toast. Certainly a dietician's nightmare; it's only drawback is that it's no longer available at an hour when it could be used as an attempt to preempt a hangover.

There are lesser variations, minus the cheeseburger patties, and of course the chili is available solo or on tamales. No matter how much a diner eats, he'll come out with change from a $10 bill.

Hodge's does breakfast, which is fine but not as exciting without the chili. We'd be happier if the toast came with real butter, but there are serious biscuits and sausage gravy that doesn't taste like it came out of a plastic barrel, and those good potatoes.

If there's a handwritten sign on the wall announcing blackberry cobbler, by the way, make sure you get some. The filling is only so-so, but the crust is a wonder.

Pat's Bar & Grill
Closest Bar/Restaurant to Turtle Park

6400 Oakland Avenue
647-6553
Lunch and Dinner, daily
Credit cards: All major
Wheelchair access: Passable

More softball sorrows have been drowned here than at almost any other place in town, and these days, with Bob Cassily's wonderful, whimsical turtle sculptures just across the street, Pat's, like Joe, has discovered that one can find a new life outside of sports.

And that life can be enjoyed equally at this traditional Dogtown spot, once called McDermott's and now known as Pat's. It's a place where large parties, crowded around small tables, commiserate or cheer with one another on softball nights. Excellent hamburgers, sizzling hot and crisp at the edges, come off a plain flat grill, and fried chicken livers reach levels unmatched anywhere in town. We're not sure what does it, but the livers are covered with a thick, crisp crust that is best with a snappy, horseradish-laced red sauce that is much like shrimp sauce. Inside, the livers are tender and rarely dried out, and many even show pink touches of rareness.

Chicken gizzards wear a similar batter, and are similarly good. Ordinary chicken, breasts and wings and drumsticks and such, also are first-rate. Cornmeal is the batter of choice for catfish and jack salmon, both winners.

Our grandchildren like the hamburgers at Pat's, and most of them don't play softball. But we just cannot envision any of our relatives growing up without exposure to the whimsical charm of Cassily and the legends of the turtles.

Paul's of Clayton
Franco-Italo-American

7814 Forsyth Boulevard, Clayton
721-3311
Lunch Monday-Friday, Dinner Tuesday-Saturday
Credit cards: All major
Wheelchair access: Impossible

Truly only a stone's throw from the Government Center, and a short walk even for politicians, lawyers and lobbyists, Paul's does a busy lunch business, not so much the zip-in, zip-out kind as the let's-sit-down-and-catch-our-breath kind. Couples meeting for lunch, class-mates catching up on news, pleasantly gossipy business visits all go on, receiving superior meals in attractive quarters. All is so comfortable that we decided to join in one day.

Paul and Sharon Arnot have been operating Paul's for the better part of a decade, while other restaurants have come and gone in their neighborhood. There are nice touches, with standard items for both lunch and dinner. Dinner entrees are served with a choice of two among appetizer, soup and salad, and include London broil, broiled quail, veal saltimbocca and salmon encrusted with sesame seeds. A full meal is in the neighborhood of $25 a person.

At lunch time, there are several pastas, all about $8 with salad or soup, but salads and sandwiches seem to be favored. Paul's also serves friands, puff pastry shells filled with ham and cheese, smoked turkey, bacon and tomato and other favorite combinations. All have a bechamel sauce, making them perfect for a chilly day, and they're a little less than the pasta luncheons.

Seafood salad ($8.25) was bay scallops, small shrimp and calamari in an excellent vinaigrette. It was heavy on the vegetables—yellow and green peppers, tomato, red onion, carrot dice and small peas, even a couple of broccoli bits—but the vinaigrette helped so much, they were as tasty as the seafood. Alongside were a couple of boiled egg halves, a little superfluous lemon and lots of fruit.

The fruit, of good quality, is available as an alternative to fries with the sandwiches, and seemed to be very popular, a fine example of grown-ups doing the right thing even when no one is watching. We were surprised to see falafel ($6.25) on the menu, and leaped at the chance. Falafel, made of ground chickpeas (garbanzos, if you prefer) rolled into balls and deep-fried until crisp, were superior, with lots of cumin for seasoning and lots of crunch in the mouth. Falafel is a popular street food in Israel and other Middle Eastern countries, and keeping everything in the pita can be a neat trick. Ours came with lettuce, good tomatoes, a yogurt-dill sauce and tahini. The latter is a slightly sharp sesame sauce that is a popular Middle Eastern garnish and seasoning, and a common addition to falafel. The serving was far too generous to roll up in the pita. The house knows this, and the plate arrives with a smile and a knife. We also tried some tuna salad that was extremely standard.

Nobody seems to have dessert at lunch these days, though one customer at Paul's polished and ate a shiny Delicious apple. Nevertheless, we went for the chocolate mousse ($3). "Award-winning," said the waiter. And sure enough, in the corner is a collection of ribbons, and attached to the hostess stand is a rave review from a one-time *Post-Dispatch* restaurant writer. It looks like chocolate ice cream, thick, but not impossibly so, and very good, and tasting of a high grade of milk chocolate. We're normally dark chocolate folks, but this was really good, and a portion large enough to share, thereby easing a pair of consciences by now in tattered shreds.

Peppercini's Italian Cafe
Italian Cuisine
7910 Bonhomme Avenue, Clayton
727-2075
Lunch Monday-Friday, Dinner nightly
Credit cards: All major
Wheelchair access: Impossible

At the site of Clayton's longtime, fall-back dinner spot, Candicci's, Peppercini's has what looks like the same front room. It's full of old photographs and prints and advertising signs, with a low ceiling and a near-bare-bulb sort of lighting that actually feels pretty right, given the space. The prices seem to match, too, seeming to be almost pre-inflation, with a three-course meal about $14.

The menu is full of the traditional lasagna, spaghetti and meatballs, fettucini Alfredo, green salads and fried mozzarella. There are also a few nightly specials, both pasta and meat. A bowl of minestrone featured lots of different vegetables and orchiette pasta, although not as dense as it might have been. The Mayfair salad flaunts shredded, not powdered, Parmesan cheese, extremely fresh croutons and a dressing that tastes like the real Mayfair, not the Caesar that the menu claimed.

Spaghetti with meatballs deserves its title as a comfort food, and Peppercini's is a good example of why. A slightly sweet tomato sauce carried a lot of fresh basil, cradling rather dense meatballs with a note of green pepper in them, just what's expected. Al dente pasta completed the triple play to make it just the thing for a cold wet night. On the other hand, an oversauced fettucini Alfredo was so wet it came in a soup bowl and was remarkably free of any taste of cheese, carrying instead an odd note of something trying to be garlic.

Hank's cheesecakes, always reliably good, are the primary dessert. However, there's something they describe as a "peanut butter mouse" that a visiting feline might love.

Servers know many of the regular customers, but fresh faces are made welcome, and things click along well. A new wine list was reportedly on the way. Good news, Clayton.

Pho Grand
Vietnamese Cuisine
3191 South Grand Boulevard
664-7435
Lunch and Dinner, Wednesday-Monday
Cash only
Wheelchair access: Passable

Do not think that the name of Pho Grand, this pioneering Vietnamese restaurant, is a pun on "faux grand." It's not false anything; it's exceptionally good and truly amazing, and the story of its success is that it's on the verge of expanding and moving to the house next door at 3195 South Grand Boulevard. This sturdy little place is a combination of the American Dream and The Little Engine That Could.

They've not raised prices in the decade or so they've been open, but they redecorated within the last few years, leaving the near-glorious tin ceiling, now painted gold, added wallpaper and painted the arched window frames in a harmonious dark green, adding a degree of elegance. But the prices remain mind-bogglingly reasonable, drawing droves of eaters for bowls of noodles and soups, and the plate-lunch-type dishes that set them apart from later arrivals on the scene. Beer, tea and soda, too.

Vietnamese appetizer rolls take a little getting used to, being served cold, wrapped in a translucent rice crepe that shows the noodles and meats and fresh cilantro as impressionistic blurs of color and shape. Dipping sauces come, a sweet-sour vinegar and a thicker one, topped with chopped peanuts. Try each; we can't decide whether they are better than the tangy rolls, which vary mainly in the type of meat inside. There deep-fried rolls wrapped in lettuce, and a lotus root salad is also offered.

The food here is served individually, rather than on platters, so sharing takes a little reaching. It's not hard to imagine diners sitting with a protective arm wrapped around a bowl of noodles, as though they were guarding test answers from a wandering eye at the next desk, though the servings are generous enough that such precautions are superfluous. Thirteen types of soup are offered, with things like charbroiled pork, medium rare- or well-done beef, meatballs or pork, shrimp and crab sticks.

We were very impressed with the chicken with lemon grass and hot chili, ga xao xa ot, small pieces of chicken with green and white onion, only mildly hot but full of wonderful flavors. With it came a ball of rice, not steamed but sticky and dressed in what the proprietor describes as "lemon sauce"—lemon grass, we believe, rather than lemon fruit—with shredded carrot, green onion and fresh cilantro. The rice is, in a word, wonderful, both solo and with the meat, and we could make a meal of it alone.

Based on the St. Louis experience, Vietnamese curries are not far from the style of those found in Thailand. The curry pastes and coconut milk that form their base taste very similar, exotic and enticing. The squid curry, cari muc, is one of the two most expensive single dishes on the menu at $5.95 (a $9 campfire pot serves two), and would be worth twice the price with lots of tender, tasty squid in a coppery sauce.

We always end Vietnamese meals with their iced coffee, thick and sweet and rich. Pho Grand's is so good that it seems to have overlays of chocolate.

Snappy service and good English (for clients who might be hesitant about that sort of thing). Dinner is less than $8, and may be the best bargain in the city.

Portabella
Modern American Cuisine
15 North Central Avenue, Clayton
725-6588
Lunch Monday-Friday, Dinner Monday-Saturday
Credit cards: All major
Wheelchair access: Comfortable

Perhaps the reverse of the Bermuda Triangle is the Clayton Rectangle, where new restaurants appear like mushrooms, springing up when your back is turned. One of the first of this surge may not be a mushroom, but it's named for one—the fat, succulent portobello. The Del Pietro family, veteran purveyors of family-style Italian food at numerous locations, put Portabella in the space once occupied by Port St. Louis, and turned the family style accordingly.

One thing that has remained is the happy uproar of people, often in large groups, having a good time. It is, admittedly, a very noisy restaurant, particularly for those seated near the bar on a Friday night, when the Bright Young Things of Clayton gather for what looks like an immense cocktail party from the 1950s, little black dresses and all. (The giveaway is that none of those martini glasses contain gin.)

Don't let the uproar fool you. This is a place for serious food. Sensitive patrons should pretend they're in New York, where nearly all restaurants are loud.

The menu is wide-ranging, with designer pizzas, house-made ravioli which lead an imaginative pasta selection, and entrees different enough to be interesting without tending to cutesiness. Somewhere on the menu there are always portobello mushrooms. One of the most successful uses is a first course where it's grilled, along with some asparagus, and topped with a balsamic vinaigrette. The dressing is very intense, used in small quantities to avoid overwhelming the vegetables, which are perfectly cooked. The sweetness of balsamico is well-balanced, and the remnants of it often get mopped up with one of the small cubes of focaccia that populate the bread basket. Like most Italian restaurants these days, there's a flask of olive oil on the table, and a waiter pours some into a dish, then grates Parmesan cheese into it, making a delicious, but treacherous combination for dunking bread. Treacherous? Certainly—the first drop to fall always hits the center of a newly purchased, light-colored tie.

Both seafood salad and crab cakes are excellent, but on a recent visit, we tried the oven-roasted mussels. A small pan brought more than a dozen, hot and puffy in a fine broth seasoned with tomato and garlic. The broth, so fragrant and tasty, was so good with the focaccia that we didn't realize that the crostini promised on the menu had been forgotten

Risotto also is a winner here, dazzling in combination with porcinis, asparagus, leeks and thyme, but a recent special that was truly special involved roasted walleyed pike served with scallops and a little pasta, penne dressed with garlic oil and capers and garnished with tomato. It was outstanding, with the sweet fish and shellfish standing up nicely against the tang of the capers. The oil and caper brine, plus the fresh tomatoes, combined to bring forth a pasta that was very different, and remarkably good.

Calf's liver is a standard on the menu with roasted onions, pancetta, and a balsamic vinegar pan sauce. The liver is cut thickly enough to be cooked rare, and though it was tasty, we'd probably ask for medium rare next time. Two large slices arrived with the savory accompaniments, and our only quibble was that it wasn't trimmed well, resulting in more chewiness than we prefer. Table mates seem unable to keep their hands off the matchstick potatoes that accompany the liver, so the kitchen sends out a mountain of them.

Desserts range from simple to grand in concept, but when it comes to flavor, everything was grand. We had a blueberry cobbler, more of what we would term a crisp, in an individual gratin dish with a crumble top and large fresh berries that weren't oversweetened or overcooked and had kept their tang. A fine piece of work. Tiramisu goes beyond what St. Louis has been seeing for the last decade, and Portabella's version, a major improvement, brings it nestled in a free-form cup made of phyllo dough. Sprinkled on top and alongside are crumbs of amaretti, the crunchy Italian cookie. The textures of pastry and crumbs provide marvelous contrast to the creamy, cool tiramisu, and make it almost a brand-new dessert. Someone in the kitchen was really thinking.

The wine list is strong on Italian imports and on Italian grapes—"Cal-Ital" is the word among West Coast growers. Service is smooth, and when the restaurant isn't jumping—late on a Friday evening when the bar is still roaring and the dining room is slowing down—the Del Pietros have the grace to let people linger over dessert and coffee in a style that would make their Old World forebears approve. And since we mentioned New York restaurants above, we might add that these aren't New York prices—about $30 a head, which will barely get you seated at Balthazar or Le Cirque.

Posh Nosh
Jewish Delicatessen
8115 Maryland Avenue, Clayton
862-1890
Breakfast, Lunch and early Dinner, Monday–Saturday
Credit cards: All major
Wheelchair access: Difficult

Jammed with memorabilia, and with people crunching pickles and sloshing through sauerkraut, the Posh Nosh is a Clayton stalwart in the Jewish delicatessen class. Lots of adventurous combinations here, like cole slaw on pastrami and we're sure that someone in the Clayton Quadrangle is probably ordering mayonnaise on corned beef, and getting it (to Woody Allen's dismay).

Ice cream chairs surround every table, even those in the alley on the east side of the shop, and every table has a tub of pickles and one of sauerkraut for nibbling throughout the meal. It's been part of the Posh Nosh experience for as long as we've known the place, and it's a pleasant touch that makes customers happy.

Entering the Posh Nosh, there are samples of the available breads, and a long list of things to put on them. Joe is a pastrami fan, and also likes the version made with turkey as something lighter in fat. Unfortunately, they lack some of the flavor and spicing. Better to eat the real stuff, and do it less often.

Time was when the photos on the Posh Nosh wall acted as a kind of living museum talking about Claytonians and how they grew, and we wish it were still here to keep us posted.

Protzel's Delicatessen
Jewish Delicatessen, What else?
7608 Wydown Boulevard, Clayton
721-4445
Breakfast, Lunch and early Dinner, Tuesday-Sunday
Cash only
Wheelchair access: Satisfactory

Bob and Evelyn Protzel stood out as St. Louis' delicatessen mavens for many years. Bob knew his pastrami, but he also was fast with a quip, turning a profit at it by writing comedy routines and radio commercials. Evelyn was the great earth mother; she had her own children in Ron and Alan, but Joe had the feeling that all her customers were her children—and some were her grandchildren. Joe talked and visited and bought smoked salmon and salami sandwiches and knishes at Protzel's for years, and nothing pleased him more than to see the boys take over after the all-too-sudden deaths of Bob and Evelyn.

In recent years, Protzel s has become more of a sandwich shop than a delicatessen, with more tables both inside and out.

You get almost as much advice from Ron and Alan as you did from their parents (but not nearly as much humor), and we swap stories about New York and Las Vegas and restaurants in between. Smoked salmon and pastrami and salami still are wonderful, but they come from commercial delicatessens in Chicago and New York. But gefilte fish (ground, spiced and baked, best with horseradish) and chicken soup and knishes and a variety of other dishes from Joe's childhood remain favorites. Alan has learned to slice lox properly, but only after creating a lox-and-cream-cheese spread from his mistakes.

The best in town for snacking and schmoozing.

Pueblo Nuevo Mexican Restaurant
Mexican Cuisine
7401 N. Lindbergh Boulevard, Hazelwood
831-6885
Lunch and Dinner, Monday-Saturday
Credit cards: All major
Wheelchair access: Passable

For old times' sake, and for familiarity, there's a rule of some sort that a meal at Pueblo Nuevo begins with one of the best guacamoles in town, completely ripe and lumpy in texture but smooth as silk in flavor, with garlic and a hint of pepper adding to the richness of the avocado itself. Pueblo Nuevo's is brilliant, but this small, spare Mexican restaurant, on a corner in a small strip mall north of the airport, also provides many things most folks haven't tried, so the decision-making starts straightaway. Whatever decisions are made, however, it's difficult to spend more than $13 a person for dinner.

Chicharrones are deep-fried nuggets of pork with lots of fat—"cracklin's, wonderful cracklin's," says the gallbladder—for a little finger snack. Chorizo with cheese is like chili con queso but with spicy sausage, like a pizza top without a crust, gooey and delicious. It's outstanding on fresh, warm chips that arrive with two sauces, a traditional but only passable red and a mo' better, mo' hotter green.

The meat here is significant. The beef is hamburger style, not shredded, but pork and chicken are tasty chunks and shreds with well-seasoned juices, and well worth trying. Tamales are fat and the masa cooks up fluffy; and they're available Christmas-style, with both red and green sauce. A delicious mole sauce, rich and with hints of cinnamon, improves enchiladas. We sampled a pork and a chicken, and picking the better was a toss-up. We've also tried their carne ranchera with red sauce, a very good pork stew, highlighted by splendid refried beans. Several vegetarian dishes are available, like enchiladas and calabaza con elote, a dish of squash and corn.

Vegetarian dishes, and other specials, go to the back of the menu. This is more authentic, they say, and we believe it, even though we also have to admit that fajitas are a Texas dish. It's always a big choice between pozole, the mild and wonderful main-course soup with pork, chicken and hominy, and the traditional toss-ins of a lime wedge and chopped onion, or birria, goat's meat in a red stew. People who like lamb will probably like this, too; it's extremely tasty, and of medium heat, if that's a concern.

We almost never have dessert here, because we're already stuffed. The flan is dense with a cream cheese-like ingredient; the capotirada also is dense. Sopapillas are always fun, though Joe thinks they should be a little lighter.

They make their own margaritas, which arrive in cactus-themed plastic glasses. From first glance to final exit, it's obvious that Pueblo Nuevo is about good food, not fancy trifles.

Pueblo Solis
Semi-Nuevo Mexican Cuisine

5127 Hampton Avenue
351-9000
Dinner Tuesday-Sunday
Credit cards: All major
Wheelchair access: Difficult

There's no way to resist saying this: This is Mom's home cooking, and we wish our moms cooked as well. Neil Solis' mother is in the kitchen of Pueblo Solis, slicing and dicing and working kitchen witchery (everyone knows that kitchen witches are good witches), helping him turn out a marvelous combination of traditional Mexican foods and contemporary dishes conceived with an eye to new uses for old ingredients.

So while there are guacamole and tacos and enchiladas and the like on the menu, there's a cilantro vinaigrette dressing for a green salad and roast chicken with achiote, a seasoning that uses annato and cumin and such to give it a distinctive flavor and color, too.

The wine list is nothing to get excited about, but this is a house that draws our cheers by making margaritas by hand, one at a time, and serving them in real glass (even though the stem is green and looks like a cactus. Whoever thought a cactus could give a better grip on a glass wet with condensation?) There's beer, of course, and some Chilean wine, and even Yago sangria, a name we haven't seen since Laclede Town was in flower.

Chips were hot, fresh, thin and perfectly drained. Four salsas came alongside. We found the bright green one excellent, the bright red one a little bitter. The other two were similar in color, but one seemed quite distinguished in its taste, a slight note of sweet punching up the other flavors. None were habenero-hot, but all were spicy.

The waiter's opening remark was that the salsas were as spicy as it got—everything else was cooled down for St. Louis palates, but they would be willing to turn the thermostat up on request. And for the most part, that was true. The guacamole, though, was the best we've had in years—chunky and smooth by turn with onion and tomato and avocado bits in it, and, yes, some heat. It came out so quickly, it must have been made beforehand, but it couldn't have been more than five or ten minutes old. A masterful version, we say.

Instead of appetizers, we asked for a few tamales to sample before our main courses. They're thinner than those at many Mexican restaurants, and an order comprises a large handful. They come filled with bean, pork or cheese and jalapeno, but don't quiver because the jalapenos are well-cooked, and therefore mild. The pork was delicious, but the bean tamale lifted tamales to another level. The combination of beans, masa (cornmeal) and seasoning is superb, not needing even a drop of salsa to enhance it. A serendipitous finding.

The menu lists roast chicken and chicken mole, but we tried a special of grilled beef with mole sauce and potatoes. The beef was rare and very tender, the mole sauce exciting. Moles are sometimes called chocolate sauces, but a little grated unsweetened chocolate is a minor ingredient in a proper mole, which combines chiles and other aromatic seasonings. Their pungency varies as much as the recipes do—like poultry dressing, everyone does it a little differently—and this one, while spicy, was far from hot and a fine piece of work. The potatoes, alas, were mostly undercooked, but the ones that weren't were delicious—and they benefited from the mole, too.

Pueblo Solis has menudo on the menu every day, a brilliant deep red broth punctuated with yellow hominy. Dishes of chopped onions, a couple of lime wedges, and pickled jalapenos and carrots come alongside. Menudo is like oxtail soup in that it is an extremely rich, flavorful soup, the broth so rich it's almost sticky in the mouth. The redness comes from pureed chiles, but the heat was minor; something this mouth-filling doesn't have to be spicy. Yes, the meat is tripe, but we urge a reluctant eater to try it. Maybe even skip the tripe itself if the texture is bothersome. Tripe is tender, but its texture is different from that of muscle meats like steaks or chops. It takes time, too, and we can cite Joe as an example of someone who sampled it several times before it won him over. Menudo is the sort of dish that another generation would characterize as putting meat on your bones. It's wonderful.

Dessert is mango cheesecake or Mexican rice pudding. We went for the cheesecake. It isn't very mango-ey, but the texture is wonderful, fluffy rather than buttery, with a graham cracker crust that tosses in its own bit of flavor and texture. Tabs will be somewhere in the $15-$20 range.

Mom does a great job.

Ramon's El Dorado
Mexican Cuisine
1701 St. Louis Road, Collinsville, Ill.
(618) 344-6435
5924 North Illinois, Fairview Heights Ill.
(618) 628-11648
Lunch and Dinner, every day
Credit cards: AE, MC, V
Wheelchair access: Difficult

The first time one of us visited Ramon's El Dorado (where Collinsville Road divides just east of Fairmount Park) it was necessary to walk carefully around the steps to the grease pits in this former service station. But Ramon Otero persevered, expanded into first one and then a second back room, enjoyed success, and opened a branch in Fairview Heights. The restaurant has been around for thirty years. It's had its ups and downs, and the current status seems to show evidence of a little bit of both. Tabs run under $20 a head.

Guacamole has slipped badly. Time was when it was fresh, chunky and pebbled with tomato and onion and other good things. The current version is quite smooth, underseasoned and tasted faintly of bacon, or more likely, bacos. Chips, on the other hand, were hot and crisp; the red salsa that accompanied them displayed tongue-tingling heat.

Uncommon items pop up here and there on the menu. A few of them are just different names for familiar items—a taco suave is a soft taco, tastier than the crisp, fried ones. A gaucho is a fat, soft corn tortilla piled with beef chunks in a spicy sauce, some refried beans, a little guacamole, lots of shredded iceberg lettuce, some chopped tomato and some powdery cheese. It's a good combination, the crunchy-chewy-soft and hot-cold textures and flavors bouncing through your mouth. A sope (pronounced SO-pay) consists of another of those fat tortillas, split open like a pita and stuffed with shredded chicken in a rich, lightly spiced sauce, and more of the lettuce, tomatoes and cheese. The two of them made for a substantial entree, and offered solid evidence that corn tortillas have more flavor and texture than those made from flour. (In Mexico, flour means "wheat flour," and was once a class distinction because wheat was more expensive and more difficult to obtain than corn.)

Flautas, those cigar-shaped, tightly rolled, deep-fried tortillas, were excellent, but taquitos were greasy—the deep fryer was acting silly, the waitress reported just before they arrived—with a pleasantly spiced ground beef filling. Closer to chewy than crispy, they were accompanied by a little more guacamole, the requisite lettuce, tomatoes and cheese, and the rice and beans that are ubiquitous on Mexican dinners around here. Carnitas came with the same sides, plus lots of sliced fresh onion, a nice touch, but the carnitas were just large chunks of pork that had been deep-fried. Sadly, they hadn't been allowed to reach the state of chewy brownness that comes when they've been carefully cooked down so the meat juice almost caramelizes on the surfaces.

Both the beans and rice run near the head of the local pack; the former well-seasoned but not hot-spicy, the latter topped with a little of that beef in red sauce. The split ends on the rice were a sure sign of overcooking, but the beef rescued it from anonymity quite well.

Unsweet margaritas, made with a mix but with an adequate amount of tequila, the usual assortment of imported beers, and a bartender who poured white zinfandel when white wine was ordered about covers the liquor department. The restaurant is a local favorite, and you can eavesdrop on some amusing conversations.

Remy's Kitchen & Wine Bar

Modern Mediterranean-American

222 South Bemiston Avenue, Clayton
726-5757
Lunch Monday-Friday, Dinner Monday-Saturday
Credit cards: All major
Wheelchair access: Satisfactory through garage

One of the marks of a real city is that you can eat at some kind of restaurant at any hour of the day or night. How big the city is, and how sophisticated it is, is marked by how late you can eat well. St. Louis, thank goodness, is moving right along that road. On a weekday night, we arrived at Remy's just before 9:30. The place was jumping. The inquiry "Dinner for two?" came without the faintest lift of an eyebrow. And best of all, we weren't the last to arrive for a full meal.

Once-sleepy Clayton is finally admitting it wants to be known as more than just a county seat, or as a small Midwestern town that is home to fewer than fifteen thousand souls. It is becoming a hip social spot. People work late in offices. Hardly anyone wants dinner before an early movie, and the meal can be the focus of the evening, in the European style. In Paris, restaurateurs of the higher style will sneer and concierges will smile sadly at reservation requests earlier than 8 p.m..

So hooray for places that stay open late.

Like its siblings, the Blue Water Grill and the Big Sky Cafe, Remy's offers small plates, both hot and cold, and larger ones. These can be mixed and matched, and servers are always careful to ask diners exactly the order of the order. A stack of plates is on every table for easy divvying up.

Like many of the newer restaurants, the menu is in a near-constant state of change. Change is good. Persevere. You will be rewarded. Remy's kitchen, under the deft hand of Lisa Slay, has a particular gift for combining flavors, not only the Mediterranean ones that are sort of a theoretical framework for the restaurant, but other, slightly quirky ones. It's a good example of the modern truth in restaurants that just because a combination sounds peculiar doesn't mean it won't taste good.

One of our openers was scallops on a bed of shredded, steamed spinach. The scallops, about an inch across, were grilled and removed just in time to keep their characteristic sweet tenderness. Lemon, and probably a little garlic, punched up the spinach, which had barely been wilted, so quickly and lightly had it been cooked, a perfect tangy contrast to the seafood. Stuffed grape leaves had the traditional filling of lamb and rice, heavy on the lamb and easy on the oregano. Grape leaves are always chewy, and varying textures, plus the flavor of tomato sauce, blended nicely.

A salad of Belgian endive, red cabbage, black mission figs and feta cheese carried a minimal amount of a balsamic vinegar reduction, barely coating the vegetables. This is an excellent example of those odd-sounding combinations that make you go "Huh?", but it certainly works. If endive, pear, Roquefort and walnuts can, why not this? Every bite sought out another, a cardinal sign of a fine dish.

There seems to be a meat loaf lover in every family, and Remy's version reciprocates perfectly. Mediterranean flavors predominate, with a slight hint of garlic, a definite presence of what seemed like cayenne pepper, and perhaps a hint of cumin. Mashed potatoes, a side dish that has thankfully returned to dinner tables around town, are kept simple here. The flavor is pure potato, with perhaps a little garlic, but not enough to drown out the main flavor.

And then there's a blissful sandwich of beef tenderloin, feta cheese, tomato and hummus on what's basically a focaccia bun. It was a little messy to eat, but a clear example of the way Tim Mallett, Slay and friends do things. The waitress said it was probably going to become a permanent fixture on the menu, and it should. The beef was tender, nicely rare, and the combination perfect. The second half of it was even better the next day, cold from the refrigerator.

Bread pudding has been a semi-regular on Remy's menu. We'd be happier if it were a little moister and the apples more tender, but diners love it. The chocolate mousse in puff pastry with berries is wonderful, the mousse fluffy and rich with chocolate, the pastry crisp and the berries counterpointing the flavor with sharpness and notes of their own. The newest chocolate dessert is a bittersweet chocolate tart. It has a chocolate cookie-crumb crust and it's filled with very good ganache, the chocolate-cream mixture that would make your old Nikes taste good. This is very simple and very chocolate, mainline stuff for chocoholics. Always the carpers, we'd have liked a little more of the port wine reduction that serves as its garnish.

The wine list here, particularly the immense by-the-glass selection, is among the best—and best value—in town. These folks are four-plus serious about the art of the grape, not just the pretty stuff that goes with it like posters and witty sayings. The wine guy—this place is too relaxed to call him a sommelier—knows every bit of his stock and talks about it with excitement and significant knowledge, on anyone's level. Well-written descriptions on the wine lists, and three demi-glass flights of related wines widen the tasting experience. The restaurant is big in the wines from Bonny Doon Vineyard, where Randall Grahm is not only a great winemaker, but also a man of great literary discernment. After all, the late Stanley Elkin was his all-time favorite author, and they enjoyed an evening of food, wine and literature on one of Grahm's visits.

Bonny Doon's famous Rhone-style wines are winners, with good prices, and now Grahm has property in France, and is making dark, almost-black wines of great flavor and depth. Good values by the bottle or by the glass, and some exciting food and wine combinations.

Maybe it's minor, but Remy's makes one statement that grates. Small, but like wearing unshined shoes to a formal wedding. That's the tacky plastic table covers, which would be more at home in a diner. They give a poor initial impression, because they're the first thing a guest sees upon sitting down. Condensation from water glasses forms puddles, small spills are not absorbed. They're unsightly, and in a restaurant where Mallett and Slay are so careful to make what's on the plates look attractive, the plates themselves look like Tiffany diamonds in Wal-Mart settings.

Riddle's Penultimate
American Eclectic
6307 Delmar Boulevard, University City
725-6985
Lunch and Dinner, Monday-Saturday
Credit cards: All major
Wheelchair access: Passable

Andy Ayers has been filling our stomachs and bending our ears for close to two decades, and both areas are better for the time spent with him. Bulky, bearded and gravel-voiced, Ayers is a die-hard Cardinal fan and fighter for civil liberties and personal freedom. A battered Red Bird newsboy's cap (instead of a traditional toque or trendy gimme cap) puts his baseball feelings on his head, and though you can't see them, they also are worn on his sleeve and in his heart. So are his political and social feelings, which can often be read as letters to the editor in local newspapers.

Ayers and his wife, Paula the Dessert Queen, are right at home in the University City Loop, the last bastion of hippie costume and attitude in the area. It's all a natural feeling, too. Joe lived in the Loop when he first came to St. Louis in 1955, when it boasted a wonderful book-and-record store, two hardware stores, two movie theaters, Mac Brown's Shell station, Rinaldi's Italian restaurant and other exciting enterprises, including Pratzel's Bakery, where a post-midnight shopper could walk into the back room, pick bagels fresh from the oven, put them in a bag and leave payment (exact change, please) on the counter. The area has gone through good days and bad ones, but it has retained its all-natural flavor. Individuals riding their dreams, not committees studying flip charts and making reports, gave the community its start and kept it vibrant and interesting through the years.

We first met Andy when he and Paula had a small sandwich and pizza shop on Natural Bridge Road in Bel-Nor, near the University of Missouri-St. Louis. It was successful, and in 1985, when Bobby's Creole left the Loop and Ayers had a chance to move in, he took it.

His irrepressible spirit, plus his imagination and talent in the kitchen overcome the casual and laid-back—sometimes too much so—attitude of the furnishings, staff and customers, have made him a success. Ayers, who admits to having lived in a pickup truck in Columbia, Mo., during his most-hippie days, was the first restaurateur in the area to push a wine-by-the-glass program, and his wine list is among the city's best, largest and most accurately priced. When it comes to Missouri wines, it is the city's best and largest. He knows Missouri wines, too, having served numerous times as a judge in the State Fair competition.

Riddle's opened as a Cajun-Creole restaurant, much in the style of the spot it replaced. But times have changed, and "eclectic" fits the menu to perfection. It fits his family, too; he has relatives who pickle his herring, and the tangy little fish, filleted beautifully, are delicious, with lots of spices and some lightly cured, still-crunchy onions adding the right balance to the vinegar and dill and finishing with a fine pop in the aftertaste. And speaking of Andy's relatives, his aging ice cream maker is kept in top shape by another, whose skill at repairing small machinery matches his absence of same at pinochle.

That ice cream, with about a half-dozen flavors usually available, is a glorious dessert, improved when it accompanies Paula's spectacular pies. Her fruit pies are our favorite, but she does a superior job on pecan, not overpoweringly sweet, but hearty and delicious, with lots of plump pecans and a lard-based crust that practically melts in the mouth. There are real red-hots in his cinnamon ice cream (great with apple pie), and nationality designations like Belgian chocolate and French vanilla ("the red hots are American," said a waitress one night), plus superior coffee and spectacular fresh strawberry and peach in season.

The menu also is heavy with fresh, local vegetables, fruit and herbs, and the Ayerses encourage area farmers and diners to be experimental and organic. Appetizer, entree and dessert at Riddle's is about $25 a person.

Riddle's Penultimate (the name, Andy says, means he may still have one more restaurant to run) is sometimes an off-putting experience for first-time diners. The entrance is cluttered and dark, and there can be a great deal of noise from both musicians and customers in the front room. It sometimes takes courage to walk past the bar and find someone at the desk. The back room is feebly lit, neither attractively dim nor brain-surgery bright, and when the rest room doors swing open, there's an occasional aroma of disinfectant/air freshener that is disconcerting.

But a menu that offers white, shiitake, oyster and portobello mushrooms in different dishes shows promise, and the promise is fulfilled on the plate. Mushrooms stuffed with crawfish have been around for a long time and are delightful, with a shot of pepper awakening the taste buds.

In season, a mess of sauteed shiitakes is a delightful appetizer, and jerked chicken, smoked trout and the aforementioned herring are solid. The trout is smoked, as the herring is pickled, in the kitchen.

Most entrees come with either soup or salad, and the garden vegetable soup is a longtime favorite. Chilled fruit soups are a summer spectacular; just as good as a dessert as it is as an appetizer. The house salad is topped with a major pile of shredded carrot and thinly-sliced red onion, and is standard.

A pair of entrees, shrimp Sara and chicken Major Grey, go back to the early days, and are proven. The chicken breast, tangy with the chutney, is a delight. A new specialty, a solid probability to gain the same classic status, is barbecued pork, Memphis style. The pork butt is rubbed and slow cooked, and comes out just right. Scallops, salmon and other seafood dishes also are winners from a menu that changes daily. Beef and pasta dishes are good, and the roast beef sandwich is accompanied by a superior remoulade sauce.

The Loop attitude demands casual, and Andy Ayers' service and decor fit right in. Diners, however, demand excellence, and Ayers delivers again— few of his beloved Cardinals get two hits a night.

The Ritz-Carlton—The Grill

Modern American Cuisine

100 Carondelet Plaza, Clayton
863-6300
Dinner nightly
Credit cards: All major
Wheelchair access: Satisfactory

Why does the Ritz in St. Louis never quite seem to get it all together? The chain historically has been among the leaders in returning first-rate food to hotel dining rooms. They clearly aim to be the best, and show it both with their pricing and their general aura of luxury. In other cities, notably San Francisco, they have succeeded beyond the dreams of anyone forced to eat in an American hotel during the '70s, the nadir of hotel dining.

In St. Louis, the superb wine list and elegant room point toward the sort of experience they want guests to have. But when a restaurant charges $44 for a Dover sole and $50 for a bottle of red wine from St. James, Mo., it has an obligation to deliver near-perfection. The Ritz doesn't.

It comes close with a crab cake, however. A nearly two-inch-high cylinder of crabmeat, very lightly browned, seemed to be nothing but the essence of utter crabbiness. No green pepper, no trendy seasonings, just crab flavor. We wonder if it wasn't helped along with some sort of a reduction of crab stock. A Baltimorean like our curmudgeonly chowhound, Uncle Jack, might not consider the shape to be a crab cake, but to us, it was wonderful.

A squid and bell pepper salad had some greens with it and wore a citrusy dressing (lime according to the menu), but we got hints of other fruits as well. It was, as described, spicy, but the squid was mushy, a texture unknown to us in our squid experience. A tenderizer? Days in an acid marinade? Watercress, jicama and beet salad had curly endive but no jicama, and the tarragon-mango emulsion didn't carry much flavor of either. Inoffensive is the kindest way to describe it.

First courses also include things like juniper rubbed squab, corn bisque with grilled prawns, and a Caesar salad. Prices go from $6.50 to $12.

Striped bass, unusual on St. Louis menus, arrived in a soup bowl with the promised mashed red potatoes, still lumpy as promised and wonderfully tasty. The menu described it as being in a roasted garlic and fennel broth, but there was no garlic, no fennel, and no broth in sight, only a little steamed spinach. The fish was poached or quickly roasted, and quite moist, but one of the three pieces tasted strangely metallic.

Pork tenderloin adobo was accented with a piece of polenta with sweet onions and a relish that had some chipotle chiles in it. The pork was requested medium and arrived rare. It was very tender and juicy, a fine tenderloin cut in inch-thick pieces. Adobo sauces may or may not be smoky, depending on their heritage. This one, a deep siena color, expressed something odd in its smokiness.

Some of the other choices among the entrees are strip steak, sea scallops and mussels on pasta, a lobster and prawn tempura, and yellowtail tuna. Prices begin at $20, and top out with the $44 sole.

Individual souffles are available for dessert ($9). The raspberry Grand Marnier floated in, accompanied by a thick sauce that was streaked with raspberry coulis. The waiter opened the souffle's top and spooned in some sauce. When he left and we cut through the top, we discovered an immense air pocket and not much souffle. It tasted good, although nearly overcooked. The remaining desserts are all $7. A Napoleon had been in damp air long enough to be soggy. The sabayon between the layers was pleasant and the fruit was good, but the caramelization discussed in the menu had been overlooked.

The omission was not crucial, but far too many details are being overlooked in a restaurant that is probably the city's most expensive restaurant, a price statement which tells us it claims to be the best.

The Ritz-Carlton—The Restaurant
Sunday Brunch

It's too much to hope that the Ritz has finally ditched its stiff trademark phrase, "It is my pleasure to serve you." But we didn't hear it once during a visit to the Sunday brunch. The Ritz should be ritzy, naturally, but that canned-sounding phrase has provoked reactions from irritation to giggles from us. What's wrong with "I was glad to help"? or even, "You're welcome"?

The atmosphere, once hinting at tea with the queen, also seems to have relaxed, and the result is an improvement. Guests dress in their best casual clothes, people at the door smile, and one feels encouraged rather than intimidated.

To be sure, the price is a stiff $40 a head to carry your own food through a buffet line. By Pollacks' first law, this should be the finest brunch in town. It isn't, although it's particularly strong in seafood and desserts.

Happily, the coffee is great. The coffee-urn-scrubbing elves have been hard at work, producing a fine, deeply flavored brew. Orange juice is indeed icy cold and fresh-squeezed, though it comes from one of those whole-orange machines.

In what is labeled a Champagne brunch, the Ritz serves Cook's, an old St. Louis brand. The restaurant poured Cook's version of spumante, sweet enough for a decent Mimosa cocktail but hardly a match for the seafood. When we discovered its sweetness, we declined, and the server found some drier, and more palatable, Brut. Still, to serve a bottle of wine that retails for less than $4 as a beverage at a $40 meal seems cheap in such an elegant dining room.

The seafood table has cold shrimp and oysters on the half shell, lots of smoked fish, sushi and two kinds of caviar. The oysters suffer from being opened in advance, but the shrimp is good, fresh and briny, with a fine proportion of horseradish in the sauce. The sushi seemed lackluster. Smoked fish includes a wonderful mackerel wearing crushed black peppercorns and mustard seeds and some fine, very simple smoked tuna, as well as mussels and shrimp. The smoked salmon has a platter to itself. Caviar is small black lumpfish and red salmon, the latter easily the best reasonably-priced caviar. There's an omelet station directly opposite, and this gives us a chance to create one of our favorites, a sour cream and salmon caviar omelet.

Traditional breakfast items rest in chafing dishes near the omelet site. Bacon is thick and crisp; the sausages are almost too ungreasy. The other egg dish was a Benedict variation with a marvelous bearnaise sauce. Stuffed French toast came from real French bread, hollowed out slightly and filled with a cream cheese and blueberry mixture, sliced, soaked and sauteed. A strawberry sauce was served in lieu of a syrup, and it was well above average.

Lunch dishes included roast pork tenderloin, a penne with peppers, grilled vegetables, chicken breasts with an Alfredo-like sauce, and grilled mahi-mahi with a tarragon sauce that was tasty, despite the fish having been too long in the chafing dish.

While the Ritz-Carlton chain should be complimented for its position at the forefront of the movement to reintroduce fine dining to hotels, its weakness here had been desserts. But no longer. At brunch, the dessert table looked wonderful, almost too perfect, but our suspicions proved very much unfounded. The magazine-cover triple-layer chocolate cake was moist and rich with chocolate; some raspberry was hiding somewhere in the recipe. A cassis mousse, unmolded to resemble a cheesecake, was creamy-fluffy and delightfully flavored. And an almond cake-look-alike turned out to be a dacquoise, layers of crisp meringue layered with creamy filling, a sure winner.

In the slightly-changed Ritz service, it remains crisp, rapid and painstaking, mostly. And there was live music, too, a luxurious accent, and no less than what one would expect.

Riverport Casino Center—Town Square Buffet
Show-Me Las Vegas—Food, not Showgirls

Riverport Casino Center, 777 Casino Center, Hazelwood
533-7777
Breakfast, Lunch and Dinner, every day
Credit cards: All major
Wheelchair access: Satisfactory

Note: All the gambling boats in the St. Louis area have large and inexpensive food service, serving three or more meals a day. We chose Riverport as a representative sample.

Brace yourself. This isn't like eating at Denny's. We suspect this place must be constantly busy. Even early on a week night there was a line, although it moved well. It's a considerable bargain, but people who say they go to casinos for the food are like those who say they buy Playboy for the articles. Still, the food was surprisingly good, and other casino visits have brought very acceptable meals, as long as one does not expect gourmet delicacies.

The format is strictly buffet, except for drinks. Diners pay in advance, and are shown to tables. A waitress takes drink orders; non-alcoholic ones are included in the price, beer is extra. And suddenly, it's open season on the tables. The food is arrayed at various stations, some with formal lines and some without. People seem polite, however, and we hope they remember it on the all-you-can-eat-crab-legs nights. The number of items is staggering. We counted fifty-six entrees and side dishes, plus more than a dozen soups and salads with their toppings, and then you get to the various breads, and a huge circular station that's just desserts.

In an operation this big and this popular, food moves quickly. The customer is the one who benefits. Fried food doesn't stay around long enough to get soggy. In addition, it arrives from the kitchen crisp and well-drained and tasting of catfish or chicken, rather than just breading. The other major meats are roast turkey—we saw only breasts being carved, but it's the real thing, not extruded stuff—roast beef, which is the least successful, being cooked until gray and rather tough, and a roast pork, moist and flavorful.

The pork is part of the Southern food area, one of the most successful. Between it and the New Orleans-style food, they offered prime Americana, red beans and sausage that were well spiced and not dried out, mashed sweet potatoes that showed the white foam of marshmallow but weren't sickly sweet, little new potatoes cooked in crab boil to make them spicy. Cornbread muffins were fresh and tender.

The pasta station featured the thicker pastas, which take the heat without getting too soft. An Alfredo wouldn't have passed in Rome, but was okay here, with mushrooms adding an acceptable accent. There were mashed potatoes, small bakers, oven-roasts and others, all acceptable. Asian food was basic, simple stuff like sweet and sour chicken, a vegetable stir-fry, and some deep-fried dumplings and spring rolls. The filling in the latter two were distinctive and well spiced, also crisp and fresh and well-drained. Barbecue is the oven-baked stuff, although people seemed excited over the ribs and pleased with the pizzas.

The dessert station had ice cream, scooped by hand, and with various toppings; four kinds of pie, including a couple that were also available sugar-free; five different cakes; Belgian waffles; bananas Foster; and two similar-looking kinds of bread pudding. The one without raisins was by far the more successful of the two, being moist and tender and pairing up well with a bourbon sauce or the Bananas Foster. The pies showed evidence of mass-produced crusts.

Service is rapid and affable, and a return from a foraging trip usually shows a clean table, refilled water glasses and fresh silverware. As for decor, well, it reminded us of a long-ago department store tearoom, except for the exuberant vegetable salt and pepper shakers. The visit was an experiment that bears repeating.

R.L. Steamers
Seafood
1227 Tamm Avenue
644-0101
Lunch Tuesday-Saturday, Dinner Tuesday-Sunday; Brunch on Sunday
Credit cards: MC, V
Wheelchair access: Passable

The writing's on the wall at R.L. Steamers, and customers should pay attention to it if they enjoy bad puns. The otherwise generally restrained decor at this Dogtown fish house wouldn't lead one to expect long blackboards near the ceiling. Foot-high letters make pronouncements like, "Frankly, Scallop, I don't give a clam."

There's often a long list of off-the-menu specials, and they, too, deserve attention. This is probably the only place in town that offers smelt, small fish fried up whole, sweet and crispy and impeccably drained. Fish lovers can dispense with the tartar sauce with red onion. A squirt of lemon, a sprinkle of salt, and down they go—the heat of cooking softens the bones so that they seem to disappear.

Oyster nachos have been on the menu since the door swung open, and they're winners, the oysters beautifully fried in cornmeal and resting on quarters of crispy tortilla with a little cheese cushioning them. A dribble of chipotle and avocado cream add the right note. The salsa is more of a fresh corn relish, spiced like a pico de gallo. Crescent City egg rolls, filled with crawfish, alligator sausage and red beans, ended up in a moderately hot Thai peanut sauce. Surprisingly, the rolls didn't swing, but the sauce sure did.

In fact, R.L. should consider offering it as a salad dressing. The salads were of mixed greens, the modern kind, not just iceberg and romaine, but they were tired. A Caesar dressing, described as mild, was downright meek. How can a seafood restaurant slight the hallowed anchovy? And a Greek vinaigrette was heavy on the vinegar, light on the oregano, and absolutely begged for a little feta cheese.

One night a special of petrale sole, the tasty fish often featured in San Francisco, was a winner, perfectly cooked and served with artichokes and capers. The blackened mahi-mahi was spicy, not overcooked, and nestled in a Worcestershire and sherry butter sauce. The tilapia, one of the tastiest of the milder fish, had a lemon caper sauce that worked adequately, but next time we'd have it just with a wedge of lemon. Crab cakes, on every menu these days, were a major disappointment with mostly claw meat and filler, and not much flavor. We're generally big fans, but only if they're made right, with lump meat. There's also a chicken breast, a steak and a pork tenderloin for the landlocked heart.

The standard side dishes here always include a strange rice mixture that has little orange and green lentil-sized things that chew like pasta. The mixture is innocuous, although occasionally undercooked. The other vegetable on the plate varies—one night it was stir-fried celery, a commendable effort to leap past the multiple squashes found in so many restaurants.

Desserts appear to come from Truffes, Helen Fletcher's laudable company, so you're probably safe with anything. A dozen wines by the glass, a barely passable list, not even up to a gentleman's C, and certainly not what you'd expect where a dinner check can pass $25 a person.

Royal Chinese B.B.Q.
Seafood and Chinese-style Barbecued Meats
8406 Olive Boulevard, University City
991-1888
Lunch and Dinner, every day
Credit cards: DSC, MC, V
Wheelchair access: Passable

There is, simply, no other Chinese restaurant in St. Louis like Royal Chinese B.B.Q. No egg foo yung, no fried wonton, no egg roll. But the joint is jumpin' seven days a week with people who want something Chinese—and different.

Right inside the door is a confrontation with hanging ducks dripping their subcutaneous fat away, strips of pork loin, red from spices and doing the same indolent act, and a large, active cutting block where a cleaver is taken to hunks of meat en route to hungry diners. It's the most San Franciscan of St. Louis restaurants, and the crowd itself is varied—solo diners to a table that can, and often does, seat ten; most ethnic and economic backgrounds; chefs from some of St. Louis' finest restaurants seeking new tastes on a night out; and several different languages bouncing across tables. Two familiar fish tanks are functional rather than aesthetic; one for fish, another for lobsters and crabs.

There are two menus; one a single sheet in English backed with Chinese characters, the second a small folder with markings to indicate new prices and items no longer offered, but still full of exciting things. Two menus should be enough, of course. But wait—there's a board covered with Day-Glo pieces of paper. Specials are written in black marker; mostly, but not entirely, bilingual. It's extremely adventurous (frog legs satay), and might well be passed by on the first visit. The two menus provide a surfeit of choices. The board may bring dizziness.

There are no traditional first courses here. Remember? No egg rolls. No dumplings. Just plunge right in, maybe splitting a vegetable platter for two, or dividing two things for four. Whether 'tis better to face the roast meats from the window or the fresh fish from the tank is as tough a choice as Hamlet ever had. Wok-cooked shrimp with salt and pepper have Szechuan pepper, aromatic and tangy, and arrive in the shell. Heads remain, but intrepid eaters know merely to yank them off. Many diners don't shell the shrimp beyond that and just crunch away.

Many seafood dishes come with either black bean sauce or ginger and scallion. The ginger is a little spicier, the beans are rich and show a texture that contrasts nicely with oysters or clams. None of the dishes flame with red peppers; a sharp ginger tang is as spicy as it gets. We're particularly fond of either of the crab variations, but then we're quite happy eating with our fingers. The ginger-scallion sauce also works for an oyster pot and a fish head pot. The same earthenware pots—and be careful; they really hold the heat—also are used for other stews to be spooned, a little at a time, over the rice. We were blown away by a seafood eggplant pot with garlic sauce. Squid, shrimps and scallops were interspersed with chunks of lavender-skinned Chinese eggplant in a succulent sweet gravy, sweet the way onions and garlic get when cooked a long time. Eggplant is notorious for soaking up liquid, and here it acts as a sponge for this luscious juice; in other words, it's a perfect dish for the eggplant. Crispy shrimp Peking style are close to sweet and sour, but sauteed rather than deep-fried, with a very thick, bright red sauce studded with garlic and surrounded with a wreath of broccoli florets. Extremely old-fashioned.

Yes, there's meat, too. Begin with the roasted meats, solo or in the various noodle dishes. It's a battle which is better—the honey grilled B.B.Q. pork or the roast duck. The duck has paddled in a marinade with soy and anise, and comes out with a sweet, crisp skin and very little fat. The pork is incredibly lean and tender, the sort of morsel you can't keep from nibbling when it arrives sliced over a little cooked cabbage and some meat juices. Roast quail and chicken are outstanding, and there's a crispy-skin pig that crackles lovingly from the kitchen (or at least we thought it did).

There are some things on the menu that are familiar to St. Louisans (on the lunch menu are beef and broccoli and cashew chicken, for instance), but they can be found anywhere. On the other hand, this is the only place in town with the frog legs, or the fish head pot, or a ground shrimp mixture packed into cigar-shaped tofu skins. And in the early spring, ask about snow pea vines. Yes, pea vines, tender young shoots, quickly sauteed and seasoned who-knows-how but absolutely thrilling. And we're not just saying that because we had them here before New York food writers started gurgling over them last year.

The menu also shows congee, the soup-like rice dish that is often an Asian breakfast, and certainly is an Asian comfort food, plus various noodles, sea cucumber, chicken with jelly fish and many other dishes of fascinating ingredients. With one or two exceptions, entrees are under $15. Service can be exemplary and is always friendly, but if there are occasional language problems, speak slowly and don't be afraid to point at a plate on another table, or at a fish in the tank.

The choices are wide-ranging and exciting. Enjoy! Indulge! We certainly do at this thrilling place. No fortune cookies, either, but one is not necessary to see into the future of several young pigs being carried in through the back door as a couple of older ones lurched out the front.

Sadie Thompson's Bistro
Modern American with Hints of Hungary
6347 North Rosebury Avenue, Clayton
863-4414
Dinner Tuesday-Saturday
Credit cards: All major
Wheelchair access: Difficult

Tucked back just off DeMun Avenue near Concordia Seminary, Sadie Thompson's really feels like a little bistro, although perhaps with an airier decor than you'd find on the Left Bank. Always small and cozy, the bistro recently has been brightened with light wood chairs and tables, new carpet and lighter walls. At the same time, Erv Janko has expanded and tweaked his menu and wine list quite a bit, and the results are extremely pleasant.

With a surname like Janko, you know there's sour cream and paprika in the air. But except for seasonal appearances of certain dishes like fruit soups and goulash, it's not a primary theme. And Janko's smart enough to know that sour cream strikes terror in the coronary vessels of many a customer, so he cuts back on fat as much as he possibly can.

On the appetizer list, the salmon mousse pate has a layer of dill-flavored sour cream. The mousse is good, too, a real flavor of the fish coming right along. But the other pate, a "country pistachio," is chicken, turkey and pork, baked in a terrine with rosemary and thyme as well as the occasional nut. It's a little firmer than the classic French pates, but not crumbly and dry, with a superb control of the herbs to give a flavorful, classic-tasting result, and with considerably less fat than its full-pork cousins.

There's also a caponata, coarsely chopped eggplant, tomatoes, peppers, onions and olives. It's seasoned with balsamic vinegar, making it slightly sweet. (Could the sweetness of balsamico be one reason it's been such a hit in America?) We like ours a little less so, but this one is good.

Sadie's soups are always an important part of the meal. The earthy Hungarian mushroom shows off shiitakes grown locally, portobellos and the standard white mushrooms, all rich and filling. There are often a couple of cold ones in the summer, as well as one hot. A cherry soup had hints of cinnamon and lots of sour cherries bathed in the creamy pink liquid, quite usable as a light dessert as well as a first course—or as both. A melon soup also has been a winner.

There are always several kinds of fish on the menu board, and these are handled well. A grilled pork tenderloin was wonderful, very tender, full of the hickory smoke and served with a merlot and cherry sauce. But be warned: This is very rare pork, a fact that came unannounced. Grilled new potatoes, a few mixed vegetables, and a fresh corn succotash came with it, but the plate wasn't overflowing, just a pleasant few bites of each.

A boned leg of lamb was stuffed with spinach and pine nuts, roasted and served over what was called a Cumberland sauce. This wasn't quite the classic English sauce, which involves melted red currant jelly, but a brown merlot-based sauce that included dried currants. Non-classic, perhaps, but tasty and a good match with the tender, lean lamb. Sides were the same, though three ovals of excellent mashed potatoes replaced their roasted cousins. These were studded with bits of carrot, giving a little change of texture and a slight added sweetness. Again, the plate didn't overflow. Even though we both love to eat, the huge servings, especially of side dishes, that we've been seeing as we visit restaurants seem either wasteful or greedy. Restaurateurs say St. Louisans want big servings, but it looks piggish and outdated to us.

The expanded wine list is a delight. Janko has added pear cider, a drink that is sweeping the community. It's alcoholic, ranging from 3 to 5 percent, and it ranges from dry to sweet. It's on draft at some places, in bottles at others, and we've tasted varieties from California, Washington and Idaho. In addition, there is a good-sized list of half bottles, always a welcome sight when we want a white wine with one course, a red with another, or we just feel like less wine with dinner. Fine choices, good prices.

Desserts nearly always include a strawberry-rhubarb pie. It's a fairly unsweet filling, although we've never managed to get there when the pie hadn't been refrigerated, so the crust is invariably soggy. Fruit crisps also are first-rate. The lemon mirror torte is a great idea, but we'd encourage them to make it more lemony. Perhaps the most indulgent-sounding dessert on the menu is a triple-layer chocolate cake with raspberry puree between the layers and a chocolate mousse icing. It's good chocolate, great texture in the cake, a rich, thin layer of icing—but it arrives so precisely sliced it looks like it came from a factory, and not nearly as luscious as it should. It's coldly excellent, without passion, and the result is that it takes a couple of bites before you decide that yes, it has great taste, and if it also is more filling, so what?

Service is good, with a verbal description covering the menu board that goes into things in considerable detail. Dinner should be in the $25 neighborhood, and Erv Janko has always been an asset to the neighborhood.

Saigon Cafe and Deli

Vietnamese Cuisine

8237 Olive Boulevard, University City
994-9929
Lunch and Dinner, every day
Cash only
Wheelchair access: Difficult

One reason people buy a book like this is to find a secret place. It may be a new restaurant or one they've driven by every day for years and never tried. It might even be an older spot they gave up on in despair, and now discover that new owners and a new menu offer a renewed sense of fun—which does not necessarily mean a loud happy hour and a staff parade with sparklers and a tuba with every birthday cake.

We have such a one. This will, of course, cause those who already know about it to chuckle at their own cleverness or complain that it'll be ruined. The former is preferable; small, hard-working restaurant owners deserve success, especially when they put out tasty food for a reasonable cost, less than $10 a head.

Vietnamese food is burgeoning in the St. Louis area. It's a cuisine that seems to be heavy on the soups, known as pho. Pho appears to be addictive. At least that report is what we get from Washington, D.C., where magazine and newspaper columnists discuss at considerable length the sites to find the best pho in town. By the way, pho is heavy on the cilantro, like a lot of southeast Asian food is.

We had seen the Saigon Cafe many times. Joe had even stopped in, a year or so ago, and reported a successful lunch. But when we visited together, it turned out to be exciting.

A spring roll was wrapped in the chilled rice paper sort of covering, full of fresh vegetables and served with a peanut sauce. It was crunchy and tasted like—well, fresh vegetables. The meat roll is deep-fried, and comes with a sweet vinegar sauce whose orange accents look like pepper, but are not.

The bowl of pho was huge, nearly a quart (or so it looked). It's a clear, spicy-hot broth with noodles, vegetables and meat. Some phos have bowls of bean sprouts and other condiments served alongside, but the roast pork we chose did not. The pork was lean and had obviously just been added to the broth, because it retained its distinctive taste. The sprouts were already in the broth, along with celery, sprigs of fresh cilantro, and other good things. Delicious, with flavors of all sorts running riot in the mouth.

Vietnamese sandwiches are an example of colonial cuisine. The French Indo-China period left a significant legacy, led by the sandwiches. The baguette was fresh and crunchy. A mixed sandwich included pate, but was mostly vegetables, along with some thinly-sliced meat. It wasn't stuffed thickly, but it was full of flavors, with thin slices of jalapeno and carrot and the inevitable cilantro, and at no time did the mouth feel neglected.

The western eater is usually confused by Asian sweets; Saigon Cafe's are no exception. Individual plastic cups are in a refrigerated case for you to inspect, and they're labeled in English. Expect variants of sweet beans and coconut with other things thrown in. After staring a while, we asked the cook to choose one for us; she gave us the three-color dessert. Red and white beans were in sweetened coconut milk under a layer of tiny celadon-green dice of something that was much like gelatin. Agar, we guessed. Encounters with sweet beans nestling in the bottom of Hawaii's shaved-ice had prepared us for this, and we finished up happy.

No alcohol, but the wonderful Vietnamese coffee is available—cold, strong and sweet, black or with condensed milk.

Saleem's
Middle Eastern Cuisine
6501 Delmar Boulevard, University City
721-7947
Dinner Monday-Saturday
Credit Cards: DC, MC, V
Wheelchair access: Passable

Saleem's is one of St. Louis' quiet success stories. From humble beginnings many years ago on South Grand Boulevard, long before the current crop of ethnic restaurants, owner—then and now—Salim Hanna took a chance on a move to the U. City Loop and has chugged along, introducing eaters to the pleasures of the Levant.

And introduce he does. On a recent evening, a family consisting of a kindergarten-aged boy, a preadolescent girl and parents, sat quietly eating. Then came a small birthday cake and a troupe of servers—no sparklers or silly stuff, but enough fuss to make the honoree feel properly saluted. And who was the guest of honor? The young lad, obviously dining at the place of his choice. This guy shows promise.

A varied group of eaters chow down here. The menu may look intimidating, but the exotic words refer to very approachable food with few truly off-the-wall tastes. In fact, this is a particularly good place for the timid eater to approach other ethnic cuisines.

Appetizers can't get much simpler than feta cheese, mild and salty, tangy olives and pita which is slightly warm and similarly crisp. We added a dish of hummus and some roast garlic to this. Hummus is pureed chickpeas, the Middle Eastern equivalent of onion dip, and comes in versions from mild to spicy. Most, though, are mild to downright timid. This one is just right, with a touch of garlic and a generous dose of tahini, the sesame version of peanut butter found throughout this part of the world. Scoop it up with the pita or—better still—the grilled pita. Roast garlic is best handled by pulling a clove from the head and squeezing the creamy contents onto some pita, or onto a spoon. Garlic, like jalapenos, loses much of its heat when it is cooked, and becomes quite friendly. Unfortunately, the garlic was slightly underdone, so it resisted the squeeze and still had some bite. Salads, which come with main courses, are simply and lightly dressed with lemon juice, not much oil, and some chopped red onion to provide a refreshing interval after the appetizers.

The easiest main course is the shish kebab. It comes as beef or lamb, two good-sized skewers, over rice. The lamb, more authentic, was high-quality meat, well-seasoned. The rice underneath is tasty and interesting, a step beyond plain rice with the addition of a little grated radish and sweet spice.

Maybe the best vegetarian sandwich in the world is falafel (usually pronounced with emphasis on the middle syllable). Patties of ubiquitous chickpeas, mashed and seasoned with garlic and cumin, are fried until crisp, popped into a split pita and topped with a drizzle of tahini and vegetables. The nearest thing to a salad bar in much of the Middle East is a falafel cart with a mind-boggling assortment of toppings. Tomato, lettuce and onion come with these, and the generous serving makes the pita give way about halfway through eating, when a knife and fork come into use.

Dessert called for baklava, crispy pastry with chopped nuts. Saleem's version is not soggy at all. We also had Turkish coffee, which is not made with sugar here, as it is in Greek restaurants, but rather with cardamom, giving it a somewhat orange-like aroma. Very authentic, strong but not lethal, and a fine finish.

Saleem's doesn't have belly dancers. There's a good wine list, however, that includes, among other things, Greek wines that go beyond roditys and retsina—a glass of red Demestica that was raw on its own became magnificent with the food. Dinner is usually less than $20 a person for appetizer, entree and that splendid baklava.

Sam's St. Louis Steak House
Steaks
10205 Gravois, Affton
849-3033
Dinner every night
Credit cards: All major
Wheelchair access: Difficult

What do people want in a steak house? Great decor? A cigar bar? Nah. They want the best red meat they can get. And Sam's St. Louis Steak House is the place for it.

The appetizers here include a grilled portobello mushroom, and a salad topped with fried artichokes. There's even a shrimp cocktail, described on the menu as "A Classic ... made with shrimp." We were shocked-shocked, and we wondered what ingredients went into the non-classic. The appetizer price range is $3-$8, and a full meal is about $30 a person.

Several kinds of broiled soft fish, like swordfish and salmon, and seafood like lobster tail, dot the menu at Sam's, and there's a nod to chicken and such. But this is first and foremost a steak house. Dinners come with a salad, baked potato or vegetable, rolls and an ice cream scoop of butter. No kidding. In the dim light, it looks like really rich vanilla. Restraint has no place in a steak house.

The house salad dressing is a rice wine vinegar, and was described as sweet and sour. Sweet dressings have become extremely popular in St. Louis, but we don't care for them. We chose a Mayfair and some oil and vinegar for a do-it-yourself turn. The Mayfair was close to perfect, with a good balance (no overwhelming celery, for instance) and the tang of fresh lemon. We added some anchovies. Like blue cheese, they add a dollar to the cost of the salads. Our only quibble is the handful of sliced California black olives tossed on the good assortment of greens. They add nothing to a salad except eye appeal, because they have no taste.

Beef comes as prime rib, filet, and sirloin, each in two sizes, a porterhouse, and a pepper steak, running from $24.95 to $29.95. The beef was, in a word, superb. The prime rib arrived as a boneless cut with a minimal amount of fat, extremely tender and flavorful. Joe, a veteran of far too many athletic banquets, is not a fan of prime rib, but found this among the best ever. The sirloin was as good. Like all the beef cuts, it is brushed before cooking with the house steak sauce it shares with Andria's in Fairview Heights, Ill. It was slightly more resistant to the teeth than the prime rib, but it was firmer, and certainly not tougher. And, as that exceptional cut of beef should be, it was more flavorful than the rib. The sauce is somewhat like a barbecue sauce, a little sweet at first taste, but quickly retreating so that it does not distract from the great beef flavor.

No foil-wrapped baked potatoes, thank goodness. They arrive in a twist of brown wrapping paper and are opened with a flourish to produce a small cloud of steam. The brown paper leaves the skins tender but not damp. With a typical St. Louis vegetable choice of cauliflower or broccoli, we tried cottage fries and were disappointed with chunks of potatoes, seemingly deep-fried with a little coating and topped with some powdery, cheese-looking material. Cheese on everything—that's become the food motto here in our town.

Desserts include cheesecakes and layer cakes, pleasant but unexciting. Wine by the glass included about four reds. A good-sized, standard wine list, however, has sections arranged by price and then by color. An interesting system.

Schneithorst's
German-American
1600 South Lindbergh Boulevard, Frontenac
993-5600
Kaffeehaus: Breakfast, Lunch and Dinner, every day
Dining room: Lunch Monday-Saturday, Dinner every day; Brunch Sunday
Credit cards: All major
Wheelchair access: Satisfactory

The name Schneithorst has been associated with food in St. Louis since the days of making sauerbraten out of T rex. more or less. At this last remaining outpost, there's a coffee shop, an upstairs outdoor area, a bar, and the main dining rooms, each with its own menu. The dining rooms, known as the Hofamberg Inn, have the feeling of Olde Bavaria, but are not overdecorated to the point of utter schmaltz.

Arrival was slightly chaotic. There's a large station with the usual reservation book and telephone, where we were told there'd be a wait of ten or fifteen minutes. This was our fault because we ignored our own advice to phone ahead. However, we were told, if we wanted to go "over there," to a doorway six feet away, we could be seated immediately. The available dining room lacked tablecloths, but we were assured it was the same menu.

What was not volunteered was that it was a smoking area, to the point of four ashtrays on our table for four. On the other hand, a diner in a wheelchair with an assist dog was waited on with great calm and professionalism.

The waitresses we saw were what someone once called Maytag washer employees—not, we hasten to clarify, referring to their sizes, but to their efficiency and reliability. Despite the empty tables, they were flying, shorthanded perhaps, but not missing a thing.

One of the few places in town with a German menu that goes further than sauerbraten, there are sausages, short ribs, sweet and sour pot roast, pork roast and other items. It's very traditional, nothing of the contemporary interpretations some restaurants in Germany have been doing for the last couple of decades. Over half the fairly large menu, though, is American food, with steaks, fried shrimp and baked fish.

The filet mignon was not bound in bacon, but was quality beef, grilled as ordered. It came with a baked potato, aluminum foil-free, and an order of French-fried onion rings, extremely lightly breaded, speckled with black pepper and cooked rather briefly. They weren't very brown, but they were extremely crisp and with a lot of onion flavor, tasting far better than they looked. Roast pork, from the German part of the menu, was slices of loin, fork tender, covered in a pale gravy that could have had more flavor. Creamy-soft mashed potatoes with a little green onion were alongside, real comfort food and extremely good. The third item on the plate was an apple dumpling, not what you'd expect with an entree. The pastry itself was merely adequate, but the sauce, probably apple-apricot, was golden with fruit, slightly sharp and great with the pork. The apples, diced and therefore easier to eat, were tender and had a pleasant tart edge that made it less dessert-like.

Sauerbraten, with the traditional apple sauce and potato pancake, had been nicely marinated to give the thin slices of pot roast a satisfactory sweet-and-sour flavor, but avoided an overdose of vinegar which can destroy the dish. The pancake was good, but if it had begun as raw potatoes it would have been better.

Schneithorst's holds a long and honorable tradition among St. Louis restaurants. The current generation does nothing to disturb it.

Seki
Sushi and Japanese Cuisine
6335 Delmar Boulevard, University City
726-6477
Lunch Tuesday-Saturday, Dinner Tuesday-Sunday
Credit cards: All major
Wheelchair access: Difficult

The multinational society that is exemplified in the University City Loop focuses tightly on the corner of Delmar Boulevard and Westgate Avenue, where practically everything edible is available in an extremely small area. Middle Eastern delicacies come from Al-Tarboush, on Westgate, while Saleem's offers similar fare across the street. On Delmar, around the corner to the east, there's Tomatillo for rapid Mexican, and St. Louis Bread Co. and Riddle's Penultimate. To the west, the Red Sea, Brandt's and Blueberry Hill can satisfy almost any urge, and then there's Seki, somewhere in the middle, offering alluring Japanese fare.

Bright lights and bare wood, with traditional dolls and paintings on walls and shelves, give Seki a definite Oriental air, and a television set with Japanese programs on makes the aura even stronger. There are occasional language problems, and service starts slowly, but once connections are made, things move steadily, with a fine sense of pace.

One of the things Seki does well is the bento box—small, open boxes divided into three or four sections, then stood on end to create shelves, each holding a lovely bite or two of an elegant, delicate appetizer. A sushi roll or a taste of sashimi, a beautifully crisped piece of tempura, a delicious sample of crispy fish topped by a slice of marinated cucumber. All are wondrous.

Sushi is fresh and tasty, perhaps a little short on variety, or maybe wise to St. Louis tastes, but tuna, salmon, yellowtail, mackerel, squid, shrimp and others are available. The various rolls are handsome, but some are not truly sushi because the fish is cooked, as in a soft shell crab roll, a delightful idea that didn't quite work, mainly because of a flavorless crab. All the sushi looked good, too, as did the sashimi and various rolls. There is something so appealing about the look of Japanese appetizers, each practically ready for framing.

Miso soup warms all the way down, and the variety of vegetables in the tempura was a delight. Shrimp is always a favorite, as are mushrooms, and Seki also offers eggplant, okra, sweet potatoes, onions, zucchini, broccoli and other vegetables.

Small plates are available to sample and to share an exciting variety of tastes, colors and views of food. Potatoes—summer potatoes—boiled and served in slightly sweetened potato water, were interesting, but had little unusual flavor. On the other hand, salmon, marinated in saki lees and grilled to perfection, was a delight, with the salmon extremely tender and the skin crisp and delicious and redolent of soy. Cow intestine stewed with tofu, and onions displays a soft texture, not unpleasant but rather bland, like most other dishes. Egg custard with black mushrooms showed a very hot custard with smooth, superior texture. Texture, rather than flavor, may be the key to Seki's success. Each dish has its own texture, and they all complement one another through a delightful meal.

Shu Feng
Chinese and Korean Cuisine
8435 Olive Boulevard, University City
997-7473
Dinner Wednesday-Monday
Cash only
Wheelchair access: Difficult

Tucked away in a small strip mall, looking for all the world like a fried-rice joint, Shu Feng flies along at a mad clip, greeting, seating and feeding people before the next cluster arrives. The frenetic pace comes from its popularity; it's a small place, and it's packed on weekends and holidays, steamy with people jammed into the tiny foyer, waiting patiently for a glimpse of some of the best Asian food in the Midwest.

The menu is primarily Chinese, but with some Korean dishes like the kim chee, pickled turnip that appears on the table as a condiment and predinner nibble for the bold. Kim chee is wildly, flamboyantly hot, addictive for the metalmouths.

Among the first course offerings are the best dumplings in town. Called water dumplings, the thin covering bulges with a generous amount of the gingery pork filling. We eat them on every visit, and they're always hot, perfectly spiced and cooked until the filling is barely done, leaving them juicy. Soy sauce and cider vinegar are on the table; mix them about fifty-fifty, and dip the dumplings. The covering is far lighter than those seen in any other Asian restaurant, and the fact that they are steamed, not fried, keeps them that way.

Among the soups, the hot and sour is outstanding, dark and thick and rich. It teems with bits of vegetables and mushrooms, a little tofu and stout red pepper adding their flavors to the already complex broth.

Another don't-miss is the string beans with (or without) meat in hot sauce. It's the end of the boring bean, glistening green and steaming hot, just tender and covered with a spicy sauce that obliterates any lingering childhood prejudice. They're equally good cold the next day, too. Mongolian beef, that standby of the last twenty years, is lean beef, tender and full of the green-onion flavor, a classy version of the standard. Crispy beef is another hot-and-spicy dish, the texture of the beef carrying the flavor a little further than the shrimp version of the same dish.

Shu Feng is particularly strong on seafood, with sauteed shrimp and sea scallops, beautiful in presentation and succulently cooked, leading a large number of particular delights. We also love the fried crisp squid in hot garlic sauce in the Korean section of the menu. There, too, you will find bulgoki, the Korean barbecued beef. While it's marked as being spicy, it's fairly mild, the same lean, tender beef broiled and piled on thinly shredded cabbage to catch the meat juices. The vegetable wilts slightly from the heat, becoming an integral and very pleasurable part of the dish.

Quite frankly, we've never had a dish at Shu Feng that we didn't like. At less than $20 a person, it's a wonderful bargain, and the wine list has bloomed recently, with some pleasant Alsatian wines to complement the meals. This is a terrific little restaurant, also favored by many Symphony musicians, physicians, lawyers, politicians and, the greatest of all bon vivants, Senator Thomas Eagleton.

Sidney Street Cafe
Modern American Cuisine
2000 Sidney Street
771-5777
Dinner Tuesday-Saturday
Credit cards: All major
Wheelchair access: Passable

The Sidney Street Cafe is one of the quiet dependables of the St. Louis dining scene. Located near the busy south side intersection of Jefferson and Gravois, the restaurant is almost unchanged after more than thirteen years of operation. The front room, dominated by a large bar and friendly bartenders, offers the first of many warm welcomes with a number of open bottles of wine standing at one end of the bar. They're ready for examining, and serve as a delightful by-the-glass wine list.

The inner room, laid out on two levels, is a warm one, with brick walls. Tables wear green tablecloths and bear small chalkboards, with appetizers on one side and entrees on the other; a technique that has been followed at other restaurants in town, and which allows for weekly, or even daily changes. The aura of this room is such that it would fit comfortably in the Central West End.

An intelligent staff knows the dishes and their preparation, and begins the evening with beignets, tender but not sweet, and an excellent beginning to a relaxing evening. The menu displays touches of French, Creole and general American fare, and starts with a pair of appetizers that are as good as anything in the city because someone in the kitchen has a talented hand with spicing. Veal dumplings resemble Asian pot stickers but surpass most produced at Asian restaurants because of a very thin skin, good meat and spicing that burns both wisely and well. Alongside is a Thai sauce that tingles. Southern rolls, perhaps a bow to much of the restaurant's heritage, certainly a tribute to the imagination of the chef, are like thick egg rolls with Cajun sausage, ham and vegetables, for some varied, excellent flavors inside a nicely spiced, crisp skin.

Diners receive a choice of soup or salad with entrees. We went for salads and discovered we'd made the wrong choice—vegetables past their prime, and a house dressing with almost no flavor.

The entree list is a good, often-changing mix of meat and fish, with maybe a dozen choices on any given night. Tuscan sea bass was excellent, a fish that had been perfectly cooked, its flesh a sparkling white just past translucent, at the height of richness and flavor. The fish was barely covered with nicely seasoned bread crumbs and topped with first-rate tomato sauce. Pea pods, carrots and rice pilaf came alongside, and are listed in descending order of impressiveness.

Lamb chops were cooked right to the moment, tender and flavorful. Few meats are as good as lamb chops, and the kitchen at Sidney Street treats them with proper respect. Roast potatoes were an excellent accompaniment, their skins crispy and the inside perfect to soak up the lamb juice.

Sidney Street's full wine list is very good, with breadth and depth, and prices that make good wines affordable. Dinner (appetizer, entree, dessert) is about $25-$30 a person, and well worth it.

Desserts come from Tim Brennan's Cravings, a sufficient recommendation. The chocolate cake was rich and full of good chocolate, a two-layer classic that would make Betty Crocker think about becoming an Avon Lady.

Spiro's
Greek Cuisine
3122 Watson Road
645-8383
Lunch Monday-Friday, Dinner Monday-Saturday
8406 Natural Bridge Road, Bel-Nor
382-8074
Lunch Monday-Friday, Dinner Monday-Saturday
1054 Woods Mill Road, Chesterfield
878-4449
Lunch Monday-Friday, Dinner every night
Credit cards: All major
Wheelchair access: Varies by location

Spiro's may not be the place for someone on a low sodium diet, but it's full of good and easy-to-understand tastes. We're both fond of Greek food, finding its rowdy, uncomplicated flavors comforting and rewarding.

Spiro's is a family-owned place, with some non-Greek food on its menus in case someone is into the safe stuff. But we'd encourage sampling a few ethnic tastes from appetizers like the traditional taramosalata, the tasty pink dip made from fish roe, and so tasty on warm pita bread. Saganaki, slices of grilled kasseri cheese, is flamed at tableside with a little brandy, sometimes with an enthusiastic "Opa!" to make it a little more so. It had enough lemon with it, although we like it cut more thinly and thus more runny, but who doesn't like a little gooey melted cheese?

Squid, on the other hand, is probably an acquired taste. The appetizer serving was pan-fried, with a great deal of oregano, enough that its texture in the mouth was annoying. The squid, however, was a pleasure, with tasty, chewy tentacles and tender slices of the body. Avgolemono, egg and lemon soup, one of our favorites, was heavy on the salt, especially in the rice, but the broth was rich and full with the classic balance of chicken and lemon.

Greek salads come tossed with the classic ingredients—feta cheese, red onions, black olives, a little green pepper and a wedge or two of tomato. A simple vinaigrette ties everything together happily.

There are pasta dishes and things like broiled chicken and, of course, shish kebab with pork, beef or lamb. Lamb is the most traditional, but can be tough; pork accepts the marinade best, just as it does with barbecue sauce; beef is the most familiar to American tastes, and Joe's favorite, especially if it's charcoaled at the edges. When they're available, we're very fond of smelts, especially if the smaller ones are in stock. The tiny fish are lightly floured and quickly fried, providing one or two bites each, chewy on the tails, mildly fishy and very satisfying. Mezedakia, liver and sweetbreads, were given the same treatment, but with more oregano. We asked that it be undercooked, and that's how it came, tender and aromatic and flavorful. Alongside were a twice-baked potato and freshly steamed vegetables with a frosting of grated cheese their only seasoning. Wedges of lemon lay on the plates for use as desired, a common condiment in this food

Greek desserts are traditionally very sweet. The baklava was crisp, and only lightly syruped, not at all overwhelming, with some cloves adding their own particular flavor. Galactoboureko, the same phyllo dough with a custard filling, hadn't maintained the crispness, but was even less sweet and particularly delicious. Greek coffee is prepared tableside, with inquiry into the desired degree of sweetness before the process begins.

Service comes without a patronizing air, and another nice touch is menus that give both Greek and English names of dishes. The wine list has no vintages, but no one should be interested in anything but roditys, the ideal match.

Spotted Dog Cafe
Bar Food
3221 Olive Street
533-5263
Lunch Tuesday-Friday, Dinner Tuesday-Sunday
Credit cards: DSC, MC, V
Wheelchair access: Passable

Laclede Town and Park alumni, which we both are, can't help but feel a tug as they drive along Olive Street now. The evidence of our past is nearly gone, just a faintly remembered tree here and there that once marked a playground or a fire lane or a window carrying the faint sounds of a saxophone out into the summer dusk. We know the sad and inglorious end, and hope the land will some day hold happy people again. In the meantime, however, there are some happy people not far away.

In a converted firehouse on Olive Street, we found some good bar food, just the thing before or after an event at the Fox or Grand Center, or even in the other half of the building, a music venue that's been handsomely redone by owners Kaylene and Christian Brewer. Check the beams and the immense chandelier. Glorious.

Chicken wings here come in a chipotle sauce (which means smoky) and in your chosen degree of hotness, a considerate thing. Lots of beers, and the exciting Spanish Peaks pear cider, are on tap to cool off after the wings. Chicken taquitos arrive with a savory green hot sauce, well-seasoned and not at all greasy. There are grilled vegetable sandwiches and BLTs as well as the standard burgers, all accompanied by an unusual gingery oil-dressed coleslaw. Good onion rings that haven't been living in a warehouse freezer.

Yes, there's a jukebox and televisions for sporting events, and an immense bar. Cement floors mean the racket on weekend nights might be in trouble with the EPA, but it's fun and usually for less than $20 a head.

Station Grille
Modern American Cuisine
Hyatt Regency, Union Station, 1820 Market Street
231-1234
Breakfast, Lunch and Dinner, every day
Credit cards: All major
Wheelchair access: Comfortable

Too many St. Louisans have forgotten about Union Station, it seems. That's too bad. The Grand Hall is surely one of the most glorious rooms in the United States. Every St. Louisan should drop by once or twice a year to pay respects and to realize just what beautiful places our city possesses. Some day we're going to take our binoculars along and get even more of the detail.

Happily, not far away, at the end of a corridor that's furnished like a real, old-fashioned hotel lobby, with a card table, sofas, checkerboard, and a grandfather clock, there's a good meal waiting.

The Station Grille hasn't always been such a great experience for us. It's a handsome room, all copper and brass and lamps, but the food never came up to the standards set by the architecture. Now, things are looking up. The menu, with first courses averaging $6.50 and entrees about $20, covers a wide range of American eating habits, with things from crab cakes to hummus and prime rib to salmon on Asian noodles.

One of the few dishes remaining from early menus is the lobster bisque. It arrives crowned with puff pastry that is crisp on top, buttery throughout, and with a bottom that remains soft from the rising steam of the soup. That creamy liquid is essence of lobster, carefully seasoned. However, many small white lumps and one large white one streaked with pink were in the bisque. All of them dissolved in the mouth. Were it not for the pink streak, we'd assume it was thickening that hadn't been beaten in well enough. Could the large piece have been surimi, the stuff they make fake crabmeat with? Puzzling. And yet, it did taste good and not floury.

Sauteed wild mushrooms came in a deep brown sauce redolent of Cognac and Marsala, not so much of the roasted garlic mentioned on the menu. It was rich and succulent, full of autumnal flavors and served on two thin slices of bread sprinkled with blue cheese and melted under the broiler, creating an excellent contrast of piquant cheese to the resonance of the mushrooms.

A salmon fillet was rubbed with chili oil before being grilled slightly underdone, and the oil enhanced it well. Hong Kong noodles, fettuccine-sized, came dressed with a soy and chili dressing that tended to flow to the bottom of the plate. At first bite the noodles seemed bland, although not overcooked. A good stir-up cured the blandness quickly, and the noodles, laced with a few strands of vegetables, were almost as tasty as the fish.

A rib steak arrived sizzling and smoking in a fajita pan, surrounded by julienne of red and green peppers and onions. Rib steak isn't a remarkably lean cut, but that adds to the flavor, as did the peppery marinade the steak wore. It was an extremely good piece of meat, considering the cut, juicy and full of the savor one expects. The vegetables continued to sizzle for several minutes after their arrival, leaving them charred, a little crispy, and succulent, some of the best we've had in a long time. The whole effect was of one giant fajita, waiting for a tortilla the size of a dinner plate, and it was delicious. Side potatoes can be baked, a baked sweet potato or a potato du jour. We declined the garlic and dill mashed potatoes for a sweet potato, which was so huge it hadn't cooked through. Frankly, though, it left more room for the steak and sizzling vegetables.

Desserts are cheesecake, ice cream, chocolate cake and a peach Melba torte, along with simpler, elegant things like superior sorbet and fresh fruit.

Service here is another pleasant thing. Once this dining room was almost vicious to women dining alone or in pairs, but we saw several receiving respectful, almost solicitous, care.

Forget the good old days. The best of times is now.

Summit

Italian-American Cuisine

200 North Broadway
436-2770
Lunch Monday-Friday, Dinner nightly
Credit cards: All major
Wheelchair access: Comfortable

We've never asked Jeff Daniels if he made Frank Sinatra the theme of his restaurant, the Summit, as a marketing decision or as a personal tribute. But the tipped fedora is in blue neon outside, videos of Sinatra concerts run as an adult-style MTV, and the pictures on the walls are Sinatra, his pals, his movies, his record covers, his records, his clippings. We couldn't find a copy of the birth certificate.

The menu is influenced by the '50s and '60s, when the post-Ava Gardner Sinatra turned into the Swingin' Sinatra. It's Italian with some steaks thrown in as further ballast for those martinis and Scotch. The tariff is fairly hefty, with three courses averaging close to $30 before drinks and tips.

First courses are as simple as a shrimp cocktail or minestrone. Fancier choices could be a grilled portobello mushroom with a Gorgonzola Marsala sauce, or calamari misto, with rings of calamari, very tender in a spicy, quite chunky tomato sauce with capers (a plus) and sliced California black olives (a minus). Overall, though, it was a generous serving of succulent seafood.

Salads include grilled asparagus and red peppers or a hearts of palm with tomato, anchovy, Gorgonzola and feta cheeses, and red onion. A Caesar had good lettuce, slightly stale croutons, mushrooms and bacon bits, odd additions to this salad, but not unpleasant. The dressing, though, was nowhere near what one expects from a Caesar, with a strange, stale taste that drifted away when eating the mushrooms and bacon.

Among the menu choices were veal Summit, with white wine, lemon, broccoli, mushrooms, cheese and tomatoes; shrimp scampi, a spicy garlic sauce with tomatoes; and chicken dolce, with tomatoes, white raisins, walnuts, balsamic vinegar and brown sugar. There are steaks and veal chops, too, and a 14-ounce strip steak, beautifully rare and well-seasoned, a glistening, sizzling piece of meat that was juicy and reasonably tender. The baby red potatoes that came alongside were more like toddlers, but oven-roasting kept them crisp outside and creamy inside, a nice change from the ubiquitous baked potato.

Pasta is fairly traditional, with fettuccines Alfredo and carbonara, linguini and clams, even spaghetti with meatballs. A beef burgundy linguini sported slices of beef tenderloin, some of which were quite tender and tasty, and others not so much. The oyster mushrooms were great, a splendid, earthy idea with the pasta, which was sauced with the juices from the beef and mushrooms. The pasta was rather past al dente, alas, but it wasn't swimming in sauce, certainly a virtue. The wine list is standard, with some good choices and fair prices.

Desserts are cheesecake and a couple of other baked things. The espresso torte was a two-layer cake with chocolate chips and chocolate icing. The mocha-colored filling, though, turned out to be flavored with coconut, and there didn't appear to be even a hint of coffee in it.

Service was obliging, although the check came unrequested on a very quiet night.

Surf and Sirloin
Steak and Seafood

13090 Manchester Road, Des Peres
822-3637
Lunch Monday-Friday, Dinner every day; Brunch on Sunday
Credit cards: All major
Wheelchair access: Satisfactory

Remember the chopped sirloin steak that was served in the Tenderloin Room for several generations, when everyone who was anyone stayed at the Chase-Park Plaza Hotel and ate in what might have been Hack Ulrich's house? Ulrich among hosts was like Stan Musial among baseball players. The chopped sirloin, coarsely ground and topped with a dark, bordelaise-style mushroom sauce, heavy on the A-1, arrived black and crispy on the outside, juicy on the inside. Only the extremely literal-minded would see a resemblance to a hamburger.

Larry Karagiannis, eldest son of a large family who served countless meals at the Tenderloin Room and other local restaurants, has it on the menu at his Surf and Sirloin, and serves it in a way that would make Hack proud. A similarly coarse grind of similarly excellent meat, it's like eating steak without quite so much jaw action.

Of course, there are many other choices on the menu in the large, cool room with some too-pretty-to-eat fish in a large tank just inside the front door. Karagiannis, by the way, opened the first of the family's Spiro's on Natural Bridge after he graduated from the University of Missouri at St. Louis and discovered less demand for history majors than for restaurateurs. The crab cakes, available as a first course or as an entree, were crisp on the outside, naked on the bottom, and an unusual combination of really large lumps of meat and a compound very much like deviled crab. The taste, however, was almost wholly crab, with no filling to interfere with what your palate wanted when it made you order them. A remoulade on the side was mild and superfluous to the joy of the crab. Oysters, farmed and "aqua pure purged,"(the menu's phrase) arrived both huge and handsome. But they apparently had been washed too long and purged of flavor, since there was none of the tang of the sea that is vital to fresh oysters. They also were awfully close to room temperature, despite being served on ice. The horseradish-heavy red sauce, just right in taste, helped them go down.

"A little Greek salad?" asked the waiter. We nodded. A huge bowl arrived. Ingredients were cut, dressed, tossed, cut a little more, and served. The salad plates were piled high, freshly dressed with creamy feta, the obligatory oregano, red onions, a couple of good olives and green pepper. Maybe a little overdressed, but the overall satisfaction level is high, and it's an extra pleasure to have a salad tossed at tableside. Many of the city's better restaurants made it a practice for a long time, but speed seems to have replaced comfort and style.

Besides that chopped steak, if soft-shell crabs marked "whales"—a size designation, not a species—are available, get them, too. And get them deep-fried, rather than sauteed. That's not our usual advice. Soft-shells are delicate, and usually a little flour and a run through sizzling butter is all they need. But these were dipped in a delicate batter and fried to a golden brown, drained within an inch of their lives, and served as crisp and dry as a potato chip. We haven't found a better soft-shell crab in town. Baked potatoes don't come in aluminum foil, but they have tender skins, so we assume they were baked in a container. Still, they were properly mealy, with no skimping on butter or sour cream. The butter, in fact, looked like about a third of a stick had been cut off and plonked on a plate.

There are unchopped steaks, of course, a few chicken and pasta dishes, some veal and pork and lamb, with entrees running $10 to $18, except for a steak marked Diamond Jim Brady, 32 ounces for $25. The menu is essentially American in the style of decades past, no dust on the plates, no cilantro allowed. A few of the desserts are a little more contemporary, but there's cheesecake and rainbow sherbet, too. We settled for Greek coffee, not on the menu, but where there's feta…

Tachibana
Japanese Cuisine
12967 Olive Boulevard, Chesterfield
434-3455
Lunch Monday–Friday, Dinner every night
Credit cards: All major
Wheelchair access: Passable

Joe likes vegetables a lot, maybe more than most people, but he and most people disagree when they discuss favorites. Joe likes Brussels sprouts, and beets, including their greens, and spinach and leeks and cooked celery. He doesn't like broccoli and cauliflower and zucchini.

At Tachibana, however, he'll make an exception for zucchini, as long as they keep the slices thin and fry it with a tempura batter. Then it's exciting, as are all vegetables, from sweet potatoes to green beans and from eggplant to asparagus and bell peppers.

Tachibana is a veteran West County Japanese restaurant that shares space in a strip shopping center with many other restaurants. Like many Japanese places, it's largely American-ized, though its sushi is splendid, with a wide variety of both traditional and modern tastes. Americans, not yet accustomed to the fishy flavor of some fish (mackerel comes to mind) or to the texture of many other denizens of the deep (sea urchin, for example), seem to prefer "rolls," and Tachibana obliges with many types and styles, from the California roll to tastes more wide-ranging, like the "dynamite roll," with real heat, though no explosives.

Mackerel, octopus, tuna, yellowtail and salmon roe are among our favorites, and we have a real weakness for the salmon skin roll.

There's a key question about the meals at Tachibana and other Japanese restaurants, as well. "Are the dishes too bland? Or are they extremely subtle?"

We got one answer on the chicken teriyaki, which didn't taste of much except the fuel that fires the grill. Japanese spare ribs were better, and sukiyaki had definite, if light, flavors. Fried rice was past its prime. Another problem at Tachibana is erratic service, exaggerated by language difficulties. We think we don't get a sufficient explanation on the ingredients and cooking process of some dishes, and find waitresses pushing us toward old favorites. And once we order, the push is to get us fed and out the door, with comfort a secondary consideration.

St. Louis Tap Room & Brewery
Brew Pub

2100 Locust Street
241-2337
Lunch and Dinner, every day
Credit cards: All major
Wheelchair access: Impossible

Despite a long and honorable history of brewing, but in true St. Louis fashion, our city was among the last in the nation to open a micro-brewery, or a brew pub. The Tap Room helped rescue our reputation a little, and its success has spawned some imitators. Still, the city's first is definitely worth a visit, and not necessarily just for beer. Nibbles and sandwiches and entrees all present finger-chewing scenarios of decision-making. There is, of course, no question of dessert, which we'll get to in due time.

First courses run around $4, sandwiches $6, main courses $9 and desserts $5. And of course there are a number of Schlafly's beers, fermenting before your eyes, which run $3.25 for a pint. They range from light lager to dark porter, and include a superior wheat beer.

Appetizers are mostly simple, including the exemplary French fries, made from real potatoes and tasting the way they did so many years ago, before restaurant kitchens even had freezers. The spicy ketchup the menu speaks of doesn't seem to come automatically any more, but is a necessity as far as we're concerned. While Joe is a ketchup-on-fries person, Ann isn't— except in this case, when the sweet-spicy ketchup tastes something you'd find in one of those joints in Northern California where everything they serve is touched by gold. It's great.

Pate is earthy and mouth-filling, soups can be excellent, with potato at the top of the list, and the white bean chili, in a serving that should be an entree, is thick and very spicy, its quiet appearance belying the fire inside. The lime wedge on the side isn't just for looks; the flavor bounce it brings is impressive.

We're suckers for the G & W liverwurst, available here as a sandwich with tangy pickled pub onions, some slaw and a dill pickle spear (which seems to have amazing tranquilizing properties on fussy toddlers, to judge from a recent visit). There are a couple of vegetarian sandwiches, as well as the expected burgers and chicken breasts, bratwurst and a schnitzel sandwich.

Entrees star the incredible fish and fries, a superlative rendering of British fish and chips, except that these fries are better than anything we've ever found on the green and pleasant isle. The fish itself is thick and moist, the batter fairly thin and yeasty from beer. The result, delivered shimmeringly hot, is dry and crisp outside and meltingly tender inside.

Desserts for us here begin and ends with the thrillingly immense portion of STP. We're not talking automotives here; this is sticky toffee pudding, the old English dessert that is a hunk of dark, very tender, slightly spiced cake, covered with a sauce that tastes of brown sugar and butter and served with a scoop of whipped cream that never felt aerosol. The cake and sauce are hot, the cream is cold and the rendition is platonic. It says a lot that the only version in town that comes close is at Zinnia, a restaurant that takes its food very seriously indeed.

And so does the Tap Room, which scores high on all counts.

Thai Cafe
Thai Cuisine

6170 Delmar Boulevard
862-6868
Lunch Monday-Friday, Dinner Monday-Saturday
Credit cards: All major
Wheelchair access: Passable

We always smile when we walk into the Thai Cafe. The wood paneling and plants remind us of a restaurant we visited in Bangkok. It was called "Cabbages and Condoms," and was run by a public health group much like Planned Parenthood, and the decor was much the same. However, there was a gift shop attached, and posters on the walls, and at the end of the meal, instead of an after-dinner mint—yes, that's right.

No such affiliation or practice at the Thai Cafe, of course, where the food seems more delicately spiced than at some of the other Thai restaurants. Dinner is under $20 per person, unless someone has many of the tropical drinks that seem to come flying out of the kitchen.

This is a young group, both customers and staff, with the latter moving at the pace of an emergency room on a Saturday night. We find it interesting that jungle goddesses are more popular than Singha, the good Thai beer, although we're the first to admit that a pina colada is a superb, if somewhat dangerous, antidote to near-lethal amounts of chiles.

That won't be a problem here, though. We asked for our usual somewhere-between-medium-and-hot, and got what we consider a medium-to-mild. A soup with coconut, mushrooms, galangal (a root related to ginger that adds its own flavor) and white meat of chicken was tart with kaffir lime leaves and had specks of chile floating atop it. It was pungent rather than incendiary, a fine piece of work for the lover of hot-and-sour soup. Another appetizer, mee krob noodles, are tiny crunchy rice noodles that taste faintly like Cracker Jack. They arrive with a few shrimp, a little sliced green onion and a handful of large bean sprouts. Interesting, certainly, but more of a snack food than what Americans think of as a first course.

Thai curries, and there are many here, are sometimes named for their color, which relates to the ingredients, or their background—Penang, for example, is for the city; or Mussaman, which acknowledges the Islamic culture existing in Southeast Asia. Most of the curries we've tried have been more like soups than stews, but a stir-fry with pork, eggplant, holy basil and red curry bore only a small amount of liquid. It was fragrant and flavorful with a slow-rising burn, the lean and slightly chewy pork contrasting with the creamy eggplant. The pork wore anise, not a common flavor in Thai cooking, but the eggplant didn't, increasing the contrast. A yellow curry, the name arising from the amount of turmeric (the spice that makes American hot dog mustard so yellow), with potatoes, onions, carrots and a mixture of seafood was considerably less hot. The liquid, as in many curries, was coconut milk, but the large number of carrots had added its own significant sweetness and the result was sadly unbalanced.

Thai coffee, slightly less strong than its Vietnamese counterpart, is the after-dinner drink, although anise lovers should investigate the Thai iced tea, a lovely color but apt to stain the clothing of the butterfingered.

Service is nothing if not zippy, but food tends to arrive when it's ready, leaving tables laden with entrees and half-eaten first courses.

Tony's
Contemporary American and Italian Cuisine

410 Market Street
231-7007
Dinner Monday-Saturday
Credit cards: All major
Wheelchair access: Passable (use building lobby on Broadway)

For those new to St. Louis, let us briefly retell the story of Tony's Restaurant, a bright and shining light for more than forty years. When Joe arrived in St. Louis to be a sports writer for the Globe-Democrat, in 1955, Tony's was among the best in town. It still was a spaghetti house, serving on checkered tablecloths, in a downtown neighborhood that included a number of Italian enclaves. But it had a tone, and there were good signs, and it had Vince Bommarito. Vince and his brother, Tony, worked together for a long time at Tony's on North Broadway. Then Tony opened Anthony's in the Market Street location, and eventually (please don't be confused), Tony became a wine importer and Vince opened Tony's on Market Street. Tony's on Broadway closed to make room for the Ugly Dome, named after an airline.

Bill Price, a great table tennis player and a fine tennis coach (Chuck McKinley was a student), first took Joe to Tony's. The young restaurateur and the young sports writer, both ardent softball players impressed by high standards of professional expertise, got to know one another. In the fullness of time, they became friends. They have lunch together from time to time, and each worried a lot when the other had serious health problems in the last few years. When Joe was writing about restaurants for the Post-Dispatch, he called Tony's the best restaurant in town on a few occasions and was highly critical on a few others. Joe also told his readers how to dine very inexpensively at Tony's.

Since we became a couple, we've dined handsomely at Tony's; it's a place where we celebrate, just as thousands of other St. Louisans do. And although we've had meals at other St. Louis restaurants that were better than some we've had at Tony's, it remains our first choice for a festive occasion. For those who dine at Tony's, whether it's once a week or once a year, it's a site of celebrations. Not a night goes by without an anniversary, a birthday, a promotion to mark. Hundreds of proposals have been made here. The birth of our youngest grandson, the estimable Benjamin, was announced to us one February night while we were dining at Tony's to celebrate Joe's birthday. Courtly Herb Cray, recently retired maitre d', did the honors.

Just what is the Tony's experience? First of all, it's the food—with outstanding raw materials, prepared with style, imagination and uncanny consistency. There are those who argue that service is the defining factor. But we're eaters, and we vote for the pleasures of the palate.

Service, however, is a close second. It's not a restaurant for a fast, pre-game sandwich, and that's not how customers are treated. Expect to be spoiled, not intimidated. Ask questions. They have answers.

The restaurant itself is very restrained, almost severe, in its decor. Some of the world-class wine cellar lines one wall of the smaller dining room, red wines gleaming softly through the bottles. The larger room now sports a couple of plants, a nice touch, but it's essentially a cream-colored room where the tuxedoed staff offers contrast and the customers supply the color. However, this is not an austere restaurant. The ladies' room here is among the most luxuriously outfitted in town.

Oh, yes, let's eat. What should it be? The first courses may be the hardest choices of the meal. This is a marvelous soup kitchen, to use an incongruous phrase. Someone back there spends all day tending stock kettles and thinking up new recipes. The wild mushroom, for example, is dark and earthy enough to make one look for a troll hiding behind the sugar bowl. We're indecently fond of the scallops, huge and perfectly seared, served with black truffle shavings sprinkled over them in a reduction of the scallop juices. Stuffed squid come in a tomato sauce piqued with basil, the interior packed with more squid. Steamed, chilled mussels carry a variety of sauces; roasted peppers with mozzarella is simple and classic, as is perfect prosciutto with melon, even better with fresh figs in the proper season.

Salads involve tomatoes and anchovies in season; Caesar at the Ides of March—and other times, too; spinach hard to beat.

Tony's most popular dish is lobster albanello, generous chunks of lobster in a wonderfully creamy pale yellow sauce with mushrooms. The best way to have it served is with a little spaghetti in the middle, the better to utilize the wonderful sauce without having to lick the plate. Osso bucco, always on the menu, is served with long, narrow marrow spoons imported from France, so as to safely remove the succulent but very shy marrow from the veal bones. It comes with its classic partner, risotto Milanese, flavored with saffron. Vince Jr., is of the very al dente school of risotto, so those who prefer it softer should say so. And if you differ, don't fear. Tony's is not a kitchen to refuse requests based on some silly principle.

Interestingly, in this house which still considers pasta a specialty, there's superb steak. Served with butter and a little garlic, it's a strip to equal any in town. Perfectly boned Dover sole, chunks of tuna, a looming veal chop are other top entrees. Of the pastas, besides the one that rides shotgun with the lobster albanello, our favorite is probably the one with mixed seafood in a dark, rich marinara sauce. While the pasta is sauced in the Italian style (or just enough), the mussels and clams and shrimp are in American quantities (enough to satisfy the biggest appetite).

Side dishes with entrees are usually "a little pasta with that?", meaning your choice of shape, and a marinara sauce or something creamier. We usually opt for a large pasta, like penne rigate, with the red sauce. Unless, of course, we decide on the spinach, which is steamed in a pan with just a little olive oil and some garlic, incredibly tasty. And there's always an order of Italian potatoes, not on the menu, but no secret. They're great fried potatoes with lots of onions and some good black Italian olives, a reminder that all this good food came out of the inspiration of somebody's home cooking.

Desserts? You must. We insist. The best chocolate dessert in the state of Missouri is the chocolate cake—three layers, with mousse in between—with homemade banana ice cream. Birthday party ice cream and cake for kids were never like this. Deep, dark, serious chocolate, creamy banana. It's heaven. The creme brulee is superb, browned enough, flecks of vanilla bean on the bottom, a high crust-to-custard ratio to enhance every bite. Cheesecake, of course. Fresh berries or whatever fruit is in season. Zabaglione can be made at tableside to go over the fruit, and we sometimes see Bananas Foster in the works. A superb dessert spot, no doubt about it.

Service seems to have relaxed slightly, perhaps just a touch more casual in tune with the times. At certain points in the meal, a table will have four or five staff members clustered around as food is finished and plated at tableside, which is how it's done here. Chairs are held, napkins re-folded, fresh water glasses show up midway through the meal. Everyone is treated well. Tony's is smart enough to know that high-school prom kids turn into customers a few years down the road, and keeps corsages in the refrigerator during dinner. Tony's knows the investment, as in superb ingredients and skilled employees, will pay off sooner or later. Probably sooner.

Top of the Riverfront

Modern American Cuisine, Mississippi River Basin Division

Regal Riverfront Hotel, 200 South Fourth Street
241-3191
Lunch and Dinner, every day; Brunch Sunday
Credit cards: All major
Wheelchair access: Comfortable

It's our general contention, as well as a lot of other traveling eaters, that the higher the dining room, the lower the odds on excellent food. There are exceptions, of course. Joe recalls a memorable Thanksgiving dinner at Windows on the World in New York; Ann once had a decent-enough meal at the top of the John Hancock Building in Chicago not long after it opened (which was probably about twenty-five years ago). But as a general rule of thumb, the tops of tall buildings are meant for drinking, not eating.

The most spectacularly-situated restaurant in St. Louis is trying to change that image. Max Taouil, the restaurant director of the Regal Riverfront, and John Santangelo, the chef de cuisine, who came here from the Arizona Biltmore (no small credential), are creating Huckleberry Finn cuisine in the revolving room atop the Regal.

Food of the Mississippi River Valley is the general theme, an idea whose time may well have come. Some of it is a reach, like the St. James broiled lobster (lobster in Maramec State Park?), but other things make a certain amount of gastro-geographical sense. Shrimp Orleans and grilled andouille, for example, certainly have their feet deep in the Big Muddy.

First courses include a "Bogalossa" crab gumbo, Maine lobster beignets, and a St. Croix Forest mushroom strudel. The strudel was slightly underdone and slightly gummy inside, but the mushrooms were generously used and only lightly seasoned to let their own flavor reign. Missouri baby field greens become a field for marinated asparagus and a roasted tomato.

Entrees include the safety of St. Louis' traditional pepper steak, a tenderloin, and a roast prime rib with Collinsville horseradish. Beyond that, they begin to show more vision, like chicken stuffed with artichokes and sauced with Seyval blanc wine, one of Missouri's best whites. Shrimp ride atop pasta, helped along by artichokes and mushrooms. "Pine Bluff pistachio crusted pheasant breast" was better cooked than grammatically composed—pheasant is wonderful when it's not dried out—although the blackberry remoulade sauce was not as spicy nor as full of blackberries as we would have liked. We think the pheasant, not the pistachio, comes from Pine Bluff; we don't know the home of the menu writer. Striped bass is stuffed with crab, a little overcooked and under-seasoned, but accompanied by delicious leeks.

The wine list is chosen to match the foods, and there are some excellent matches, even though prices are generally on the high side.

We've tasted Santangelo's cooking away from the hotel, and he's been more insistent in his spicing then, so we know he has the imagination and knows how to use it. We wonder if he's making too much of St. Louis' legendary conservatism, and is reluctant to let go and run with his talent. We hope he tries, or the hotel lets him try, depending on whose call it is. This is a good concept, and he has some fine ideas. With dinner checks running near $40 a head for three courses before adding wine and service, diners are entitled to the best a chef can do, whether there's a gorgeous view or not.

And yes, it really is gorgeous, especially at dusk.

Trainwreck Saloon

American Bar Food

9243 Manchester Road, Rock Hill
962-8148
314 Westport Plaza, Maryland Heights
434-7222
720 North First Street
423-1006
Lunch and Dinner, daily
Credit cards: All major
Wheelchair access: Passable

Railroad buffs aren't the only patrons at the Trainwreck Saloon. Take the original, on Manchester Road. It's filled with people who don't give the great photos a second look, nor do they seem to care much about the model trains or even the caboose parked in the back.

It does seem a waste of memorabilia, but the food is good enough that it's okay for people to visit just for lunch. Sweet potato fries are cut shoestring size and cooked until they're the color of mahogany, full of flavor when they're piping hot and crispy, equally as tasty slightly cooler when the sweetness is more noticeable. This is the only place in town we know of that serves two chilis, one mild and the other pungent. Not surprisingly, we prefer the latter. It bears no resemblance to the soup-like things that bear the name at many restaurants. Thick with meat and pungent with cumin, oregano and, of course, chiles, a cup is a great starter. A bowl would melt the snow off the Trainwreck's porch.

This is burger country, but the Trainwreck goes two better. Not only are there half-pound hamburgers, they offer both ostrich and bison burgers, third-pound babes that don't shrink much because they're so low in fat. The bison burger is our favorite, meaty and rich with a slight gaminess that reminds you it's meat, not just something that holds up the condiments. Served rare at our request, it was moist enough, but not so much that the juice made mush out of the bun.

A Cow Catcher—we do wish the names were a tad less cute—was a roast beef sandwich on a French roll. Well-done beef, pleasantly seasoned, came with a cup of meat juices that certainly tasted good, without that fake beef-bouillon cube flavor. Sandwiches come with a choice of potato salad, cole slaw or cottage cheese. We tried the former two, and preferred the cole slaw, a sprightly vinaigrette version. Desserts are pretty ordinary.

There's a large selection of draft beers and Fitz's Root Beer in longnecks, for the abstainer who would be unnoticed.

Trattoria Marcella

Close to the Old Country

3600 Watson Road
352-7706
Dinner Tuesday-Saturday
Credit cards: All major
Wheelchair access: Difficult

Trattoria Marcella is almost certainly the closest thing St. Louis has to a restaurant in Bologna, which is the second-best eating town in Italy, according to most Italians. The best one, of course, is the hometown of whomever you're talking to. We love Bologna passionately for just that reason. Trattoria Marcella isn't Bolognese-style food, of course. It's Komorek-style food, in the passion of brothers Steve and Jamie, who named their place for their mother, Marcella Slay, who belongs to another distinguished restaurant family.

Opened in the summer of 1995, the restaurant has been a hot enough ticket from Day One to have expanded shortly after its third anniversary. It's simply decorated, full of people who, having lucked out and secured a reservation, are busy enjoying themselves. Italians love to talk, too, but maybe they stop while they eat. Trattoria Marcella is, to be sure, noisier than any Bolognese equivalent.

An herb garden grows behind the restaurant, letting arriving diners know that the Komoreks are serious about their food. And it shows from the start of the meal. Bruschetta is wonderful, with the best tomatoes, homegrown herbs, and some asiago cheese, which we leave off. The fritto misto a la Komorek is calamari and spinach deep-fried, dusted with Parmesan cheese and served with lemon. It's the sort of thing the whole table keeps nibbling on, saying "I've got to stop eating this, I'll be too full," until it's gone, except for a couple of little crumbs someone picks up surreptitiously. It's crispy and hot, full of textures and flavors, and irresistibly good.

Pizzas are done by hand, little ones maybe 10 inches across. The four-cheese version arrives topped with salad greens and tomatoes, the heat warming and slightly wilting the greens to make them crunchy-chewy. The addictive spinach salad sports rather strange toppings, like smoked salmon bacon, onions, tomatoes and shoestring potatoes, another stuff-yourself dish. (Smoked salmon bacon, like smoked salmon pastrami, refers to techniques for preparing the salmon, rather than the meat.)

Choices don't get any easier when it comes to entrees. Creamy risotto appears in various styles, with wild mushrooms or roasted chicken, asparagus and sun-dried tomatoes, all still slightly al dente and delicious. The sun-dried tomatoes, or if the season is right, fresh ones, partner with fresh clams, escarole, red pepper and garlic in an olive-oil-based sauce for spaghettini, many different tastes and textures weaving together to dazzle the tongue. Clams join mussels and shrimp in a tomato broth with toasted bread on the side, a wonderful soup-stew. We sigh over the calf's liver with onions, pancetta bacon and a Marsala sauce, so rich that one can barely finish half the dish. Pastas are brilliantly prepared, imaginatively sauced, and presented with a simplicity that emphasizes the food and its flavors, not the garnishes.

Desserts also are classic, with tiramisu, creme brulee, cannoli and others, all delivered in proper style, sometimes improved with a Komorek touch.

The wine list is outstanding, too, with many interesting bottles at often-reasonable prices. Service is rapid, but willing to explain the menu in extensive detail and mediate discussions about who should order what. Dinner, before drinks, tax and tip, will be in the $25-$30 range, and given the quality of the meals and the size of the portions, Trattoria Marcella could almost be considered a bargain.

Tribeca
Italian Cuisine
16 North Central Avenue, Clayton
721-5307
Lunch and Dinner, Monday-Saturday
Credit cards: AE, MC, V
Wheelchair access: Passable

Another sapling of the Racanelli tree, this green-walled bar-restaurant offers a brief and to-the-point menu of tapas, pizzas, pastas and a few more solid hunks of meat. Since wine is considered the correct drink with tapas, there's a lengthy list, with proper pricing, but in terms of spelling and locations, the early versions looked as if they had been translated and spelled by someone who spoke Bronx, rather than Italian or English. Joe grew up in Brooklyn, and learned early that the Bronx, where the Racanellis lived after emigrating from Bari, was different. But he didn't know it was that different.

Another problem in the early days was slightly confused service, as if the creative spirit in the kitchen was moving at the rhythm of an authentic trattoria rather than a spot in the heart of Clayton.

The bread at the table is a focaccia with some tomato on top that the waitress referred to as pizza bread. It was almost addictive, despite the fact that it was room temperature or a few degrees less. Room temperature should be minimum on focaccia; less is difficult to forgive.

Clams semicasino (without bacon) were small, pungent and tasty; fried oysters were more erratic, some flavorful and some not. A seafood salad, however, was superior and full of briny specimens. Quite properly, special attention was paid to the tomatoes, probably plum tomatoes, which were excellent.

Pizzas were 10-inch individual ones, led by a classic tomato, cheese and fresh basil that suffered a little from someone's generous hand with the buttery cheese, but otherwise looked, smelled and tasted much like the classic pizza Margherita you get in Italy. However, with some Bronx logic, there's the Racanelli version of pizza Margherita with radicchio and fresh Parmesan, extremely tasty with the slight bitterness of the radicchio standing tall. Other choices were a spicy chorizo sausage and some delicious rock shrimp, bolstered with a hit of pepper. The pizzas are preceded by East Coast-style shakers of crushed red peppers and cheese.

The bread pudding was the homemade dessert on a night we visited, and while it's a far cry from Bari (or from the Bronx), it was first-rate.

Tropicana Market
Food of The Americas, with a Little Eastern European

5001 Lindenwood Avenue
353-7328
Lunch every day
Credit cards: MC, V
Wheelchair access: Passable

Years ago, little corner grocery stores in St. Louis were referred to as delicatessens. They sold groceries and sandwich-fixings, and were mostly found in south St. Louis. The name may have come from the braunschweiger, cervelat and other lunch meats doled out from the butcher's case. Delicatessens with lox and cream cheese, or those with meatballs and peppers, were different phenomena in different parts of town.

The Tropicana Market, in the heart of traditional south St. Louis, manages to be both a neighborhood grocery and an outstanding lunch place, offering foods and flavors of the Caribbean and Latin America and, to a lesser degree, eastern Europe.

A couple of blocks northwest of Kingshighway and Chippewa, Luis Trabianco and his family stock masses of fresh and packaged ingredients for the other American cuisines, the ones less familiar to St. Louis. We shop for plantains and chile peppers and a lot of other dandy things. But mostly we head there for lunch. Behind the canned goods and produce are several tables, and a deli case of major interest to the eater. Their version of a Cuban sandwich is sliced roast pork, not the pressed ham-and-pickle thing sometimes found elsewhere. The pork is tender and garlicky, juicy enough to handle its fat roll, and a fine place to sample a little of the several kinds of off-the-beaten-path hot sauces that are table condiments.

Week to week, the items in the case vary, but it's nearly impossible to spend more than $10. The counter help, which often includes Luis' mom, happily answer questions, but with the number of questions increasing by leaps and bounds, Luis has begun displaying sample lunch plates, with cards explaining their contents. Soft tacos can be made with shredded chicken and cilantro, or the other meat fillings waiting in the case. We've had heavenly tamales and empanadas, too, fascinating in varied flavors, but never fiery-hot until an eater shakes on the sauce, or adds some fresh salsa.

There's a wide choice of beverages chilling in a cooler, from the tropical sodas like pineapple or guava to the delicious Taiwanese iced coffee in a can. Pastries are in a case by the front door, for picking and choosing. Some of these, as well as some of the groceries, give indication of the neighborhood's increasing Eastern European population and Luis' sensibilities about including them in the Tropicana mix. There's a rich and very dense Cuban bread pudding, various pastries and cakes, and some rice pudding.

The dining area inside is tiny, only four tables. In good weather, there are tables outside. And Luis is talking about taking out a back wall for more tables. That's fine. Just don't change the cooking. Tropicana is like nowhere else in town. We like it a lot.

Tucker's Place

Traditional St. Louis, with an Emphasis on Steaks

Soulard, 2117 South 12th Street
772-5977
Lunch Monday-Friday, Dinner every night
West, 14282 Manchester Road, Manchester
227-8062
Lunch Monday-Saturday, Dinner every night
South, 3939 Union Road
845-2584
Lunch Monday-Saturday, Dinner every night
Credit cards: All major
Wheelchair access: Impossible (Soulard); Passable (Manchester and Union Road)

If there's a better place for an inexpensive steak in St. Louis, we haven't found it. Tucker's Place, which began at the Soulard address and has expanded west and south, is a perfect place for splurging young lovers—brick walls, fireplaces and simple food. In the first rush of love, uncomplicated food is often the best, not demanding too much attention away from awareness of the sublime nearness of The Other.

It is, however, basically a hearty eating house, the sort of place you might go before a basketball game with a group of friends. The appetizers are nearly all deep-fried, led by toasted ravioli (of course), chicken wings, potato skins, mushrooms and jalapeno pepper-and-cheese poppers—perfect ballast for the second and third beers. And this is basically a beer house, with a satisfactory selection, but a lesser one for the wine.

The entrees are served with salad and baked potato. The salad is as expected—iceberg lettuce, a little onion, a cherry tomato—but it's fresh, with no brown lettuce edges in sight. The house lemon pepper dressing is slightly sweet, and there's brand-specific Hidden Valley Ranch for the nostalgic and a few others, all at an extra charge. The salads arrive with a generous handful of ersatz, rather powdery "bacon" bits that surprisingly, blended nicely with the ranch dressing, and their slightly odd taste covered well by the other ingredients. The persnickety palate scarfed it right down.

Steaks lead the way, of course, with a pair of top sirloins, a filet mignon, a 16-ounce New York strip, and a 22-ounce T-bone ranging from $7.95 to $14.95, and there's a big (one-and-a-half-inch thick) pork loin chop for $10.95. Some fish items, too, but Tucker's made its reputation on steaks, and steaks are the way to go.

The T-bone and the pork chop were excellent, and super-excellent values. The steak is advertised as 22 ounces, although bone and fat count for some. Nevertheless, for a steak that missed being chosen for the hallowed halls of places like Morton's or Ruth's Chris, this was good, tender, tasty meat, perfectly cooked to the requested medium rare—which, to us, means the interior is red but still warm.

The pork chop was blissful. If you're in barbecue withdrawal, this hunk of grilled pig meat will stave your crave for a while. The server asked how we wanted it cooked, an unusual request for a pork order, but one we've recently heard more often. Medium well is our answer, a little pink is okay and well over the kill point for bacteria. And that's how it came—crispy around the edges, moist and tender. The baked potatoes, too, passed the biggest test: no aluminum foil. They were big, not the double-fist size, but a good single serving. They come with butter; sour cream was extra. No broccoli, no parsley, no twisted orange slice. This place means business, and delivers it at dinner for less than $25 a person.

Dessert was cheesecake. We passed. We were full.

Turvey's on the Green

Modern American

255 Union Boulevard
454-1667
Lunch Tuesday-Friday, Dinner Tuesday-Sunday
Credit cards: All major
Wheelchair access: Satisfactory

One of St. Louis' warmest and loveliest restaurants, Turvey's offers a gracious dining room, with lots of glass offering a usually serene view of Union Boulevard. The bar, in an adjacent room, is a long, classic oval, and another dining room, to the south, is on a glassed-in porch. In this stylish pre-World War II building, the general effect is what Ralph Lauren can only yearn for.

Basically a steak, chop and seafood house, with a handful of specials and a couple of pizzas, Turvey's entrees run about $15-$20, and a full meal is about $30. They are accompanied by a superior wine list, long and deep. There are very good values in the $25-$35 range, and the list is heavy on California, with well-known and less-familiar labels. Kenwood wines are good values, and there may be some of the excellent 1995 Storybook Mountain Zinfandel remaining. Many solid cabernet sauvignons are on hand, and some very good pinot noirs from California and Oregon.

Service is smooth, though we ran into one of those Oops! situations when the waiter put the next table's wine order—and charge—on our check. The problem was rectified speedily, however.

Bread and rolls are first-rate, especially the focaccia, with olive oil bolstered by fresh-ground Parmesan cheese on the side, and salads display a wide variety of greens and satisfactory dressing.

Among the appetizers, hummus with red bell pepper shows a pinkish cast and superior flavor from a softball-sized serving atop excellent, fresh mixed greens. The whole package was topped with some finely diced red pepper and egg whites, adding color as well as flavor, and the hummus had a good influence of garlic and pepper. It was among the best hummus we'd tasted in a long time; its only shortcoming was overtoasted pita triangles, crisp and tough. The Turvey's salad offered the same greens as the house version, red onion rings, three colors of pepper strips croutons and a couple of tomato wedges. House dressing was fit for a Caesar.

Roast chicken was outstanding, marinated in buttermilk and herbs, arriving in an exemplary sauce, scented with tarragon and flavored with that herb, mushrooms and cream. Green beans, carrots and state-of-the-art traditional mashed potatoes came alongside. Loin lamb chops were thick and delicious, cooked as ordered and served atop a melange of roasted vegetables and fruits. It's rare when the side dish overshadows the main course, and it wasn't easy to outdistance the lamb, but small dicings of potato, eggplant, a few small zucchini slices, red bell pepper, fruits, raisins, plums and other stone fruits added a glorious contrast, sweet but not too sweet. The lamb was delicious, the vegetables even more so.

The dessert tray is small but eminently satisfactory, led by a lemon gooey butter cake with a rather tough crust, but the filling was so good and so tart that all criticism was forgotten. A good chocolate cake, and a couple of cheesecakes round out the choices.

The Village Bar

Classic Bar Food

12247 Manchester Road, Des Peres
821-4532
Lunch and Dinner, Monday-Saturday
Credit cards: MC, V
Wheelchair access: Passable

Before there were sports bars, or fern bars, there was the Village Bar. Before the Village Bar, we're afraid, there was just a big, black, hole. No light. No air. No beer. No hamburgers. No nothin'.

One of the area's finest flat-grill hamburgers, and probably its best fried mushrooms and second-best onion rings, come out of a small corner of the Village Bar, where visitors sometimes feel they have been pulled into the long-ago radio serial, "Duffy's Tavern." Not many of us remember "Duffy's Tavern, where the elite meet to eat. Archie the manager speakin', Duffy ain't here."

Duffy was never there, of course, existing only as a silence at the other end of an imaginary telephone line. Archie relayed his words

The Village Bar looks like a roadhouse, and the wig display in the window next door heightens the image. Inside, the shuffleboard game keeps up a constant chatter, and several television sets, tuned to different sporting events at the same time, hold the attention of the other customers.

Beer and burgers are the traditional fare—the burgers juicy and dribbling a little grease. They're thicker than the ones at, for example, Carl's Drive-Inn, and thinner than those at O'Connell's. Onion rings feature very thin, fall-away batter that gets very crisp, and rings that are thick and sweet. Big, fat mushrooms, again with a light batter but clean frying oil and a high temperature, are piping hot, but juicy and delicious. Best onion-mushroom combination anywhere. Fries are crisp and hot, and the Better Burger, a larger hamburger with Swiss cheese and a kaiser roll, is a delight.

Time was when lunch was strictly on the honor system. You ordered, you ate, and you went to the bar and rattled off what you had eaten. The bartender, working a register like a pre-electronic grocery checker, provided the total.

Unfortunately, time passes and things change. Duffy's is gone, and so is Archie, and the waitresses at the Village Bar carry pads.

Wei Hong Bakery & B.B.Q.

Chinese, with pauses in Viet Nam and Singapore

3175 South Grand Boulevard
773-8318
8148 Olive Boulevard, University City (carry-out bakery only)
993-6208
Lunch and Dinner, Wednesday-Monday
Cash only
Wheelchair access: Comfortable (South Grand)

What goes around, comes around, and in this case, it's pigs' feet for sale in the old and once very German neighborhood south of Grand and Arsenal. The trotters are steamed, not pickled, and they're at Wei Hong, across the street from Jay International, one of our favorite stores, and next to the Holy Land Market, where Halal meat and other important Middle Eastern food products are sold. Jay is a landmark, but the other two are 1998 arrivals, adding to the lengthening and increasingly interesting list of places for food and fun on South Grand Boulevard.

"CHINESE FOOD" glows a neon sign, but the window is full of porcelain statues and vases. Inside, a tall case of roasted meats—duck, pork, chicken—faces the visitor, hanging quietly and dripping their way to excellence. Behind it is a row of bakery cases, filled with unfamiliar, but delicious-looking, pastries of all colors and shapes. Next to the roasts, a handwritten sign gives prices per pound for the various meats. And there they are—pigs' feet—back home again.

We somehow doubt these pigs' feet will ever be sold in neighborhood bars, but beer isn't a bad idea with this sort of food (someplace else, however, there's no liquor license here). The pigs' feet aren't available on the handwritten, bilingual menu, but there are many surprisingly fine dishes, both expected and unexpected.

Before heading for a seat, the curious diner is encouraged to inspect the meats and bakery items, usually marked in English, and make mental notes. The bakery has savory buns, either deep-fried or baked, but seldom the white steamed ones that seem to put off Americans unused to their pale exteriors. There might be ham and egg bun (quite Hong Kong, this combo) or roast pork, sweet and juicy, and a longtime favorite.

The menu shows lots of soups and noodle dishes, including rice noodles. Familiar dishes to us are things like fried rice, wonton soup and kung pao chicken. It's the other things we'd encourage. Singapore noodles, or mai fun, are just beginning to be seen around here. Singapore, with its polyglot ethnicity, usually means spicy. And Singapore noodles are curry-spicy, not killer-hot but definitely curried, and jammed with extras, not unlike a mega-deluxe fried rice. Red and green pepper strips, onion slices, green onion, scrambled egg, shrimp, barbecued pork bits, flavor every bite of noodles. An immense platter is $6.25, near the midpoint of the menu. The most expensive thing, "seafood combination," under Chinese Casseroles, is $8.50.

Squid dishes are popular, and there are a couple of styles of beef tripe for the adventurous. Spare ribs and green pepper, stir-fried and seasoned with black bean sauce, are alluring, and so is soy chicken and beef with satay sauce. Salted shrimp with black pepper came out as large, incredibly fresh shrimp, deep-fried in a batter so light you could see through it, lightly salty but with no apparent black pepper. Instead, a handful of onion and hot pepper slivers, both red and jalapeno, were added. The vegetables were spicier than the shrimp, which were cooked in the shell with most of the head attached. We differ on shrimp-in-shell—Ann likes it sometimes, Joe doesn't—so let the diner decide. The heads, by the way, taste very much like lobster roe.

We had a bun apiece for a first course, two entrees, iced tea (which is Chinese and not American standard) and a Coke, finished with the luscious Vietnamese iced coffee and spent $17.

Sounds good, certainly, but then we got the fortune cookies. These are orange-flavored fortune cookies, unusual enough. Turns out they come from one of the most wonderful-sounding companies we've found lately—the Ha Ha Fortune Cookie Company of Brooklyn, N.Y. No wonder they're good.

Woofie's
The Hot Dog Place
1919 Woodson Road, Overland
426-6291
Lunch and Dinner, Monday-Saturday
Cash only
Wheelchair access: Passable

"Serving the hot dog with dignity," is the motto of Woofie's. The dogs, at least to two non-Chicagoans, are worthy of the slogan. Hot dogs in Chicago are practically a religion, and people argue over them like they do over pizza in St. Louis. Joe doesn't; he insists nothing beats real Nathan's at Coney Island, with sauerkraut and mustard, and anything else is an imposter. He brooks no argument.

These are indeed of the Chicago school, and the basic dress for these all-beef dogs from the Vienna company is mustard, ketchup, diced onion, a long spear of dill pickle, electric-green relish and a "sport pepper," a small green pickled pepper that can really sizzle from an unexpected mouthful. To spread the heat around, break the top off the pepper and sprinkle juice and seeds the length of the bun.

The death last year of the founder Charley Eisen and the subsequent sale of Woofie's left the customers, a large group with an inordinately high percentage from the media, watching things closely, but all seems to be continuing steadfastly.

There are plenty of variations on the theme—foot-longs and fat dogs, Polish sausage, bratwurst and the corn dog, which was perhaps the first Missouri food that a young Joe Pollack ever fell for. You can get sauerkraut on the dogs, but you can't get that other New York street condiment—stewed onions. Hamburgers are available, according to the menu, but no one seems to be that wasteful of an opportunity for a good dog. The very first seasoned fries in St. Louis were made here. Topped with what tastes like Lawry's seasoned salt, they're always hot and good.

This is a Coca-Cola house, although there's root beer for those who need that combination because of a misspent youth at Dog 'n' Suds.

Seating inside is at chrome stools; the place holds perhaps a dozen close personal friends. There are some tables outside, and a drive-through window, although the sign cautions that hamburgers aren't available there. Lots of folks get their food to go, milling around while they wait and inspecting gazillions of photos and newspaper clippings on the wall. Everybody comes to Woofie's, from Bob Costas to the cashier at the gas station down the road, and even the hungriest get out with change from a $10 bill.

Yemanja Brasil
Brazilian Cuisine

2900 Missouri Avenue
771-7457
Lunch Tuesday-Friday, Dinner Tuesday-Saturday; Brunch on Sunday
Credit cards: All major
Wheelchair access: Extremely difficult now,
but plans are for better accommodations soon.

The Benton Park neighborhood is named for the wonderful little park at the corner of Jefferson Avenue and Arsenal Street. It's old south St. Louis, row houses with cement steps. In some cases, the original brick paving shows through streets and sidewalks. It's not always fashionable. But it sports a number of good restaurants, even as it perpetuates the memory of the Missouri Bentons, artists and lawmakers.

Yemanja (YEE-AH manzhah) Brasil (the natives spell it with an "s") is three years old. It has prospered quietly, expanding into the attached building next door and making plans for a small patio to provide wheelchair access. The small storefront dining room is now the bar, still with a sofa and footstool and a couple of tables. Be warned about the bar. It dispenses the near-lethal caipirinha (kai peer EEN yah), the insidiously delicious cocktail made of lime juice and a Brazilian rum called cachaca served on the rocks. We love them, but they carry a great deal more alcohol than it would seem.

Brazilian food reflects both the Portuguese and African parts of the culture and the tropical climate for much of the country. Yemanja Brasil's menu leans toward seafood, although there's a beef entree, a pork tenderloin and a couple of styles of chicken, one a Latin American risotto (spelled risoto here). Three vegetarian main courses also are available.

Roasted red sweet peppers always are tasty. They're pimentao (pee men tom) jundiai here, a first course that combines them with onions, oregano, anchovies and a pinch of hot red pepper. The combination is wonderful, only slightly warm on the heat meter, the delicious whole anchovy filets matching off with the peppers even better than the more common garlic. Another combines asiago cheese, cream and onions popped under the broiler, and ceviche comes in a small tulip glass, like a sundae. Ceviche is raw fish marinated in lime juice with seasonings, and the acid solidifies the fish enough so that it seems cooked. However, the fish must be in the marinade long enough to "cook," but not so long that it gets hard or starts to fall apart. This was perhaps slightly past peak, but still tasty. The balance of onion, cilantro, and hot pepper was splendid. Ceviche, by the way, is a perfect hot-weather food.

Dinner comes with the house salad, small but good, and based on fresh lettuce, kept chilled, under a proper serving of a sweet vinaigrette dressing. The other ubiquitous side dish is rice. We can't recall ever having had more perfectly cooked rice in a non-Asian restaurant. Just done but not overcooked, it was quite remarkable.

The rice formed the base for the camarao yemanja, big shrimp sauteed in olive oil with onions and sweet red and green peppers and sauced with coconut. The bold can punch this up with a couple of hits of hot sauce, but we found it simple and sweet and flavorful.

On most Saturdays, the special is the Brazilian national dish, feijoada (fay joo-ah dah). To call it bean soup is a gross injustice, but if you must, it's bean soup for the gods. Black beans, of course, cooked with sausage, pork ribs and a special, imported dried beef, plus lots of herbs and spices, to make a smoky, creamy magnificence that is served in a pot. On the accompanying side plate are rice, finely shredded collard greens still a little fluffy and with a wonderful flavor, a slice of orange and farofa. Farofa looks like brown crumbs, but is yucca flour browned with a little garlic to act as a condiment when the beans are spooned over the rice, adding texture as well as flavor. We're not sure if the combination—beans, rice, a little farofa and a piece of meat— or beans straight from the pot are better. This is a platonic dish, right up there with any creation out of a five-star restaurant with a Food Channel chef.

The most authentic dessert is a coconut custard, very unlike the American custard. The coconut is coarsely shredded, and the custard is translucent from the egg yolks—there may be no whites in this at all—and the sugar, not unlike the bottom of a pecan pie but deeper. The beverage of choice is the Brazilian espresso, for which the coffee is not only Brazilian, but also seems to be roasted a little less, producing a smoother taste. Sugar-in-coffee folks should try the combination before adding any.

There are a few bottles of wine on a board, and a few available by the glass. Try iced tea or beer. Under $25 a head unless you get carried away with caipirinhas, in which case you'll probably be carried off, too.

Zinnia
Modern American Cuisine
7491 Big Bend Boulevard, Webster Groves
962-0572
Lunch Tuesday-Friday, Dinner Tuesday-Sunday
Credit cards: All major
Wheelchair access: Passable

Zinnia is one of St. Louis' best restaurants. We'll brook no argument. Even stuffy folks in expensive clothes have fun with David Guempel's food. As the restaurant approaches its tenth anniversary in Webster Groves, it gradually has expanded from its gas station and grocery store beginnings. Imagination and execution in the kitchen have flourished apace, and the consistency of excellent food and beautiful presentation has remained strong. Zinnia is an excellent value with three courses, excluding drinks, tax and tip, running about $30.

The rowdy lavender exterior cools off once inside, where the decor is simple and modern. The menu, like many in town, shifts gradually and seasonally, and there's always an immense chalkboard full of additional possibilities for the evening's joy.

For appetizers, it's hard to pass the duck tacos, wonton skins folded to hold Chinese-glazed duck nuggets and chopped mangoes. A rice-vinegar dipping sauce and a few greens rest alongside. The tacos shatter immediately, of course, but the shards are so good they finally become delicious fork food along with the greens and dipping sauce. Folks who aren't quite at the sushi point in life should try the tuna that's seasoned with wasabi and pickled ginger, then tempura-battered and quickly fried to rare. Mussels Zinnia are a house specialty. Cold mussels in a honey-dill sauce may sound awkward, but it makes for a merry delight as the flavors play happily together.

Joe loves sweetbreads, and he loves them most at Zinnia. Not enough restaurants serve variety, or organ meats, although things are improving. We think most people's problem stems more from texture than from flavor. Sweetbreads, the thymus gland of a calf, are tender and subtly flavored, not nearly so "different" as, say, kidney, and are a fine platform for the sauce maker's art. These come with mushrooms, capers and a little Madeira in the sauce to compete for best of breed.

This is a good, knowing kitchen for pork lovers, and roast loins or stuffed chops are handled with style. Duck also is in good hands, with several reliable Asian-style variations. Understanding that lamb shanks are, literally, hard to handle for folks who are dressed up and en route to the theatre or the opera, Zinnia cooks them with a tomato and red wine sauce, bones them and serves the result with mashed potatoes. Trout Zinnia, another signature dish, is sweet Missouri trout breaded with chopped nuts and sesame seeds. When in season, soft shell crabs are glorious, sauteed quickly and crisply to the peak of flavor and available either as an appetizer or as an entree.

Desserts, too, work their way through the seasons. There are always sorbets, some pastry work, a cake and a mousse. They've recently begun serving sticky toffee pudding, a dark, earthy steamed cake served warm with the toffee sauce and a creme anglaise, or custard sauce, alongside. Warm and charming, it's nursery food at its very best, though not quite to the standard of the downtown Tap Room.

An outstanding, well-balanced, properly-priced wine list and service that's unerringly smooth will end a meal in plenty of time for the curtain. But two stern recommendations to a diner in this situation: First, reserve a table early enough to allow sufficient time for Guempel to do his best; and second, tell the server right away so that everyone else also is warned.

Zoe Pan-Asian Cafe
Pacific Rim Cuisine
4753 McPherson Avenue
361-0013
Lunch Monday-Saturday, Dinner every night
Credit cards: All major
Wheelchair access: Satisfactory

In the group of new restaurants that makes up the Class of '98, Zoe's Pan-Asian stands out. She's trying to give St. Louis something completely new, and is. Pacific Rim cuisine has been dancing around the country for several years, but this is its St. Louis debut.

For those who haven't been introduced, Pacific Rim takes elements from different parts of Asia, including the Pacific Islands, and melds them into California-style food. The Pacific Northwest figures into this, too, although Alaska is not yet a contender. Seattle has several excellent restaurants, like Wild Ginger. A menu may have Thai curried chickpeas in the pancakes formerly seen with moo shu pork next to stir-fried shrimp with mango sauce.

We've eaten it in California, Seattle and, most impressively, in Hawaii, where Roy Yamaguchi has taken the islands' own crossroads cuisine and expanded it to create dishes that make diners gasp. So, yes, we think it's good stuff, and St. Louis deserves to have Singapore noodles with roast duck and all its kin.

Enter Zoe Houk Robinson, formerly of Cafe Zoe in Clayton.

The Pan-Asian is handsome, celadon and black, vigorously hip-looking, and announcing that it's a spot for things done differently. More SoHo than South China Sea, it nevertheless pleases the eye. And business has been good, drawing both the voguish and the eaters. The menu makes it easy to assemble a number of little dishes for nibbling, or to go a more western direction of first course, entree, and dessert. The tab for the latter will be above $25 before service and journeys to the beverage list.

That list includes some good wines, but more amusingly, there's a burst of giddy cocktails ranging from the semi-traditional like vodka or gin gimlets and pineapple daiquiris to things like the Suzy Wong, with watermelon juice and vodka, or Tiger's Milk, which teams mango and coconut milk with rum in a lethal concoction.

It's a delicious-sounding menu. Crispy salmon rolls with citrus wasabi sauce, steamed vegetable dumplings and nine-spice spare ribs all act as openers. So does a Japanese eggplant with sweet black vinegar and tahini sauces, roasted until soft and ready for the sauces to carry it. The vinegar has thin slices of jalapeno, not as lethal as it sounds until you chew on one with seeds, but the sweet-hot is nice. Tahini brings a nutty flavor that softens the aftershock of the vinegar and offers new sensations of its own. Shrimp are seared in their very fragile shells and served with a mango and yogurt sauce. We disagree on shrimp in shell—he prefers to shell them, she plows through—but we agreed these were delicious. The sauce, a yogurt-mango mix much like raita, is good enough to eat with a spoon.

Good reports on the Asian vegetable antipasto are common, and we happily confirm them. Three or four small salad-like items may include a slaw made with beets and red cabbage and seasoned with rice vinegar. Carrots are sliced into thin sheets and marinated in a wonderfully insistent ginger. Cucumber wears an avocado-studded yogurt. Another slaw is dressed with sesame oil. The dish varies from day to day, but always is worthwhile.

Main courses include a section with noodle-based dishes that come in soup bowls. A lot of folks are hooked on noodles; those who think they're an Italian monopoly need to investigate Asian cooking. Here, linguini shines with shrimp and scallops in a coconut curry sauce. Coconut milk, by the way, often is used in Thai curries. Vietnamese beef and rice stick noodles, in a sensuous broth, are crowned with a handful of fresh herbs.

There always are a couple of vegetarian entrees. In addition, roasted sea bass might wear an orange mustard glaze. Tuna comes rare with a sesame crust. A duck breast is glazed with slightly sweet, slightly anise flavorings and served with broth over onions, celery, bok choy and spinach, a succulent dish. The only misses we encountered were a grilled chicken breast with Thai peanut sauce and spinach, and a side dish of green beans.. The breast was technically perfect, still moist, slightly crusty. But it had no seasoning. Spinach, cooked for not more than thirty seconds, was perfect, but peanut sauce was practically invisible in the low-light room and barely detectable on the tongue. It wasn't a bad dish, but it took dead aim at the unadventurous eater. The beans arrived in a light layer of a sweet glaze with crushed cashews on top, and the effect was close to candying them. It just didn't swing.

Dessert includes baked bananas with a coconut creme anglaise, a sauce that appeared in several selections. Bananas were cut lengthwise and browned, a process that makes them wonderfully sweet and rich. Creme anglaise was used as a drizzle. Toasted coconut, sprinkled on top, left more image than flavor of coconut.

In general, we think that seasoning is considerably less robust than it should be, selling St. Louis diners short. Several of our dishes were very good—the vegetable salads, for instance—but others like the duck could have gone from good to great with a stronger accent on big flavors. St. Louis diners have supported Thai, Vietnamese, Chinese, Indian and Japanese restaurants for many years, and most are familiar with the flavors and spicing. The best Pacific Rim cooking is done with courage and without hesitancy.

American

Almond's
Annie Gunn's
Anthony's Bar
Balaban's
Big Sky Cafe
Blanche's
Breakaway Cafe
Busch's Grove
Cafe Manhattan
Cafe Mira
Cardwell's at The Plaza
Cardwell's of Clayton
Carriage House at DeMenil Mansion
Colorado
Cravings
The Crossings
Crown Candy Kitchen
Delmar Restaurant & Lounge
Duff's
Duke's
Faust's
Frazer's Traveling Brown Bag
Harry's Restaurant & Bar
Harvest
Hot Locust Cantina
J.P. Field's and John P. Field's
Key West Cafe

Kirk's American Bistro & Bar
Lemmons Restaurant
Lynch Street Bistro
The Mansion at LakePointe
Molina's Wishing Well
Neruda
Oh My Darlin' Cafe in Clementine's
Once Upon a Vine
Paul's of Clayton
Portabella
Remy's Kitchen & Wine Bar
Riddle's Penultimate
The Ritz-Carlton
Riverport Casino-Town Square Buffet
Sadie Thompson's Bistro
Sidney Street Cafe
Station Grille
Top of the Riverfront
Turvey's on the Green
Zinnia

Bar Food

Blueberry Hill
Culpeppers
Fitz's
Joe and Charlie's
John D. McGurk's
King Louie's

Llywelyn's Pub
Norton's Cafe
O'Connell's Pub
Old 66 Brewery & Restaurant
Pat's Bar and Grill
St. Louis Tap Room & Brewery
Spotted Dog Cafe
Trainwreck Saloon
The Village Bar

Brazilian
Yemanja Brasil

Breakfast & Brunch
Chestnut's at the Adam's Mark
Chris' Pancake and Dining
Delmonico Diner
Goody-Goody
Harry's Restaurant & Bar
Kopperman's
Majestic Restaurant
Museum Cafe
Obie's of Soulard
Oh My Darlin' Cafe in Clementine's
Parkmoor
Pumpernickle's
The Ritz-Carlton
South City Diner
Uncle Bill's Pancake and Dinner House

Burgers
Carl's Drive Inn
Fast Eddie's Bon-Air

Chinese
Chef Hsu's Hunan Star
Great Chef Garden
Hunan & Peking Garden
Royal Chinese B.B.Q.
Shu Feng
Wei Hong Bakery & B.B.Q.

Chile
O.T. Hodge Chile Parlor

Deli
Jack Carl's Two Cents Plain
Posh Nosh
Protzel's

Everything
The Market in the Loop
Tropicana Market

French
Cafe Campagnard
Cafe de France
Cafe Provencal
Fio's La Fourchette
Malmaison

German
Bevo Mill
Schneithorst's

Greek
Olympia Kebob House & Taverna
Spiro's

Hot Dogs
Woofie's

Indian
House of India
India Palace
India's Rasoi

Italian
Bar Italia
Benedetto's
Bruno's Little Italy
Cafe Napoli
Charlie Gitto's on The Hill
Cicero's

Cunetto's House of Pasta
Dominic's
Dominic's Trattoria
Farotto's Pizzeria
Favazza's
Frank Papa's Ristorante
Gianfabio's
Gian-Peppe's
Gino's
Giovanni's
Giuseppe's
John Mineo's
Joseph's Italian Cafe
Kemoll's
Lombardo's
Lo Russo's Cucina
Lou Boccardi's
Peppercini's Italian Cafe
Summit
Tony's
Trattoria Marcella
Tribeca

Japanese
Nobu's Japanese Restaurant
Seki
Tachibana

Mexican
Arcelia's
Casa Gallardo Grill
Chuy Arzola's Tex-Mex Restaurant
El Maguey
Flaco's Tacos
Nachomama's
Pueblo Nuevo Mexican Restaurant
Pueblo Solis
Ramon's El Dorado

New Orleans
Bobby's
Frazer's Traveling Brown Bag

Pacific Rim
Zoe Pan-Asian Cafe

Pan Caribbean
Babalu's

Persian/Middle Eastern
Cafe Natasha
Saleem's

Russian/Armenian
Dvin Restaurant

St. Louis Eclectic
The Feasting Fox, Al Smith's Restaurant

Seafood
Blue Water Grill
Bristol Bar & Grill
Broadway Oyster Bar
Crazy Fish
R.L. Steamers
Surf and Sirloin

Steak
Al's
Andria's
Best Steak House
Big Chief Dakota Grill
Charcoal House
Citizen Kane's Steak House
Dierdorf & Hart's
Kreis' Restaurant
Mike Shannon's Steaks and Seafood
Morton's of Chicago
Sam's St. Louis Steak House
Tucker's Place

Thai
King and I Restaurant
Thai Cafe

Turkish
Cafe Istanbul

Vietnamese
Da Nang
Mai Lee Restaurant
Pho Grand
Saigon Cafe and Deli